Constructing a Life
PHILOSOPHY
OPPOSING VIEWPOINTS®

Other Books of Related Interest in the Opposing
Viewpoints Series:

American Values
Biomedical Ethics
Civil Liberties
Death and Dying
Euthanasia
Male/Female Roles
Science & Religion
Sexual Values
Social Justice
Suicide

Constructing a Life
PHILOSOPHY
O P P O S I N G V I E W P O I N T S ®

Sixth Edition

David L. Bender & Bruno Leone, *Series Editors*

David L. Bender, *Book Editor*

OPPOSING VIEWPOINTS SERIES ®

Greenhaven Press, Inc.   PO Box 289009   San Diego, CA 92198-9009

Library of Congress Cataloging-in-Publication Data

Constructing a life philosophy : opposing viewpoints / David L. Bender, book editor. — 6th ed., rev.
    p.   cm. — (Opposing viewpoints series)
Includes bibliographical references and index.
ISBN 0-89908-198-3 (alk. paper) — ISBN 0-89908-173-8 (pbk. : alk. paper)
1. Life. 2. Conduct of life. 3. Religion. I. Bender, David L., 1936-   . II. Series: Opposing viewpoints series (Unnumbered)
BD431.C665   1993
140—dc20
                                  92-40706
                                  CIP

Sixth Edition
Revised

"Congress shall make no law . . . abridging the freedom of speech, or of the press."

First Amendment to the U.S. Constitution

The basic foundation of our democracy is the first amendment guarantee of freedom of expression. The Opposing Viewpoints Series is dedicated to the concept of this basic freedom and the idea that it is more important to practice it than to enshrine it.

Contents

Chapter 3: How Do Religions Give Life Meaning?

Chapter 4: How Do Others Make Moral Decisions?

Chapter 5: How Should One Live?

Why Consider Opposing Viewpoints?

"The only way in which a human being can make some approach to knowing the whole of a subject is by hearing what can be said about it by persons of every variety of opinion and studying all modes in which it can be looked at by every character of mind. No wise man ever acquired his wisdom in any mode but this."

John Stuart Mill

In our media-intensive culture it is not difficult to find differing opinions. Thousands of newspapers and magazines and dozens of radio and television talk shows resound with differing points of view. The difficulty lies in deciding which opinion to agree with and which "experts" seem the most credible. The more inundated we become with differing opinions and claims, the more essential it is to hone critical reading and thinking skills to evaluate these ideas. Opposing Viewpoints books address this problem directly by presenting stimulating debates that can be used to enhance and teach these skills. The varied opinions contained in each book examine many different aspects of a single issue. While examining these conveniently edited opposing views, readers can develop critical thinking skills such as the ability to compare and contrast authors' credibility, facts, argumentation styles, use of persuasive techniques, and other stylistic tools. In short, the Opposing Viewpoints Series is an ideal way to attain the higher-level thinking and reading skills so essential in a culture of diverse and contradictory opinions.

In addition to providing a tool for critical thinking, Opposing Viewpoints books challenge readers to question their own strongly held opinions and assumptions. Most people form their opinions on the basis of upbringing, peer pressure, and personal, cultural, or professional bias. By reading carefully balanced opposing views, readers must directly confront new ideas as well as the opinions of those with whom they disagree. This is not to simplistically argue that everyone who reads opposing views will—or should—change his or her opinion. Instead, the series enhances readers' depth of understanding of their own views by encouraging confrontation with opposing ideas. Careful examination of others' views can lead to the readers' understanding of the logical inconsistencies in their own opinions, perspective on why they hold an opinion, and the consideration of the possibility that their opinion requires further evaluation.

Evaluating Other Opinions

To ensure that this type of examination occurs, Opposing Viewpoints books present all types of opinions. Prominent spokespeople on different sides of each issue as well as well-known professionals from many disciplines challenge the reader. An additional goal of the series is to provide a forum for other, less known, or even unpopular viewpoints. The opinion of an ordinary person who has had to make the decision to cut off life support from a terminally ill relative, for example, may be just as valuable and provide just as much insight as a medical ethicist's professional opinion. The editors have two additional purposes in including these less known views. One, the editors encourage readers to respect others' opinions—even when not enhanced by professional credibility. It is only by reading or listening to and objectively evaluating others' ideas that one can determine whether they are worthy of consideration. Two, the inclusion of such viewpoints encourages the important critical thinking skill of objectively evaluating an author's credentials and bias. This evaluation will illuminate an author's reasons for taking a particular stance on an issue and will aid in readers' evaluation of the author's ideas.

As series editors of the Opposing Viewpoints Series, it is our hope that these books will give readers a deeper understanding of the issues debated and an appreciation of the complexity of even seemingly simple issues when good and honest people disagree. This awareness is particularly important in a democratic society such as ours in which people enter into public debate to determine the common good. Those with whom one disagrees should not be regarded as enemies but rather as people whose views deserve careful examination and may shed light on one's own.

Thomas Jefferson once said that "difference of opinion leads to inquiry, and inquiry to truth." Jefferson, a broadly educated man, argued that "if a nation expects to be ignorant and free . . . it expects what never was and never will be." As individuals and as a nation, it is imperative that we consider the opinions of others and examine them with skill and discernment. The Opposing Viewpoints Series is intended to help readers achieve this goal.

David L. Bender & Bruno Leone,
Series Editors

Introduction

Lao Tzu is the author of *Tao Te Ching*, the fundamental text of Taoism and the basis of Chinese religious thought. Only the Bible has been translated more often. Its popularity, like the Bible's, stems from the hope it offers readers to find meaning and direction for their lives. In a sense, it is an Eastern "handbook for living." Although the book is short (about five thousand words), it is profound and can be read many times, each time revealing new lessons.

Books that promise to reveal life's meaning are valuable because they attempt to answer questions we all ask. How should we live? How should we relate to others? The answers we construct for these and similar questions determine how we live our lives. Our patterns of answers make up our life philosophies. The Greek philosopher Aristotle claimed that whether we are aware of it or not, we each have a life philosophy. The purpose of this book is to present important alternative life philosophies to help the reader identify and construct his or her own philosophy.

Where Are You Now?

The first chapter asks the question "What is your current life path?" M. Scott Peck, author of the first viewpoint, claims that one's view of reality is like a map with which to negotiate the terrain of life. He argues that we all construct our own maps and that if we are to reach our personal goals and destinations they must be accurate. In addition to having accurate maps, we must know our current positions. With hope, the book's first chapter will sensitize the reader to the necessity of carefully analyzing one's current beliefs and assumptions. The second viewpoint, by Plato, is intended to assist in this task. Plato's famous story of the cave, which invites the reader to experience life in its shadowy depths, can help to draw attention to the fact that we are all encumbered with biases and preconceptions. If nothing else, Plato's fascinating image of life graphically emphasizes the importance of an open mind and how enormously difficult it is to acquire.

The book's last four chapters provide a look at the maps others have constructed. If the reader is going to design a map, why start from scratch? Why not examine the maps of others? It makes sense to investigate how others have answered the questions that form the last four chapters of this book: What is life's meaning? How do religions give life meaning? How do others make moral decisions? How should one live? The reader may not find a particular life philosophy in the book totally useful. Perhaps only bits and pieces from different philosophies will be used—or nothing at all. In reading the following viewpoints, the reader will have a chance to scrutinize the life philosophies of famous and thoughtful mapmakers.

The philosophies presented in this book are balanced between atheist and believer, skeptic and optimist, nihilist and hopeful. Richard Robinson, in chapter two, expresses the resigned opinion that this life is all there is and that humanity's finest accomplishment is to live with courage as it awaits its final extinction. In the same chapter, Teilhard de Chardin describes a hopeful philosophy, built on the conviction that life is a divinely directed process that will only be completed when humanity finds itself in complete union with God. So the book goes, weaving a mosaic of alternative philosophies and offering the reader a wide range of choices.

The Necessity of an Open Mind

It is not the editor's intention to make a particular viewpoint appear more attractive than another. It is left to the reader to decide which viewpoint is most sensible. As editor I have tried to prevent my own beliefs and philosophy from influencing the book. I am not interested in promoting a particular set of values or beliefs. I am firmly convinced, however, that no viewpoint should be censored or excluded in one's examination of different philosophies. When in pursuit of the truth, the most common enemy is a closed mind. Even after the reader has chosen a suitable philosophy, it is still necessary to know the views of those who hold different beliefs. The quest for a life philosophy is one of life's most important enterprises. It should not be hampered by self-imposed constraints. The task is difficult enough.

There are some who claim that excessive introspection may cause more harm than good. They advise others to simply live life and not examine it too closely, to "go with the flow." The thrust of this book is in a different direction. Socrates, Plato's famous teacher, once said that the unexamined life is not worth living. Although Socrates may have exaggerated, a thoughtful, examined life is surely more enjoyable than one that is undirected and purposeless.

In addition to the alternative life philosophies presented, critical thinking skill activities have been added throughout the book to aid the reader. Each chapter is also concluded with a periodical bibliography for further investigation. At the back of the book an annotated book bibliography and list of helpful periodicals has been included to further aid the reader's search.

Some Words of Caution

One cannot construct a life philosophy by reading one book, or by participating in a stimulating discussion, or in some other singular fashion. Although every long journey begins with a single step, its successful completion requires repeated effort, patience and persistence. Also, be cautious about placing your trust in a single guru or a single viewpoint from this book. There are many false prophets who claim to know the mind of God. Lao Tzu warns us that "Those who say don't know. Those who know don't say." In his book, *If You Meet the Buddha on the Road Kill Him*, Sheldon Kopp advises his readers that the important things that each person must learn no one else can teach. He cautions about placing too much dependence on a therapist, minister, or other expert, pointing out they are also just struggling human beings.

Continue to question, especially after you think you have the answers. Joseph Needleman, one of this book's contributors, makes the following observation:

> Questioning makes one open, makes one sensitive, makes one humble. We don't suffer from our questions, we suffer from our answers. Most of the mischief in the world comes from people with answers, not from people with questions.

Questioning will lead to change. Life is not static. Maps must be continually redrawn. Everyone is confronted with change. Indeed change is the element that makes life at once both difficult and exciting. One must be prepared to constantly revise and update his or her personal map. This is the sixth edition of this book. Watch for a seventh.

What Is Your Current Life Path?

Constructing a Life
PHILOSOPHY

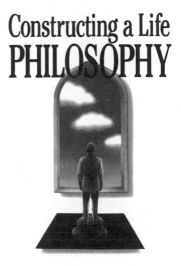

Chapter Preface

In life's continual search for meaning, it is important that you begin your quest with the knowledge of your present situation. Though many of us would like to retreat to the safety of the garden in Genesis, we have no choice but to contend with the conflict and reality we face daily where we live.

The three viewpoints in this chapter use different metaphors, a map, a cave, and a myth, each intended to help the reader explore his or her present life situation. In his books and in the first viewpoint, M. Scott Peck makes the point that life is difficult and that it takes courage to live successfully. He encourages others to face up to the task of contending with the changes we all face in life by continually revising our life maps. Plato, in his classic cave metaphor, helps the reader realize we all live in our personal caves. Each of us is fettered by our past, our present mindset, and many other factors that have shaped us. In the chapter's last viewpoint, Sam Keen maintains that everyone has a personal myth or story that provides life's meaning and purpose. One of life's challenges, he believes, is to discover this myth and to become its conscious director.

When Adam and Eve were expelled from the Garden of Eden, they were forced to face the unending challenges of life with which we are all very familiar. But more devastating than their new task of tilling the earth, they were now prevented from eating again from the tree of knowledge. This metaphor conveys an important message. The acquisition of knowledge, like life itself, is difficult and requires effort, and the most difficult knowledge of all to acquire is self-knowledge. The purpose of this chapter is to help you gain some understanding of where you are in your quest for self-knowledge.

"Our view of reality is like a map with which to negotiate the terrain of life. If the map is true and accurate, we will generally know where we are."

Choosing a Map for Life

M. Scott Peck

Since his resignation in 1972 as assistant chief of psychiatry and neurology consultant to the surgeon general of the U.S. Army, M. Scott Peck has practiced psychiatry. He is a prominent figure in the current movement toward the integration of psychology and spirituality. In the following viewpoint, Peck suggests that the actions of individuals are generally consistent with their world views. Because life's circumstances are constantly changing, we must all remain open to the challenge of revising our perceptions of reality. He points out that personal growth, like all change, can only be accomplished with honesty, courage, and dedication to truth.

As you read, consider the following questions:

1. How does the author describe the term "transference," and how does he relate it to his concept of one's perception of reality resembling a map?
2. How is Peck's description of transference similar to the situation experienced by Plato's cave dwellers in the following viewpoint?

From M. Scott Peck, *The Road Less Traveled*. Copyright © 1978 by M. Scott Peck, M.D. Reprinted by permission of Simon & Schuster, Inc.

Truth is reality. That which is false is unreal. The more clearly we see the reality of the world, the better equipped we are to deal with the world. The less clearly we see the reality of the world—the more our minds are befuddled by falsehood, misperceptions and illusions—the less able we will be to determine correct courses of action and make wise decisions.

Map of Life

Our view of reality is like a map with which to negotiate the terrain of life. If the map is true and accurate, we will generally know where we are, and if we have decided where we want to go, we will generally know how to get there. If the map is false and inaccurate, we generally will be lost.

While this is obvious, it is something that most people to a greater or lesser degree choose to ignore. They ignore it because our route to reality is not easy. First of all, we are not born with maps; we have to make them, and the making requires effort. The more effort we make to appreciate and perceive reality, the larger and more accurate our maps will be. But many do not want to make this effort. Some stop making it by the end of adolescence. Their maps are small and sketchy, their views of the world narrow and misleading. By the end of middle age most people have given up the effort. They feel certain that their maps are complete and their Weltanschauung is correct (indeed, even sacrosanct), and they are no longer interested in new information. It is as if they are tired. Only a relative and fortunate few continue until the moment of death exploring the mystery of reality, ever enlarging and refining and redefining their understanding of the world and what is true.

Revising Life's Map

But the biggest problem of map-making is not that we have to start from scratch, but that if our maps are to be accurate we have to continually revise them. The world itself is constantly changing. Glaciers come, glaciers go. Cultures come, cultures go. There is too little technology, there is too much technology. Even more dramatically, the vantage point from which we view the world is constantly and quite rapidly changing. When we are children we are dependent, powerless. As adults we may be powerful. Yet in illness or an infirm old age we may become powerless and dependent again. When we have children to care for, the world looks different from when we have none; when we are raising infants, the world seems different from when we are raising adolescents. When we are poor, the world looks different from when we are rich. We are daily bombarded with new information as to the nature of reality. If we are to incorporate this information, we must continually revise our maps, and sometimes when enough new information has accumulated, we must make very major revisions. The process of making revisions, particularly major revisions, is painful, sometimes excruciatingly painful. And herein lies the major source of many of the ills of mankind.

What happens when one has striven long and hard to develop a working view of the world, a seemingly useful, workable map, and then is confronted with new information suggesting that that view is wrong and the map needs to be largely redrawn? The painful effort required seems frightening, almost overwhelming. What we do more often than not, and usually unconsciously, is to ignore the new information. Often this act of ignoring is much more than passive. We may denounce the new information as false, dangerous, heretical, the work of the devil. We may actually crusade against it, and even attempt to manipulate the world so as to make it conform to our view of reality. Rather than try to change the map, an individual may try to destroy the new reality. Sadly, such a person may expend much more energy ultimately in defending an outmoded view of the world than would have been required to revise and correct it in the first place.

This process of active clinging to an outmoded view of reality is the basis for much mental illness. Psychiatrists refer to it as transference. There are probably as many subtle variations of the definition of transference as there are psychiatrists. My own definition is: Transference is that set of ways of perceiving and responding to the world which is developed in childhood and which is usually entirely appropriate to the childhood environment (indeed, often life-saving) but which is *inappropriately* transferred into the adult environment.

Examples of Transference

The ways in which transference manifests itself, while always pervasive and destructive, are often subtle. Yet the clearest examples must be unsubtle. One such example was a patient whose treatment failed by virtue of his transference. He was a brilliant but unsuccessful computer technician in his early thirties, who came to see me because his wife had left him, taking their two children. He was not particularly unhappy to lose her, but he was devastated by the loss of his children, to whom he was deeply attached. It was in the hope of regaining them that he initiated psychotherapy, since his wife firmly stated she would never return to him unless he had psychiatric treatment. Her principal complaints about him were that he was continually and irrationally jealous of her, and yet at the same time aloof from her, cold, distant, uncommunicative and unaffectionate. She also complained of his frequent changes of employment. His life since adolescence had been markedly unstable. During adolescence he was involved in frequent minor altercations with the police, and had been jailed three times for intoxication, belligerence, "loitering," and "interfering with the duties of an officer." He dropped out of college, where he was studying electrical engineering, because, as he said, "My teachers were a bunch of hypocrites, hardly different from the police." Because of his brilliance and creativeness in the field of computer technology, his services were in high demand by industry. But he had never been able to advance or keep a job for more than a year and a half, occasionally being fired, more often quitting after disputes with his supervisors, whom he described as "liars and cheats, interested only in protecting their own ass." His most frequent expression was "You can't trust a goddam soul." He described his childhood as "normal" and his parents as "average." In the brief period of time he spent with me, however, he casually and unemotionally recounted numerous instances during childhood in which his parents had let him down. They promised him a bike for his birthday, but they forgot about it and gave him something else. Once they forgot his birthday entirely, but he saw nothing drastically wrong with this since "they were very busy." They would promise to do things with him on weekends, but then were usually "too busy." Numerous times they forgot to pick him up from meetings or parties because "they had a lot on their minds."

What happened to this man was that when he was a young child he suffered painful disappointment after painful disappointment through his parents' lack of caring. Gradually or suddenly—I don't know which—he came to the agonizing realization in mid-childhood that he could not trust his parents. Once he realized this, however, he began to feel better, and his life became more comfortable. He no longer expected things from his parents or got his hopes up when they made promises. When he stopped trusting his parents the frequency and severity of his disappointments diminished dramatically.

Beetle Bailey/By Mort Walker

Reprinted with special permission of King Features Syndicate.

Such an adjustment, however, is the basis for future problems. To a child his or her parents are everything; they represent the world. The child does not have the perspective to see that other parents are different and frequently better. He assumes that the way his parents do things is the way that things are done. Consequently the realization—the "reality"—that this child came to was not "I can't trust my parents" but "I can't trust people." Not trusting people therefore became the map with which he entered adolescence and adulthood. With this map and with an abundant store of resentment resulting from his many disappointments, it was inevitable that he came into conflict with authority figures—police, teacher, employers. And these conflicts only served to reinforce his feeling that people who had anything to give him in the world couldn't be trusted. He had many opportunities to revise his map, but they were all passed up. For one thing, the only way he could learn that there were some people in the adult world he could trust would be to risk trusting them, and that would require a deviation from his map to begin with. For another, such relearning would require him to revise his view of his parents—to realize that they did not love him, that he did not have a normal childhood and that his parents were not average in their callousness to his needs. Such a realization would have been extremely painful. Finally, because his distrust of people was a realistic adjustment to the reality of his childhood, it was an adjustment that worked in terms of diminishing his pain and suffering. Since it is extremely difficult to give up an adjustment that once worked so well, he continued his course of distrust, unconsciously creating situations that served to reinforce it, alienating himself from everyone, making it impossible for himself to enjoy love, warmth, intimacy and affection. He could not even allow himself closeness with his wife; she, too, could not be trusted. The only people he could relate with intimately were his two children. They were the only ones over whom he had control, the only ones who had no authority over him, the only ones he could trust in the whole world.

When problems of transference are involved, as they usually are, psychotherapy is, among other things, a process of map-revising. Patients come to therapy because their maps are clearly not working. But how they may cling to them and fight the process every step of the way! Frequently their need to cling to their maps and fight against losing them is so great that therapy becomes impossible. . . .

Truth Can Overcome Transference

The problem of transference is not simply a problem between parents and children, husbands and wives, employers and employees, between friends, between groups, and even between nations. It is interesting to speculate, for instance, on the role that transference issues play in international affairs. Our national leaders are human beings who all had childhoods and childhood experiences that shaped them. What map was Hitler following, and where did it come from? What map were American leaders following in initiating, executing and maintaining the war in Vietnam? Clearly it was a map very different from that of the generation that succeeded theirs. In what ways did the national experience of the Depression years contribute to their map, and the experience of the fifties and sixties contribute to the map of the younger generation? If the national experience of the thirties and forties contributed to the behavior of American leaders in waging war in Vietnam, how appropriate was that experience to the realities of the sixties and seventies? How can we revise our maps more rapidly?

Truth or reality is avoided when it is painful. We can revise our maps only when we have the discipline to overcome that pain. To have such discipline, we must be totally dedicated to truth. That is to say that we must always hold truth, as best we can determine it, to be more important, more vital to our self-interest, than our comfort. Conversely, we must always consider our personal discomfort relatively unimportant and, indeed, even welcome it in the service of the search for truth. Mental health is an ongoing process of dedication to reality at all costs.

What does a life of total dedication to the truth mean? It means, first of all, a life of continuous and never-ending stringent self-examination. We know the world only through our relationship to it. Therefore, to know the world, we must not only examine it but we must simultaneously examine the examiner. . . .

Examination of the world without is never as personally painful as examination of the world within, and it is certainly because of the pain involved in a life of genuine self-examination that the majority steer away from it. Yet when one is dedicated to the truth this pain seems relatively unimportant—and less and less important (and therefore less and less painful) the farther one proceeds on the path of self-examination.

Beetle Bailey/By Mort Walker

Reprinted with special permission of King Features Syndicate.

A life of total dedication to the truth also means a life of willingness to be personally challenged. The only way that we can be certain that our map of reality is valid is to expose it to the criticism and challenge of other map-makers. Otherwise we live in a closed system—within a bell jar, to use Sylvia Plath's analogy, rebreathing only our own fetid air, more and more subject to delusion. Yet, because of the pain inherent in the process of revising our map of reality, we mostly seek to avoid or ward off any challenges to its validity. To our children we say, "Don't talk back to me, I'm your parent." To our spouse we give the message, "Let's live and let live. If you criticize me, I'll be a bitch to live with, and you'll regret it." To their families and the world the elderly give the message, "I am old and fragile. If you challenge me I may die or at least you will bear upon your head the responsibility for making my last days on earth miserable." To our employees we communicate, "If you are bold enough to challenge me at all, you had best do so very circumspectly indeed or else you'll find yourself looking for another job."

The tendency to avoid challenge is so omnipresent in human

beings that it can properly be considered a characteristic of human nature. But calling it natural does not mean it is essential or beneficial or unchangeable behavior. It is also natural to defecate in our pants and never brush our teeth. Yet we teach ourselves to do the unnatural until the unnatural becomes itself second nature. Indeed, all self-discipline might be defined as teaching ourselves to do the unnatural. . . .

For individuals and organizations to be open to challenge, it is necessary that their maps of reality be *truly* open for inspection. . . . It means a continuous and never-ending process of self-monitoring to assure that our communications—not only the words that we say but also the way we say them—invariably reflect as accurately as humanly possible the truth or reality as we know it.

It Takes Courage to Live

I believe it takes courage to live. In action, this means I surrender myself to life. To try to control your life is the coward's way out. It means there are no adventures, surprises, or magical turning points.

Rita Mae Brown, *Free Inquiry*, Summer 1987.

Such honesty does not come painlessly. The reason people lie is to avoid the pain of challenge and its consequences. . . .

We lie, of course, not only to others but also to ourselves. The challenges to our adjustment—our maps—from our own consciences and our own realistic perceptions may be every bit as legitimate and painful as any challenge from the public . . . which is why most people opt for a life of very limited honesty and openness and relative closedness, hiding themselves and their maps from the world. It is easier that way. Yet the rewards of the difficult life of honesty and dedication to the truth are more than commensurate with the demands. By virtue of the fact that their maps are continually being challenged, open people are continually growing people.

"Imagine mankind as dwelling in an underground cave."

Living in a Cave

Plato

Plato, the great pupil of Socrates, lived in Athens from 427-347 B.C. This viewpoint is taken from *The Republic*, in which he uses Socrates as a spokesman. In the preceding viewpoint, M. Scott Peck discusses the relationship of change to human growth and the necessity of courage and dedication to truth in becoming fully human. In the following viewpoint, Plato illustrates the difficulty of change. With his unique story of life in an underground cave, he illustrates people's predisposition to accept things as they find them and to resist change and growth.

As you read, consider the following questions:

1. Plato suggests that we are all prisoners of some sort. What imprisons us? What imprisons you?
2. Plato claims it is often easier to live with falsehoods than with truth. What example does he use to illustrate this? Can you think of an example from your life experience?
3. How does Plato show that ignorance or prejudice predisposes one to reject reality? Can you think of an example in contemporary society? In your life?

From Eric H. Warmington and Philip G. Rouse, eds., *The Great Dialogues of Plato*, W.H.D. Rouse, trans. Copyright © 1956, 1961 by John Clive Graves Rouse. Reprinted by arrangement with The New American Library, Inc., New York.

"Next, then," I said, "take the following parable of education and ignorance as a picture of the condition of our nature. Imagine mankind as dwelling in an underground cave with a long entrance open to the light across the whole width of the cave; in this they have been from childhood, with necks and legs fettered, so they have to stay where they are. They cannot move their heads round because of the fetters, and they can only look forward, but light comes to them from fire burning behind them higher up at a distance. Between the fire and the prisoners is a road above their level, and along it imagine a low wall has been built, as puppet showmen have screens in front of their people over which they work their puppets." "I see," he said.

The Bearers and Things Carried

"See, then, bearers carrying along this wall all sorts of articles which they hold projecting above the wall, statues of men and other living things,[1] made of stone or wood and all kinds of stuff, some of the bearers speaking and some silent, as you might expect."

"What a remarkable image," he said, "and what remarkable prisoners!"

"Just like ourselves," I said. "For, first of all, tell me this: What do you think such people would have seen of themselves and each other except their shadows, which the fire cast on the opposite wall of the cave?"

"I don't see how they could see anything else," said he, "if they were compelled to keep their heads unmoving all their lives!"

"Very well, what of the things being carried along? Would not this be the same?"

"Of course it would."

"Suppose the prisoners were able to talk together, don't you think that when they named the shadows which they saw passing they would believe they were naming things?"[2]

"Necessarily."

"Then if their prison had an echo from the opposite wall, whenever one of the passing bearers uttered a sound, would they not suppose that the passing shadow must be making the sound? Don't you think so?"

"Indeed I do," he said.

"If so," said I, "such persons would certainly believe that there were no realities except those shadows of handmade things."[3]

"So it must be," said he.

Removal of the Fetters

"Now consider," said I, "what their release would be like, and their cure from these fetters and their folly; let us imagine whether it might naturally be something like this. One might be released, and compelled suddenly to stand up and turn his neck round, and to walk and look towards the firelight; all this would hurt him, and he would be too much dazzled to see distinctly those things whose shadows he had seen before. What do you think he would say, if someone told him that what he saw before was foolery, but now he saw more rightly, being a bit nearer reality, and turned towards what was a little more real? What if he were shown each of the passing things, and compelled by questions to answer what each one was? Don't you think he would be puzzled, and believe what he saw before was more true than what was shown to him now?"

"Far more," he said.

"Then suppose he were compelled to look towards the real light, it would hurt his eyes, and he would escape by turning them away to the things which he was able to look at, and these he would believe to be clearer than what was being shown to him."

"Just so," said he.

Leaving the Cave

"Suppose, now," said I, "that someone should drag him thence by force, up the rough ascent, the steep way up, and never stop until he could drag him out into the light of the sun, would he not be distressed and furious at being dragged; and when he came into the light, the brilliance would fill his eyes and he would not be able to see even one of the things now called real?"[4]

"That he would not," said he, "all of a sudden."

The Cave

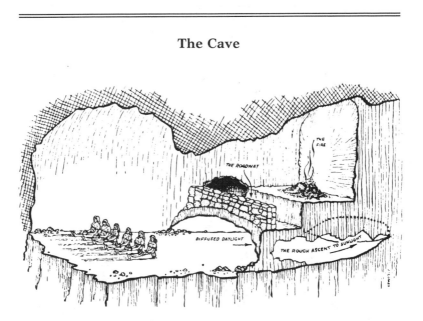

Source: *The Great Dialogues of Plato*, Warmington and Rouse, eds.

"He would have to get used to it, surely, I think, if he is to see the things above. First he would most easily look at shadows, after that images of mankind and the rest in water, lastly the things themselves. After this he would find it easier to survey by night the heavens themselves and all that is in them, gazing at the light of the stars and moon, rather than by day the sun and the sun's light."

"Of course."

"Last of all, I suppose, the sun; he could look on the sun itself by itself in its own place, and see what it is like, not reflections of it in water or as it appears in some alien setting."

"Necessarily," said he.

"And only after all this he might reason about it, how this is he who provides seasons and years, and is set over all there is in the visible region, and he is in a manner the cause of all things which they saw."

"Yes, it is clear," said he, "that after all that, he would come to this last."

"Very good. Let him be reminded of his first habitation, and what was wisdom in that place, and of his fellow-prisoners there; don't you think he would bless himself for the change, and pity them?"

"Yes, indeed."

"And if there were honours and praises among them and prizes for the one who saw the passing things most sharply and remembered best which of them used to come before and which after and which together, and from these was best able to prophesy accordingly what was going to come—do you believe he would set his desire on that, and envy those who were honoured men or potentates among them? Would he not feel as Homer says,[5] and heartily desire rather to be serf of some landless man on earth and to endure anything in the world, rather than to opine as they did and to live in that way?"

"Yes, indeed," said he, "he would rather accept anything than live like that."

Returning to the Cave

"Then again," I said, "just consider; if such a one should go down again and sit on his old seat, would he not get his eyes full of darkness coming in suddenly out of the sun?"

"Very much so," said he.

"And if he should have to compete with those who had been always prisoners, by laying down the law about those shadows while he was blinking before his eyes were settled down—and it would take a good long time to get used to things—wouldn't they all laugh at him and say he had spoiled his eyesight by going up there, and it was not worthwhile so much as to try to go up? And would they not kill anyone who tried to release them and take them up, if they could somehow lay hands on him and kill him?"[6]

"That they would!" said he.

Conclusion

"Then we must apply this image, my dear Glaucon," said I, "to all we have been saying. The world of our sight is like the habitation in prison, the firelight there to the sunlight here, the ascent and the view of the upper world is the rising of the soul into the world of mind; put it so and you will not be far from my own surmise, since that is what you want to hear; but God knows if it is really true. At least, what appears to me is, that in the world of known, last of all,[7] is the idea of the good, and with what toil to be seen! And seen, this must be inferred to be the cause of all right and beautiful things for all, which gives birth to light and the king of light in the world of sight, and, in the world of mind, herself the queen produces truth and reason; and she must be seen by one who is to act with reason publicly or privately."

1. Including models of trees, etc.
2. Which they had never seen. They would say "tree" when it was only a shadow of the model of a tree.
3. Shadows of artificial things, not even the shadow of a growing tree: another stage from reality.
4. To the next stage of knowledge: the real thing, not the artificial puppet.
5. *Odyssey* xi.
6. Plato probably alludes to the death of Socrates. See *Apology*.
7. The end of our search.

"We gain personal authority and power in the measure that we . . . discover and create a personal myth that illuminates and informs us."

Discovering Your Personal Myth

Sam Keen

Sam Keen, a colleague of the mythologist Joseph Campbell, has studied how the world's mythologies affect our daily lives. His book *The Faces of the Enemy* probes the images we create of our enemies—personal or global—and the serious implications these images have on our daily behavior. The following viewpoint is from his book *Your Mythic Journey*, a book for individuals to detect a story line (myth) that Keen believes gives life meaning and purpose. An individual's customs, traditions, and philosophies all combine to form that individual's understanding of life. Keen concludes that everyone's personal growth and maturity is attained by discovering this myth and becoming its conscious director.

As you read, consider the following questions:

1. What is Keen's definition of a myth?
2. In the author's opinion, what is a literalist?
3. Why does the author claim that it is important for individuals to continually revise their personal myths?
4. How does your myth differ from the fettered captives in Plato's cave in the preceding viewpoint? How is it similar?

Reprinted by permission of The Putnam Publishing Group from *Your Mythic Journey* by Sam Keen and Anne Valley-Fox. Copyright © 1973 by Sam Keen and Anne Valley-Fox.

It seems that Americans are finally taking seriously what Carl Jung, this Swiss psychologist, said is the most important question we can ask ourselves: "What myth are we living?". . .

What Is a Myth?

What is a myth? Few words have been subject to as much abuse and been as ill-defined as *myth*. Journalists usually use it to mean a "lie," "fabrication," "illusion," "mistake," or something similar. It is the opposite of what is supposedly a "fact," of what is "objectively" the case, and of what is "reality." In this usage myth is at best a silly story and at worst a cynical untruth. Theologians and propagandists often use myth as a way of characterizing religious beliefs and ideologies other than their own.

Such trivialization of the notion of myth reflects false certainties of dogmatic minds, an ignorance of the mythic assumptions that underlie the commonly accepted view of "reality," and a refusal to consider how much our individual and communal lives are shaped by dramatic scenarios and "historical" narratives that are replete with accounts of the struggle between good and evil empires: our godly heroes versus the demonic enemy.

In a strict sense *myth* refers to "an intricate set of interlocking stories, rituals, rites, and customs that inform and give the pivotal sense of meaning and direction to a person, family, community, or culture." A living myth, like an iceberg, is 10 percent visible and 90 percent beneath the surface of consciousness. While it involves a conscious celebration of certain values, which are always personified in a pantheon of heroes (from the wily Ulysses to the managing Lee Iacocca) and villains (from the betraying Judas to the barbarous Moammar Kadafi), it also includes the unspoken consensus, the habitual way of seeing things, the unquestioned assumptions, the automatic stance. It is differing cultural myths that make cows sacred objects for Hindus and hamburgers meals for Methodists, or turn dogs into pets for Americans and roasted delicacies for the Chinese.

People's Myths Are Primarily Unconscious

At least 51 percent of the people in a society are not self-consciously aware of the myth that informs their existence. Cultural consensus is created by an unconscious conspiracy to consider the myth "the truth," "the way things *really* are." In other words, a majority is made up of literalists, men and women who are not critical or reflective about the guiding "truths"—myths—of their own group. To a tourist in a strange land, an anthropologist studying a tribe, or a psychologist observing a patient, the myth is obvious. But to the person who lives within the mythic horizon, it is nearly invisible.

For instance, most Americans would consider potlatch feasts, in which Northwest Indian tribes systematically destroy their

31

wealth, to be irrational and mythic but would consider the habit of browsing in malls and buying expensive things we do not need (conspicuous consumption) to be a perfectly reasonable way to spend a Saturday afternoon. To most Americans the Moslem notion of *jihad*—holy war—is a dangerous myth. But our struggle against "atheistic communism" is a righteous duty. Ask a born-again Christian about the myth of the atonement, and you will be told it is no myth at all but a revealed truth. Ask a true believer of Marxism about the myth of the withering away of the state, and you will get a long explanation about the "scientific" laws of the dialectic of history.

What Is a Myth?

I use myth to mean the systematic, unconscious way of structuring reality that governs a culture as a whole, or a people, or a tribe. It can govern a corporation, a family, or a person. It's the underlying story.

Sam Keen in *A World of Ideas II*, 1990.

I suggest two analogies that may help to counteract the popular trivialized notion of myth. The dominant myth that informs a person or a culture is like the "information" contained in DNA or the program in the systems disk of a computer. Myth is the software, the cultural DNA, the unconscious information, the metaprogram that governs the way we see "reality" and the way we behave.

Myths Can Be Creative or Destructive

The organizing myth of any culture functions in ways that may be either creative or destructive, healthful or pathological. By providing a world picture and a set of stories that explain why things are as they are, it creates consensus, sanctifies the social order, and gives the individual an authorized map of the path of life. A myth creates the plotline that organizes the diverse experiences of a person or a community into a single story.

But in the same measure that myth gives us security and identity, it also creates selective blindness, narrowness, and rigidity because it is intrinsically conservative. It encourages us to follow the faith of our fathers, to hold to the time-honored truths, to imitate the way of the heroes, to repeat the formulas and rituals in exactly the same way they were done in the good old days. As long as no radical change is necessary for survival, the status quo remains sacred, the myth and ritual are unquestioned, and the patterns of life, like the seasons of the year, repeat themselves. But when crisis comes—a natural catastrophe, a military defeat, the introduction of a new technology—the mythic mind is at a loss to deal with novelty. As Marshall McLuhan said, it tries to "walk into the future looking through a rearview mirror."

Families Have Myths

Every family, like a miniculture, also has an elaborate system of stories and rituals that differentiate it from other families. The Murphys, being Irish, understand full well that Uncle Paddy is a bit of a rogue and drinks a tad too much. The Cohens, being Jewish, are haunted each year at Passover when they remember the family that perished in the Holocaust. The Keens, being Calvinists, are predestined to be slightly more righteous and right than others, even when they are wrong. And within the family each member's place is defined by a series of stories. Obedient to the family script, Jane, "who always was very motherly even as a little girl," married young and had children immediately, while Pat, "who was a wild one and not cut out for marriage," sowed oat after oat before finding fertile ground.

The Task of Tasks

I asked myself, "What is the myth you are living?" and found that I did not know. So . . . I took it upon myself to get to know "my" myth, and I regarded this as the task of tasks . . . I simply had to know what unconscious or preconscious myth was forming me.

C.J. Jung in *The Portable Jung*, 1976.

Family myths, like those of the Kennedy clan, may give us an impulse to strive for excellence and a sense of pride that helps us endure hardship and tragedy. Or they may, like the myths of alcoholic or abusive families, pass a burden of guilt, shame, and failure from generation to generation as abused children, in turn, become abusive parents, ad nauseam. The sins, virtues, and myths of the fathers are passed on to the children of future generations.

Every Individual Has a Personal Myth

Finally, the entire legacy and burden of cultural and family myth comes to rest on the individual. Each person is a repository of stories. To the degree that any one of us reaches toward autonomy, we must begin a process of sorting through the trash and treasures we have been given, keeping some and rejecting others. We gain the full dignity and power of our persons only when we create a narrative account of our lives, dramatize our existence, and forge a coherent personal myth that combines elements of our cultural myth and family myth with unique stories that come from our experience. As my friend David Steere once pointed out to me, the common root of "authority" and "authorship" tells us a great deal about power. Whoever authors your story authorizes your actions. We gain personal authority and power in the measure that we question the myth that is upheld by "the authorities" and discover and create a personal myth that illuminates and informs us.

What Do You Believe?

I began to examine my own experience at a very crucial and disturbed period in my life—when my own tenacious clinging to the Christian worldview and the Christian myth began to crumble, when I couldn't believe it anymore—and I had to ask myself the question, well, what do you believe? How do you find any rock upon which to put your feet? For a long time I was at a loss, and suddenly it occurred to me that instead of looking at the answers that myth gave, I could look at the questions. I began to interrogate my own life using those questions. Who are my heroes? Who are my villains? What is my source? Where did I come from? Who are my people? I discovered that I could find within my own autobiography, as it were, a complete but undeveloped mythology. And as I began to look at those stories and recover those stories for myself, I had a mythology that gave me a story by which I lived.

Sam Keen in *A World of Ideas II*, 1990.

What George Santayana said about cultures is equally true for individuals: "Those who do not remember history are condemned to repeat it." If we do not make the effort to become conscious of our personal myths gradually, we become dominated by what psychologists have variously called repetition compulsion, autonomous complexes, engrams, routines, scripts, games. One fruitful way to think of neurosis is to consider it a tape loop, an oft-told story that we repeat in our inner dialogues with ourselves and with others. "Well, I'm just not the kind of person who can . . ." "I never could . . ." "I wouldn't think of . . .". While personal myths give us a sense of identity, continuity, and security, they become constricting and boring if they are not revised from time to time. To remain vibrant throughout a lifetime we must always be inventing ourselves, weaving new themes into our life-narratives, remembering our past, re-visioning our future, reauthorizing the myth by which we live.

Personalizing the Metaphor of Plato's Cave

Imagine that Plato visited you and addressed his metaphor of the cave to you personally. The cave would be a description of your life and world. What insights would the story's telling give you? Understand that a metaphor is a comparison of two dissimilar things for the purpose of conveying a deeper meaning or insight. An example would be to say that a football player "is a tiger." The expression, though not literally true, conveys a more penetrating image of the football player's aggressive style of playing football than by simply saying, "He's an excellent football player."

You know you do not live in a cave. The cave is simply a metaphor for the culture and environment you live in. How can this metaphor give you a more penetrating understanding of the forces that shape and control your life? As you plan your life's journey and mark your map for continuing the trip, you must know your present position. In your life situation, what might the following items symbolize?

If you are doing this exercise as the member of a class or group, compare your conclusions with those of other class or group members.

fetters

bearers

things held up

shadows

naming of objects

guide to the surface

roadway

sunlight

35

What Is Life's Meaning?

Constructing a Life
PHILOSOPHY

Chapter Preface

"I am plagued by doubts. If only God would give me some clear sign! Like making a large deposit in my name in a Swiss bank account."

—Woody Allen

The films of comedian Woody Allen often explore the meaning of life and modern relationships. Although his conclusions may satisfy only a few people, he raises questions that confront us all. This chapter addresses the ultimate question, "What Is Life's Meaning?" Unfortunately, the reader will not be able simply to turn to the chapter's last page to find the answer. If life is difficult, as M. Scott Peck claims in chapter one, the answer to its most challenging question will not come easily.

The seven viewpoints that make up this chapter attempt to answer the question in different ways. It is the reader's task to examine each viewpoint to decide which most closely matches his or her own perspectives. Is Jesus Christ the answer as Billy Graham asserts? Or does life have no purpose as Richard Robinson, the chapter's first spokesperson, states? Does Riane Eisler make the answer clearer by claiming Western civilization must reject the current male-led model and return to the feminine values that guided us in our ancient past? Does human life exist just by chance as George Wald writes? Or is the hand of God somehow involved in human evolution, as Teilhard de Chardin believes? The chapter's last spokesperson, Arnold Toynbee, writes that love, understanding, and creating provide meaning in individual lives. Is his answer the correct one? Or is the pessimism of Woody Allen ultimately the best answer? It is you the reader who must make the final determination.

"The finest achievement for humanity is to recognize our predicament, including our insecurity and our coming extinction, and to maintain our cheerfulness and love and decency in spite of it."

Life Has No Purpose

Richard Robinson

Richard Robinson was born in Watton, Norfolk, England, in 1902. He was educated at Oxford University and taught philosophy at Cornell University from 1928 until 1946. In 1946, he returned to Oxford where he wrote the book from which this viewpoint is taken. He has also authored *Plato's Earlier Dialectic* and *Definition*. In the following viewpoint, Robinson asserts that the atheist's conception of humanity is nobler than the theist's. In his view, life has no purpose or protector, requiring the atheist to live with greater courage than the believer.

As you read, consider the following questions:

1. Why does Robinson claim that people are basically insecure?
2. How does the author suggest that people react to the question of their existence?
3. Why does the author suggest that the atheist's concept of humanity is nobler than the theist's?
4. Why does Robinson suggest that people should love one another?

From Richard Robinson, *An Atheist's Values*. Reprinted with permission of the Clarendon Press, Oxford.

The human situation is this. Each one of us dies. He ceases to pulse or breathe or move or think. He decays and loses his identity. His mind or soul or spirit ends with the ending of his body, because it is entirely dependent on his body.

The human species too will die one day, like all species of life. One day there will be no more men. This is not quite so probable as that each individual man will die; but it is overwhelmingly probable all the same. It seems very unlikely that we could keep the race going forever by hopping from planet to planet as each in turn cooled down. Only in times of extraordinary prosperity like the present could we ever travel to another planet at all.

We are permanently insecure. We are permanently in danger of loss, damage, misery, and death.

There Is No Secret to the Universe

Our insecurity is due partly to our ignorance. There is a vast amount that we do not know, and some of it is very relevant to our survival and happiness. It is not just one important thing that we can ascertain and live securely ever after. That one important thing would then deserve to be called 'the secret of the universe'. But there is no one secret of the universe. On the contrary, there are inexhaustibly many things about the universe that we need to know but do not know. There is no possibility of 'making sense of the universe', if that means discovering one truth about it which explains everything else about it and also explains itself. Our ignorance grows progressively less, at least during periods of enormous prosperity like the present time; but it cannot disappear, and must always leave us liable to unforeseen disasters.

The main cause of our insecurity is the limitedness of our power. What happens to us depends largely on forces we cannot always control. This will remain so throughout the life of our species, although our power will probably greatly increase.

There Is No God

There is no god to make up for the limitations of our power, to rescue us whenever the forces affecting us get beyond our control, or provide us hereafter with an incorruptible haven of absolute security. We have no superhuman father who is perfectly competent and benevolent as we perhaps once supposed our actual father to be.

What attitude ought we to take up, in view of this situation?

It would be senseless to be rebellious, since there is no god to rebel against. It would be wrong to let disappointment or terror or apathy or folly overcome us. It would be wrong to be sad or sarcastic or cynical or indignant. . . .

No; in a dark and cloudy day a book of humour is better than

"The Shropshire Lad"; and one of the important parts of 'training for ill' is to acquire cheerfulness.

Cheerfulness is part of courage, and courage is an essential part of the right attitude. Let us not tell ourselves a comforting tale of a father in heaven because we are afraid to be alone, but bravely and cheerfully face whatever appears to be the truth.

Life's Purpose

It is frequently argued that religion gives men a purpose for living, namely, to please some god and win eternal bliss in heaven. And many men do need some great purpose for which to live. But it would be far more socially beneficial to induce men to accept the promotion of human welfare on earth as their major purpose in life. There is no evidence that any man has ever achieved bliss in heaven, but we can observe innumerable gains in human welfare in all countries. Moreover, men can achieve far greater and more immediate personal satisfaction from success in their efforts to promote human welfare in this world than from any effort to achieve bliss in the next world. And the observation of visible success is bound to strengthen any purpose.

Burnham P. Beckwith, *American Atheist*, March 1986.

The theist sometimes rebukes the pleasure-seeker by saying: *We were not put here to enjoy ourselves; man has a sterner and nobler purpose than that.* The atheist's conception of man is, however, still sterner and nobler than that of the theist. According to the theist we were put here by an all-powerful and all-benevolent god who will give us eternal victory and happiness if we only obey him. According to the atheist our situation is far sterner than that. There is no one to look after us but ourselves, and we shall certainly be defeated.

As our situation is far sterner than the theist dares to think, so our possible attitude towards it is far nobler than he conceives. When we contemplate the friendless position of man in the universe, as it is right sometimes to do, our attitude should be the tragic poet's affirmation of man's ideals of behaviour. Our dignity, and our finest occupation, is to assert and maintain our own self-chosen goods as long as we can, those great goods of beauty and truth and virtue. And among the virtues it is proper to mention in this connection above all the virtues of courage and love. There is no person in this universe to love us except ourselves; therefore let us love one another. The human race is alone; but individual men need not be alone, because we have each other. We are brothers without a father; let us all the more for that behave brotherly to each other. The finest achievement for humanity is to recognize our predicament, including our insecurity and our coming extinction, and to maintain our cheerfulness and love and decency in spite of it. We have good things to contemplate and high things to do. Let us do them.

The Accident of Life

That Man is the product of causes which had no prevision of the end they were achieving; that his origin, his growth, his hopes and fears, his loves and his beliefs, are but the outcome of accidental collocations of atoms; that no fire, no heroism, no intensity of thought and feeling, can preserve an individual life beyond the grave; that all the labours of the ages, all the devotion, all the inspiration, all the noonday brightness of human genius, are destined to extinction in the vast death of the solar system, and that the whole temple of Man's achievement must inevitably be buried beneath the debris of a universe in ruins—all these things, if not quite beyond dispute, are yet so nearly certain, that no philosophy, which rejects them can hope to stand.

Bertrand Russell, *A Free Man's Worship*, 1923.

We need to create and spread symbols and procedures that will confirm our intentions without involving us in intellectual dishonesty. This need is urgent today. For we have as yet no strong ceremonies to confirm our resolves except religious ceremonies, and most of us cannot join in religious ceremonies with a good conscience. When the *Titanic* went down, people sang 'nearer, my God, to thee'. When the Gloucesters were in prison in North Korea they strengthened themselves with religious ceremonies. At present we know no other way to strengthen ourselves in our most testing and tragic times. Yet this way has become dishonest. That is why it is urgent for us to create new ceremonies, through which to find strength without falsehood in these terrible situations. It is not enough to formulate honest and high ideals. We must also create the ceremonies and the atmosphere that will hold them before us at all times. I have no conception how to do this; but I believe it will be done if we try.

"I am telling you that the life in Christ works. I have seen it work all over the world."

Jesus Christ Gives Life Purpose

Billy Graham

Billy Graham is a worldwide symbol of evangelism and has preached the Gospel of Christianity to more millions than anyone in history. He is the founder of the Billy Graham Evangelistic Association and leads the weekly radio program "Hour of Decision," which is broadcast around the world. In a world of human frailty and sin, Graham states that everyone needs commitment to a call or a goal to find fulfillment. For him that commitment has been Jesus Christ. In the following viewpoint, he recommends Jesus to others who are searching for meaning in life.

As you read, consider the following questions:

1. What causes human weakness, in the opinion of the author?
2. Why does Graham place so much emphasis on the cross?
3. Why does the author believe that a personal commitment to Jesus Christ makes sense?

From *The Gateway to Truth,* © 1962 by The Billy Graham Evangelistic Association. Reprinted with permission.

An outstanding mathematician visited me recently and said, "If anyone had told me five years ago that I would be coming to see you, I would have laughed. But I am at the end of myself, and I am going to commit suicide unless I find an answer to what I am facing."

His problems were neither domestic nor financial nor vocational; they were problems of emptiness that he could not explain. He belonged to the world of misfits, the world of lost people. Ours is an age of philosophical uncertainty, and we no longer know what we believe. We stand uncommitted. I ask students everywhere I go, "What is controlling you?"

Eugene O'Neill in *Long Day's Journey into Night* expresses a philosophical attitude we find so prevalent today. "Life's only meaning," he says, "is death, so face it with courage and even with love of the inevitable. Death becomes a blanket on a cold night." Jean-Paul Sartre, the French existentialist, has said, "there is no exit from the human dilemma."

When we seek to get to the root of our problems, we discover that many writers and thinkers are saying that the problem is man himself. Dr. J.S. Whale asked the undergraduates at Cambridge University, "What is man? Where did he come from? Why is he here? Where is he going? What is the purpose and destiny of the human race?" Dr. John A. Mackay told the students at Princeton, "The anthropological problem is the crucial problem of our generation."

The Flaw in Human Nature

There are psychologists and psychiatrists who are beginning to admit that something is basically wrong with human nature. Some say it is a shadow cast by man's immaturity; others describe it as a deficiency determined by heredity and environment; still others call it a constitutional weakness. *It is time to ask what the Bible has to say*—this old book that some have dismissed by saying it is irrelevant in the twentieth century.

The Bible calls the trouble inside of man by an ugly word. We don't like this old word—we prefer the new jargon—but I am going to use the old word. The Bible calls it sin. It tells us that man's soul has a disease. You ask me where sin comes from and I cannot tell you; I do not know. The Bible speaks of it as "the mystery of iniquity." God has not seen fit to reveal to us the origin of this tragic disease that has gripped the entire human race.

Suppose I visit the Auca Indians in Ecuador, as I did a few years ago. There I find people living in the Stone Age. I see them lying, cheating, hating, killing. War has almost completely annihilated the various tribes of the Auca Indians. I say to myself, "What these people need is education, economic security, better food, better clothes." It is true that they need them all. But when I come to

New York, and Paris, and London, and Moscow, what do I find? People who have all of these advantages, and who are still lying, hating, cheating and killing. The most devastating wars of history have been fought by the so-called civilized countries.

The Reality of Sin

How can a country like Germany produce in one generation an Albert Schweitzer and an Adolf Eichmann? Something is basically wrong. How could Joseph Goebbels, who secured his doctor's degree at Heidelberg University, become the man he was?

Many words in the Bible are translated "sin." A transgression of the law is sin. To miss the mark is sin. Isaiah the prophet declared, "Your iniquities have separated between you and your God, and your sins have hid his face from you, that he will not hear" (Isaiah 59:2). Jesus Christ charged the Pharisees with leaving undone the things they ought to have done, and He said, "Whosoever committeth sin is the servant of sin" (John 8:34). This thing affects the mind, it affects the conscience. It affects the will, it causes conflict with others. Sin controls the ego, which is self. Christ said we are to love God first and self last, but sin has reversed that.

Jesus Is God Made Flesh

The Bible teaches that God is actually three Persons. This is a mystery that we will never be able to understand. The Bible does not teach that there are three Gods—but that there is one God. This one God, however, is expressed in three Persons. There is God the Father, God the Son, and God the Holy Spirit.

The Second Person of this Trinity is God's Son, Jesus Christ. He is co-equal with God the Father. He was not *a* Son of God but *the* Son of God. He is the Eternal Son of God—the Second Person of the Holy Trinity, God manifested in the flesh, the living Savior.

Billy Graham, *Peace With God,* 1984.

Archbishop William Temple once said, "Sin makes 'me' the center of the world." We become selfish as individuals, as a nation, as a society. Sin, the Bible says, eventually brings judgment— "The wages of sin is death." It creates its own hell on this earth as well as in the life to come. For you see, you and I were made for God, and without God there is always an emptiness and restlessness. We quest and search and try to find fulfillment in life, but we never quite attain it.

I cannot prove to you the existence of God. I see evidences of God, and something down inside me tells me that there must be a God. Furthermore, I have never found a tribe that didn't believe in a god of some sort. If we don't have a God we make a god; anything that is higher than ourselves becomes a god. But the Bible indicates not only that there is a God, but that He took the initiative; that the mighty God of all the universe has spoken and has revealed Himself in a person, and that that person is Jesus Christ.

Why does the church put so much emphasis on the Cross? Because the Cross is the heart of Christianity. On that Cross in some mysterious way Christ died for us. God took our sins, our breaking of the law that caused us to deserve death and judgment, and He laid our sins on Christ. As the Scripture says, He was made sin for us (2 Corinthians 5:21).

When I was a student I had to face Christ. Who was He? He had made the astounding claim, "I am the way, the truth, and the life; no man cometh unto the Father but by me." I wrestled with the inescapable fact that either Jesus Christ was who He claimed to be, or He was the biggest liar, fraud and charlatan in history. Which was it? Buddha said toward the end of his life, "I am still searching for the truth." But here was a man who appeared and said, "I am the embodiment of all truth. All truth is centered in me."

One day by a simple act of faith I decided to take Jesus Christ at His word. I could not come by way of the intellect alone; no one can. That does not mean that we reject reason. God has given us minds and the ability to reason wherever reason is appropriate, but the final and decisive step is taken by faith. I came by faith.

A few years ago I was invited to lunch by the head of the department of psychology at an eastern university. He remarked to me, "We have come to believe that man is so constituted psychologically that he needs converting, especially in later adolescence. In order to find fulfillment, young people need converting." In the *New York Times* a professional psychiatrist wrote, "Unless the church gets back to converting the people, we psychiatrists are going to have to do it."

My Commitment to Jesus Christ

What Jesus Christ said about conversion was not only theologically true, it was also psychologically sound. Man does need commitment to a call, to a goal, to a flag. Does it work when a man comes, repenting of his sins, to receive Christ by faith? I can only tell you that it worked in my own life. Something did happen to me. I didn't become perfect, but the direction of my life was changed.

I was reared on a farm in North Carolina, and did not have the best of education. During the depression period my parents were unable to give me the advantages that youth has today. I grew up in a Christian home, but by the time I was 15, I was in full revolt against all religion—against God, the Bible, the church. To make a long story short, one day I decided to commit my life to Jesus Christ. Not to be a clergyman but, in whatever I was to be, to seek the Kingdom of God first.

As a result, I found a new dimension to life. I found a new capacity to love that I had never known before. Just in the matter of race, my attitude toward people of other backgrounds changed remarkably. All of our difficulties are not solved the moment we are converted to Christ, but conversion does mean that we can approach our problems with a new attitude and in a new strength.

Commitment to Christ Works

I was a poor student until that time, but immediately my grades picked up. I am not suggesting that you should come to Christ in order to get better grades, but I am telling you that the life in Christ works. I have seen it work all over the world. I have seen those converted whom I might classify as intellectuals; but they have to come as children. We say to our children, "Act like grown-ups," but Jesus said to the grown-ups, "Be like children." You are not to come to the Cross as a doctor of philosophy, or as a doctor of law, but simply as a human being; and your life can be changed.

The Cross of Christ

In the cross of Christ I see three things: First, a description of the depth of *man's sin*. Do not blame the people of that day for hanging Christ on the cross. You and I are just as guilty. It was not the people or the Roman soldiers who put Him to the cross—it was your sins and my sins that made it necessary for Him to volunteer this death.

Second, in the cross I see the overwhelming *love of God*. If ever you should doubt the love of God, take a long, deep look at the cross, for in the cross you find the expression of God's love.

Third, in the cross is the only *way of salvation*. Jesus said, "I am the way, the truth and the life: no man cometh unto the Father but by me" (John 14:6). There is no possibility of being saved from sin and hell, except by identifying yourself with the Christ of the cross.

Billy Graham, *Peace With God*, 1984.

You ask, "Does it take with everybody?" Yes, with everyone who is willing to believe. I don't find that anyone is excluded. I have become confirmed in my belief that the Bible is right in saying that God has fashioned the hearts of men alike. We are not together in today's world linguistically, culturally or racially. We are divided. We have become a neighborhood without being a brotherhood. Yet there is one area in which I am convinced we are all alike—the spiritual dimension. I believe the hearts of all of us are the same. Our deep needs are identical the world over, for they come from within. Our need is God.

Probably it sounds a bit intolerant and narrow to you for an evangelist to go around the planet preaching the Cross—and you are right; for Jesus said that the gate to the Kingdom of Heaven is narrow. But we are narrow also in mathematics and in chemistry. If we weren't narrow in chemistry we would be blowing the place up. We have to be narrow. I am glad that pilots are not so broad-minded that they come into an airport any way they want.

Why then should we not be narrow when it comes to moral laws and spiritual dimensions? I believe that Christ is different; that He is unique. I believe that He is the Son of the living God and that He did change my life.

The Kingdom of God

Many intellectuals are asking where history is going; they are speculating on what the end will be. I believe that Christ's prayer, "Thy kingdom come. Thy will be done in earth, as it is in heaven"—the prayer that you and I often pray—is going to be answered. And when the human race stands at the edge of the abyss, ready to blow itself apart, I believe God will intervene in history again. I don't believe any world leader will write the last chapter of history. I believe God will write it. I believe that the future kingdom is going to be the Kingdom of God, that there is a destiny for the human race far beyond anything we can dream. But it will be God's kingdom and will come in God's way.

Meanwhile He is calling people from all walks of life to follow His Son, Jesus Christ. I know that those who respond are a minority, but Christ used a minority while He was on earth. When He died on the Cross only 120 of His followers could be mustered. Yet within a short time, according to the testimony of the people of that day, they had "turned the world upside down."

In Moscow some years ago I saw 50,000 students gathered in Red Square, stamping their feet and chanting, "We're going to change the world. We're going to change the world!" I thought to myself, what if we could get students in the United States and all around the world, including the Soviet Union and China, to march under the banner of Christ? Why couldn't we be a dedicated minority, committed to Jesus Christ, with love in our hearts and with His flag to follow? I am asking this of students everywhere I go.

I believe that if we can light a few torches here and there on campuses on every continent, we might have a spiritual revolution that would really change the world. Here, in this dimension, lies our hope for humanity. We can argue and debate the old philosophical problems from now on, and die without committing ourselves to anything; or we can march in the army of Jesus Christ. Which will it be?

"Let us reaffirm our ancient covenant, our sacred bond with our Mother, the Goddess of nature and spirituality."

Ecofeminism Can Give Life Purpose

Riane Eisler

Riane Eisler is the author of the international bestseller *The Chalice and the Blade* and the co-founder of the Center for Partnership Studies, a research and educational center in Pacific Grove, California. In her book, Eisler reinterprets ancient history and modern archaeological findings to claim evidence for a life-style based on ecofeminism, a philosophy in which people live in sexual and social equality in harmony with nature. She calls this life-style "a partnership way." In the following viewpoint, Eisler issues a manifesto, rejecting what she calls the current patriarchal and male-dominated society that now exists and calling for a return to the ecofeminist traditions of the past.

As you read, consider the following questions:

1. What is the Gaia hypothesis, according to Eisler?
2. How does the author distinguish between dominator and partnership societies?
3. What kind of future for humankind does Eisler envision?

From Riane Eisler, "The Gaia Tradition and the Partnership Future: An Ecofeminist Manifesto," in *Reweaving the World*, Irene Diamond and Gloria Feman Orenstein, eds. San Francisco: Sierra Club Books, 1990. Reprinted with permission.

The leading-edge social movements of our time—the peace, feminist, and ecology movements, and ecofeminism, which integrates all three—are in some respects very new. But they also draw from very ancient traditions only now being reclaimed due to what British archaeologist James Mellaart calls a veritable revolution in archaeology.

These traditions go back thousands of years. Scientific archaeological methods are now making it possible to document the way people lived and thought in prehistoric times. One fascinating discovery about our past is that for millennia—a span of time many times longer than the 5,000 years conventionally counted as history—prehistoric societies worshipped the Goddess of nature and spirituality, our great Mother, the giver of life and creator of all. But even more fascinating is that these ancient societies were structured very much like the more peaceful and just society we are now trying to construct.

A Reverence for the Earth

This is not to say that these were ideal societies or utopias. But, unlike our societies, they were *not* warlike. They were *not* societies where women were subordinate to men. And they did *not* see our Earth as an object for exploitation and domination.

In short, they were societies that had what we today call an ecological consciousness: the awareness that the Earth must be treated with reverence and respect. And this reverence for the life-giving and life-sustained powers of the Earth was rooted in a social structure where women and "feminine" values such as caring, compassion, and non-violence were not subordinate to men and the so-called masculine values of conquest and domination. Rather, the life-giving powers incarnated in women's bodies were given the highest social value. . . .

The Gaia Tradition

We now know that there was not one cradle of civilization in Sumer about 3,500 years ago. Rather, there were many cradles of civilization, all of them thousands of years older. And thanks to far more scientific and extensive archaeological excavations, we also know that in these highly creative societies women held important social positions as priestesses, craftspeople, and elders of matrilineal clans. Contrary to what we have been taught of the Neolithic or first agrarian civilizations as male dominated and highly violent, these were generally peaceful societies in which both women and men lived in harmony with one another and nature. Moreover, in all these peaceful cradles of civilization, to borrow Merlin Stone's arresting phrase from the book of the same title, "God was a woman" (New York: Dial Press, 1976).

There is today much talk about the Gaia hypothesis (so called

49

because Gaia is the Greek name for the Earth). This is a new scientific theory proposed by biologists Lynn Margulis and James Lovelock that our planet is a living system designed to maintain and to nurture life. But what is most striking about the Gaia hypothesis is that in essence it is a scientific update of the belief system of Goddess-worshipping prehistoric societies. In these societies the world was viewed as the great Mother, a living entity who in both her temporal and spiritual manifestations creates and nurtures all forms of life. . . .

Dominator and Partnership Societies

Even in the nineteenth century, when archaeology was still in its infancy, scholars found evidence of societies where women were not subordinate to men. But their interpretation of this evidence was that if these societies were not patriarchies, they must have been matriarchies. In other words, if men did not dominate women, then women must have dominated men. However, this conclusion is not borne out by the evidence. Rather, it is a function of what I have called a *dominator* society worldview. The real alternative to patriarchy is not matriarchy, which is only the other side of the dominator coin. The alternative, now revealed to be the original direction of our cultural evolution, is what I call a *partnership* society: a way of organizing human relations in which beginning with the most fundamental difference in our species—the difference between female and male—diversity is *not* equated with inferiority or superiority.

The Goddess Rather than God

I used to think of the divine as "God." Now, if I think in terms of a personalized deity at all, I think more of the Goddess than of the God. I feel very strongly that our society's denial of the feminine aspect of the deity, the Mother aspect, is one of the great obstacles to having that personal relationship, that direct connection with the divine.

Riane Eisler in *For the Love of God*, 1990.

What we have until now been taught as history is only the history of dominator species—the record of the male dominant, authoritarian, and highly violent civilizations that began about 5,000 years ago. For example, the conventional view is that the beginning of European civilization is marked by the emergence in ancient Greece of the Indo-Europeans. But the new archaeological evidence demonstrates that the arrival of the Indo-Europeans actually marks the truncation of European civilization.

That is, as Marija Gimbutas extensively documents, there was in Greece and the Balkans an earlier civilization, which she calls the civilization of Old Europe (*The Goddesses and Gods of Old Europe*, 1982). The first Indo-European invasions (by pastoralists from the arid steppes of the northeast) foreshadow the end of a matrifocal, matrilineal, peaceful agrarian era. Like fingerprints in the archaeological record, we see evidence of how wave after wave of barbarian invaders from the barren fringes of the globe leave in their wake destruction and what archaeologists call cultural impoverishment. And what characterizes these invaders is that they bring with them male dominance along with their angry gods of thunder and war. . . .

The Goddess Was the Source of All Life

We have been taught that in "Western tradition," religion is the spiritual realm and that spirituality is separate from, and superior to, nature. But for our Goddess-worshipping ancestors, spirituality and nature were one. In the religion of Western partnership societies, there was no need for the artificial distinction between spirituality and nature or for the exclusion of half of humanity from spiritual power.

In sharp contrast to "traditional" patriarchal religions (where only men can be priests, rabbis, bishops, lamas, Zen masters, and popes), we know from Minoan, Egyptian, Sumerian, and other ancient records that women were once priestesses. Indeed, the highest religious office appears to have been that of high priestess in service of the Goddess. And the Goddess herself was not only the source of all life and nature; she was also the font of spirituality, mercy, wisdom, and justice. For example, as the Sumerian Goddess Nanshe, she sought justice for the poor and shelter for the weak. The Egyptian Goddess Maat was also the goddess of justice. The Greek Goddess Demeter was known as the lawgiver, the bringer of civilization, dispensing mercy and justice. As the Celtic Goddess Cerridwen, she was the goddess of intelligence and knowledge. And it is Gaia, the primeval prophetess of the shrine of Delphi, who in Greek mythology is said to have given the golden apple tree (the tree of knowledge) to her daughter, the Goddess Hera. Moreover, the Greek Fates, the enforcers of laws, are female. And so also are the Greek Muses, who inspire all creative endeavor. . . .

We also know from a number of contemporary tribal societies that the separation between nature and spirituality is not universal. Tribal peoples generally think of nature in spiritual terms. Nature spirits must be respected, indeed, revered. And we also know that in many of these tribal societies women as well as men can be shamans or spiritual healers and that descent in these tribes is frequently traced through the mother.

51

In sum, *both* nature and woman can partake of spirituality in societies oriented to a partnership model. In such societies there is no need for a false dichotomy between a "masculine" spirituality and "feminine" nature. Moreover, since in ancient partnership societies woman and the Goddess were identified with *both* nature and spirituality, neither woman nor nature were devalued and exploited. . . .

We Must Rediscover the Goddess of Spirituality

For many thousands of years, millennia longer than the 5,000 years we count as recorded history, everything was done in a sacred manner. Planting and harvesting fields were rites of spring and autumn celebrated in a ritual way. Baking bread from grains, molding pots out of clay, weaving cloth out of fibers, carving tools out of metals—all these ways of technologically melding culture and nature were sacred ceremonies. There was then no splintering of culture and nature, spirituality, science, and technology. Both our intuition and our reason were applied to the building of civilization, to devising better ways for us to live and work cooperatively.

We Must Reclaim the Great Mother

I believe that the denial of our connection with the Mother aspect, the feminine aspect of the deity, is one of the major obstacles to achieving that meaningful and fulfilling personal relationship not only with the deity but with one another. We all can observe the element of the feminine, of the Mother, of the nurturer, from our experiences of a mother. The Great Mother also has a dark aspect, however: the transformative aspect of reclaiming life at death. But to have been deprived of that motherly dimension in the deity reflects something in our dominator society: a deadening of empathy, a deadening of caring, a denial of the feminine in men, and a contempt for women and the feminine.

Riane Eisler in *For the Love of God*, 1990.

The rediscovery of these traditions signals a way out of our alienation from one another and from nature. In our time, when the nuclear bomb and advanced technology threaten all life on this planet, the reclamation of these traditions can be the basis for the restructuring of society: the completion of the modern transformation from a dominator to a partnership world.

Poised on the brink of ecocatastrophe, let us gain the courage to look at the world anew, to reverse custom, to transcend our limitations, to break free from the conventional constraints, the conventional views of what are knowledge and truth. Let us understand that we cannot graft peace and ecological balance on a dominator system; that a just and egalitarian society is impossible without the full and equal partnership of women and men.

Let us reaffirm our ancient covenant, our sacred bond with our Mother, the Goddess of nature and spirituality. Let us renounce the worship of angry gods wielding thunderbolts or swords. Let us once again honor the chalice, the ancient symbol of the power to create and enhance life—and let us understand that this power is not woman's alone but also man's.

A Renewed Understanding

For ourselves, and for the sake of our children and their children, let us use our human thrust for creation rather than destruction. Let us teach our sons and daughters that men's conquest of nature, of women, and of other men is not a heroic virtue; that we have the knowledge and the capacity to survive; that we need not blindly follow our bloodstained path to planetary death; that we can reawaken from our 5,000-year dominator nightmare and allow our evolution to resume its interrupted course.

While there is still time, let us fulfill our promise. Let us reclaim the trees of knowledge and of life. Let us regain our lost sense of wonder and reverence for the miracles of life and love, let us learn again to live in partnership so we may fulfill our responsibility to ourselves and to our Great Mother, this wondrous planet Earth.

Distinguishing Between Fact and Opinion

B.C./By Johnny Hart

By permission of Johnny Hart and News America Syndicate.

Although the advice of the Great Guru in the cartoon above is not too helpful, it does make a factual statement. Avoidance of death would certainly prolong life.

The purpose of this activity is to aid you in distinguishing between statements that are factual and those that are based on opinion. Consider the following example. "Everyone alive today will eventually experience death." This is a fact which no one will deny. But let us consider a statement which makes a judgment about death. "After death everyone will either be assigned to heaven or hell by God." Such a statement is clearly an expressed opinion. Speculating about what happens after death depends on one's point of view. An atheist will view the question of an afterlife much differently than will a Christian.

It is important to realize then even though a statement is merely an expressed opinion, it may, after study and investigation, be proven factual. However when reading, one can only judge from the evidence at hand. When investigating controversial issues it is important that one be able to distinguish between statements that are either fact or opinion from the evidence presented.

Most of the following statements are taken from the viewpoints in this book. Some have other origins. Consider each statement carefully. *Mark O for any statement you feel is an opinion or interpretation of facts. Mark F for any statement you believe is a fact.*

F = fact
O = opinion

1. The end always justifies the means.

2. The Bible contains the answers to many individuals' problems.

3. Sin is the cause of most human problems.

4. An absolute code of right and wrong exists; the difficulty is discovering it.

5. There is no God.

6. There is only one absolute moral law, to do the "loving thing" in every situation.

7. Atheism requires more courage than theism.

8. Most value judgments in our society are made in terms of money.

9. A creative life is the ultimate style of living.

10. The Christian concept of God is more correct than the Hindu.

11. Christianity is the dominant religion in the United States.

12. Astrology can indicate the pattern of the future.

13. Science has proven that traditional religions are ineffective and even harmful.

14. The Bible is the only written revelation which God has given to man.

15. More Bibles have been printed than any other book in history.

"There's no Christian path, Hindu path, Buddhist path, your path, my path. One must be free of all paths."

There Is No Best Guide for Life

Jiddu Krishnamurti

Jiddu Krishnamurti, who died in 1986 at the age of ninety, was believed by the leaders of the Theosophical Society to be the incarnation of the Lord Maitreya, a superior being who had previously appeared as Buddha and Jesus. The international society attempts to unite religion, philosophy, and science and to bring together Eastern and Western teachings. Krishnamurti broke away from the society in 1929 and became a philosopher and teacher. In the following viewpoint, Krishnamurti states that truth is discovered by rejecting all organized religions, gurus, messiahs, philosophies, and religions. The viewpoint is excerpted from an interview with Krishnamurti by *East West*, a journal of new age philosophy.

As you read, consider the following questions:

1. What meaning does the author find in the lives of Buddha and Jesus?
2. What does Krishnamurti say about following gurus?
3. In what does the author believe?

Reprinted with permission from *Meetings with Remarkable Men and Women* from the editors of East West/Natural Health, East West Natural Health Books, PO Box 1200, 17 Station St., Brookline Village, MA 02147. All rights reserved.

East West: It appears that the Buddha left a technique to practice awareness, and his influence has been very great.

Krishnamurti: He couldn't have left a technique. Buddha couldn't possibly have said, "Seek refuge in me." The systems came after he died. We think because he had attained some illumination, had suffered and gone through starvation, that we must also go through that to achieve what he achieved. And he might say, "Well, that's all childish stuff. It has nothing to do with enlightenment."

Can one person who is illumined—to put it in modern terms, free from all conditioning—affect the consciousness of all the rest of mankind? What do you think, impersonally, objectively, as you look at the world? Two thousand years of Christian propaganda, "Jesus is the savior," and the churches have burned people, tortured people, had hundreds of years of war in Europe. Christians have been one of the greatest killers in the world. I'm not against nor for—I'm just pointing out that this is the result of two thousand years of "peace on earth." It has no meaning, whether Jesus existed or not. So has all this propaganda, this programming of the brain, after two thousand years of repetition of the Mass day after day, affected man at all? Christ said, "Don't hate your enemy, love your enemy." And everything we do is contrary to that. We don't care. So, what will affect man? What will change man who has been programmed, literally programmed like a computer, to worship Jesus, to worship the Buddha, to worship other gods?

Mind Conditioning

Can the mind free itself from all programs? Is it possible to be totally free of taking in information—what the newspapers say, what the magazines say, what the priests, psychologists, and professors say? Education, television, evangelists—that peculiar breed—are all telling me what to think and, increasingly, what to do. If I have a little quarrel with my wife I go to the specialists—the psychologists, psychotherapists. Dr. Spock or some professor tells me how to raise my children. I'm becoming a slave to these specialists, my mind is conditioned and I'm limited—conditioning implies limitation—I'm in battle with everybody else for the rest of my days. And there's the future of man.

EW: Then what's the point of it all?

JK: Nothing! It has no meaning! What is the point of the Pope going to Poland, or all over South America? Is it a vast entertainment? Sustaining the faith? He says you must sustain faith, which means believe in Christ—which means do what we tell you.

It's all so absurd! So what will you do, with the world pressing

57

you all the time—they won't let you alone. I say, Sorry, I won't accept any of it. Whether it's the Buddha, Christ, the Pope, Mr. Reagan telling me what to do . . . sorry, I won't. This means we have to be extraordinarily capable of standing alone. And nobody wants to do that.

EW: Do you think there is a truth?

JK: Yes, but there is not my truth, your truth. And it has no path. There's no Christian path, Hindu path, Buddhist path, your path, my path. One must be free of all paths to find it. The Hindus have been very clever at this. They said there is the path of knowledge, the path of action, the path through devotion—this suits everybody.

Religion Must Be Rejected

EW: So you say to stand alone we find our truth.

JK: No. The word alone means all one. But people say, "I can't do it alone, so please help me to put my house in order," and invent the guru—not a particular guru but the whole idea of gurus. The world of so-called religion, whether it is the religion of Hindus, Buddhists, Jews, Catholics, the whole structure of religious ceremonies, is put together by thought, is it not? The Mass was invented by man. They may say it came directly from heaven but that seems rather absurd—it's been invented by man. The ancient Egyptians had their ceremonies to shape man. It isn't something new, the worship of symbols and figures. The guru, the mantra, various forms of yoga which have been brought over to this unfortunate country, are all authorities leading you to meditate and everything else.

We have tried Jesus, we have tried every form of person and idea, theory, system. They have not worked. So it's up to me to put my house in order—I cannot depend on anyone else. If you reject the church, the whole religious structure of the world, any kind of spiritual authority, you are free of it.

EW: Haven't these people and systems been inspiration to some?

JK: What is inspiration? To do something better—you answer it yourself.

EW: Isn't it to add to the potential of each human being?

JK: Yes, but if I am asleep . . .

EW: Then it is to wake up.

JK: Yes. And all the time I want entertainment to keep me awake. Man wants to be entertained, he wants to escape from himself at any price. This is a fact. The church has done it, and now sports—football, cricket, and so on—is a vast entertainment. I'm bored, I'm harassed, I'm weary, so I come to you and say, "Inspire me. For the moment you stimulate me. You act as a drug for the moment so I depend on you."

EW: You speak of freedom from something—from religion, from politics . . .

JK: Freedom is in itself without any motive, not from or for, just freedom. For instance, I am not a Hindu—I am free from it. But that's not freedom; I am free from a particular form of prison, but we create other prisons as we go along. The point is, suppose you have understood and have rejected, negated, all this and you want to help me. There is something unethical, if I may use the word, in trying to help me, right? Do you understand? So, then I become an example—that's the worst thing! There have been many examples of all kinds of idiocies: So-called "heroes" who have killed a thousand people in war, and saints who are half demented. Why then do you want help, to follow somebody, look up to somebody, why?

B.C. By Johnny Hart

By permission of Johnny Hart and Creators Syndicate, Inc.

When there is some kind of disease in me I go to the doctor; if I don't know the direction I seek help from a police officer; the postman is helping when he brings a letter. In the physiological world help is necessary; otherwise we couldn't exist, right? But I'm asking myself, psychologically, inwardly, will anybody help me?

Man has suffered for millenia. What will help him to end that suffering? He goes on killing, he goes on murdering, he has ambition in everything—which is another form of killing—and what will stop him? Not Gandhi—his non-violence is really a form of violence. Non-violence is an idea, right? When man is violent and you give him a fact, then fact is violence and non-fact is non-violence. And you are dealing only with non-fact all the time. Why don't we deal with the fact, which is violence? Why do you put that picture of non-violence in front of me? I say deal with what is here.

EW: Do you think we will just keep going on like this—warring among ourselves for all of history?

JK: You're asking the same question in different words

—what's the future of man. Unless we radically change, the future is what we are now. It's a serious fact. And nobody wants to change radically. They change a little bit here, a little bit there. If you want peace, you live peacefully. But nobody wants to live peacefully—neither the Pope, nor the prime minister, nor anybody. So they're keeping up the wars. I've talked to a great many politicians in my life, a great many spiritual leaders, to gurus who come to see me—I don't know why—they never talked about ending conflict, which means finding out the *cause* of conflict. Never. Let's say nationalism is one of the causes. They never talked about it. If the Pope said tonight that the church will excommunicate anybody who joins the army to do organized killing then tomorrow he wouldn't exist. They would throw him out. So he won't say, "Let's talk about peace."

I'm not cynical, I'm just looking at facts. So, what will change man? Apparently nothing from outside—no church, no threats, no wars, nothing from outside. Change implies a great deal of inquiry, a great deal of search. Someone hasn't the time so he says, "Tell me all about it quickly." But one must give one's life to this, not just play around with it. The monks think they have given their life but they have given their life to an idea, to a symbol, to somebody called Christ. The Hindus have their sannyasins, the Buddhists their bhikkus—it's the same phenomena.

EW: It appears that we are at a unique time in history.

JK: Yes, but the crisis is not in the world out there. Rather, it is inside us, in our consciousness. Which means that man has to change.

No Beliefs

EW: Do you believe in rebirth?

JK: First of all, I don't believe in anything. Secondly, what is it that is going to be reborn? Say I have been suffering for ten years and I die. Now will I in my next life go on from where I left off? Is there individuality at all? Is there the ego—my ego, your ego, a spiritual essence, the atman? The highest principle?

EW: Perhaps it's just a process.

JK: What is that? It's a process of thought. There is nothing sacred about thought, nor about the things that thought has created in the churches of the world. They worship it but it's not sacred. There is something absolutely sacred but you can't pick it up casually, you can't just believe. Do you understand? Men have searched for this in different ways and never found it, they have given their lives to it. It can't be found in an afternoon conversation or reading a book, or going to some fanciful meditation. If you don't find it what's the point of all this? One has to work on this for years to find out. It isn't just a game that you play. But people haven't the time so they worship the one who has something. Or they kill him. Whether they worship or kill, both are exactly the same.

EW: Isn't there some possibility of transmission between individuals?

JK: Now you are with somebody who is a little peaceful and who doesn't want a thing from you, and you feel quiet. But you have what? You have taken a drug for the time being and the moment you leave here it will all go. It's so obvious.

EW: But if we are climbing some mountain and we've come to see you because it seems that you are a few steps ahead . . . .

JK: I don't believe in climbing. There is no climbing, no "I am this, I have become that." There is only *this*. Change *this*, that's all.

"I think of myself as a deeply religious person. But my religion is that of one scientist. It is wholly secular. It contains no supernatural elements. Nature is enough for me."

Evolution by Chance Explains the Human Situation

George Wald

George Wald, born in 1906, is Higgins Emeritus Professor of Biology at Harvard University, where he began teaching in 1935. He is also a Nobel laureate in physiology medicine. For Wald, science gives life meaning. He claims we citizens of planet earth are not alone in the universe and that chance explains our existence. Contrary to the view of Teilhard de Chardin in viewpoint six of this chapter, Wald does not see the directing hand of God behind evolution. He sees the struggle to know epitomized in science, not the supernatural.

As you read, consider the following questions:

1. What does Wald mean when he says he is a deeply religious person?
2. In the author's opinion, how did intelligent life originate on earth?

From George Wald's speech delivered at the John XXIII Institute Conference on Theology and Ecology, St. Xavier College, Chicago, Illinois, January 31, 1970. Reprinted with permission.

Man has been engaged, since we have known him, in an unending struggle to know: whence he comes, what kind of thing he is, and at least a hint of what may become of him.

I think that the struggle to know is epitomized in science. One could add a word and say an unending struggle to know God. I think the big question is, if one added that word, would one have changed the meaning of the sentence? For me, no.

I think of myself as a deeply religious person. But my religion is that of one scientist. It is wholly secular. It contains no supernatural elements. Nature is enough for me: enough of mystery, beauty, reality. I am getting along with nature. . . .

We Are Not Alone

We are not alone in this universe. We cannot be. I think we see now that if one begins a universe or any large part of it with just hydrogen, then in many places in it life will arise. Life arises in natural conditions by natural laws; and given enough time in any of those places, one will, I think, have achieved a thinking creature with a technology, like man—somewhat like man. . . .

As far as I can see, we are not by any means alone in this universe. It is a very big universe—so big that our own galaxy, the Milky Way, has the cozy feeling of being just our front yard. Yet that galaxy is almost unimaginably big. It takes light traveling at 186,000 miles a second over one hundred thousand years to cross the Milky Way. There are now about 3.5 billion people on this earth, and we are beginning to feel crowded; but there are one hundred billion stars like our sun in this galaxy, the Milky Way. A simple rule that is easy to remember in these matters of cosmology was stated by Eddington many years ago: 10^{11} stars make a galaxy (that is, one hundred billion; we are just a run-of-the-mill galaxy—they tend to be about that size); 10^{11} galaxies make a universe. The most conservative estimate I have seen of stars in the Milky Way with planets that might bear life is 1 percent. That makes one billion of them just in our own galaxy. They may not all have life, but given enough time they should. And of the one hundred billion galaxies that Eddington was talking about as making a universe, there are already roughly one billion within the range of our most powerful telescopes. One billion is 10^9. There are perhaps 10^9 planetary systems in our own galaxy capable of bearing life, many of which should have life; and there are 10^9 such galaxies already within range of observation; so it makes the fantastically large number of 10^{18} places in our already observed universe that are capable of bearing life.

It is almost unimaginable that in many of those places life must not have started long before it started here. How long before? You think of the pace that we have reached. What our world will be like if we can keep it going one hundred years from now almost transcends our capacities to imagine. But one hundred years is nothing. One thousand years is nothing. In geological time, one million years is just a day. There is no reason that we know of why, on planets elsewhere in our galaxy and in the universe, life should not have gotten going, and should not have gotten to that contemplative creature with technology, very long before this—a million years, a hundred million years, perhaps even one billion years earlier.

Spontaneous Life

Our planet is about 4.5 billion years old. About three billion years ago, life arose upon it. That was in the cards; it arose spontaneously. There was quite a controversy that disturbed scientists for a couple of centuries between the spontaneous and the supernatural creation of life. And there came a wonderful moment in this bitter controversy in which the champions on both sides were Catholic priests: an Italian priest, the Abbe Spallanzani, on the one side, insisting upon the impossibility of spontaneous generation, and, on the other side, as the great champion of spontaneous generation, John Turberville Needham, an English Jesuit, the founder and first president of the Belgian Royal Academy. I wondered how a priest could support the theory of spontaneous generation as opposed to its only conceivable alternative, supernatural creation. Needham tells us perfectly plainly that you have only to read the opening paragraphs of the Book of Genesis. The language used, at least in the first story of the creation, is not that God made the living creatures, but that he ordered the earth and waters to bring them forth. "Let the waters bring forth" those living things. "Let the earth bring forth" those living things. Needham's view was that, such orders having once been issued and never, as far as we know, rescinded, the earth and waters were forever free thereafter to bring forth life, which is exactly what we mean by spontaneous generation.

George Wald, in a speech delivered at St. Xavier College on January 31, 1970.

These are hard thoughts. They make one ask the question, What then is our home in the universe? I think our home in the universe is the solar system—our corner of the universe. Let us talk about it a little. It is self-sufficient. Its source of energy is the sun. Relative to that, only negligible amounts of energy come in from the outside. I think the only life in the solar system is that on earth. Everything yet learned from the rockets, from space exploration, everything we have learned, is clinching that conviction: that the only life in the solar system is the life on earth. As for the position of man, I think that we are the only men in the universe. I have been talking about contemplative creatures who resemble man in their intellectual characteristics and in possessing a technology. But the chance that one of them is a man is negligible.

64

Man is the result of a long, long evolution, every step of which had a chance, a probability, of happening that way. Compound all those probabilities, and the chance of going through the operation just that way another time in another place is negligble. In fact, if you ask, Is there a chance that elsewhere in the universe there is a vertebrate—one of the great classes of vertebrates that include the fish, the amphibians, the reptiles, the birds, the mammals? I would say it is exceedingly unlikely, an almost negligible probability even for that.

Contact with Other Civilizations Is Unlikely

So we have our own special individuality. That is true of the creatures here on this planet, including man, but also of the creatures in a reasonable well-inhabited galaxy and universe. And that, of course, raises a series of strange problems. One of them is, Are we ever going to come into contact—even into communication—with some advanced technological civilization in outer space? I myself think the chances are very small. For the distances are almost unimaginably great. If you ask the question, How far would you have to go to reach a sun—a star—that is of the right kind to have perhaps a planet that has a chance of containing life? I would tell you that the nearest one to my knowledge has the beautiful name of Epsilon Eridani—and it is 10.8 light years away. That is, it takes light traveling at 186,000 miles a second 10.8 years to get from us to Epsilon Eridani. That is how long it would take a radio message to travel that distance. And then, if there were someone on Epsilon Eridani to receive it, the probability of which is almost nil—we are asking not just for life, we are asking for someone who can receive radio messages—if there were such a creature, and if he realized that he were getting signals, and if he promptly responded, twenty-two years would have passed between our sending a signal and receiving a response—a long time. It would not make a lively conversation. That is the *nearest* possibility. The others are much farther out.

So are we likely to be visited? There has been all that talk that unidentified flying objects (UFOs) are perhaps visitors from outer space. There are two things against it. First of all, one would have to perform the trick of traveling close to the speed of light. It is hard to do that and not be light. And even that would make a very long journey. There is another matter that is a little amusing. There are one hundred billion solar systems just in our galaxy. If there even were creatures prepared to travel that way, why should they come here?

"Evolution is no hypothesis. It is the key to the whole meaning of existence. It operates not through blind chance as the scientific materialists argued, but purposefully an irreversible process planned by God."

God-Directed Evolution Explains Life's Meaning

Pierre Teilhard de Chardin by John Kobler

Pierre Teilhard de Chardin, who died in 1955, was a Jesuit priest whose writings bring together the fields of science and religion. In his major work, *The Phenomenon of Man*, he describes evolution as a divinely inspired process directed toward union with God. "Man did not descend from an ape," he was fond of saying. "He ascended." Teilhard was also a noted geologist, theologian, and paleontologist. In the following viewpoint, John Kobler, a free-lance writer, presents an overview of Teilhard's synthesis, showing how theistic evolution is the key to the whole meaning of existence.

As you read, consider the following questions:

1. In Teilhard's view, what major stages has evolution already gone through and what stage lies ahead?
2. Why could Teilhard's view of evolution be called an optimistic one?

John Kobler, "The Priest Who Haunts the Catholic World," *The Saturday Evening Post*, October 12, 1963, pp. 44-46. Reprinted by permission of the author and *The Saturday Evening Post*, © 1963 by the Curtis Publishing Company.

Catholic dogma does not require believers to accept Genesis literally. It permits a variety of theories, including evolution, providing they recognize Scripture as divine revelation. Fifteen centuries ago Saint Augustine advised Christians not to consider the Bible a scientific text, and his own commentary on Genesis is often cited to show that evolution can be compatible with orthodoxy. Nevertheless, in practice evolution has long been a risky area for Catholics, because its early proponents were predominantly materialists who dismissed God from the universe. In fact, not until Pope Pius XII's encyclical letter of 1950, *Human Generis,* did the church explicitly authorize Catholic scholars to explore evolution, and then only as an unproven hypothesis.

Evolution Planned by God

In Teilhard's system, however, evolution is no hypothesis. It is the key to the whole meaning of existence. It operates not through blind chance as the scientific materialists argued, but purposefully, an irreversible process planned by God. A twofold principle underlies this process: Nothing can appear that has not been prepared from all eternity, and the universe is always at work perfecting itself.

The starting point of evolution from primordial matter Teilhard called Alpha, and the Goal, the Omega Point. Omega is, in effect, God, but Alpha also contains God. Thus, the universe began in God and will return to Him. "Man," Teilhard wrote, "is not a static center of the world, as he long assumed, but the axis and arrow of evolution, which is something finer." So far the march of evolution has advanced through three major stages—pre-life, life and thought. Hyper-life, for which Teilhard believed man to be now ripe, lies ahead. ". . . humanity has just entered what is probably the greatest transformation it has ever known. . . . Something is happening in the structure of human consciousness. It is another species of life that is just beginning."

From hyper-life, Teilhard prophesied, with the boundless optimism that colored his vision, humanity individually and collectively will eventually enter into ultimate, perfect union with God at the Omega Point, and so will conclude the epic drama of evolution. Nothing, he felt, could prevent that final consummation.

Two Kinds of Energy

As the main forces of evolution, Teilhard posited two kinds of energy. The first kind, "tangential" energy, acts upon what he termed the "Outside of Things." Scientists see the growth of the universe as a sequence of combinations: atoms forming molecules, molecules forming cells, cells forming plants and animals.

But the physical and chemical forces that bring about these changes manufacture no new energy. According to the laws of thermodynamics, the new organism expends its energy in heat and

Teilhard's View of Evolution

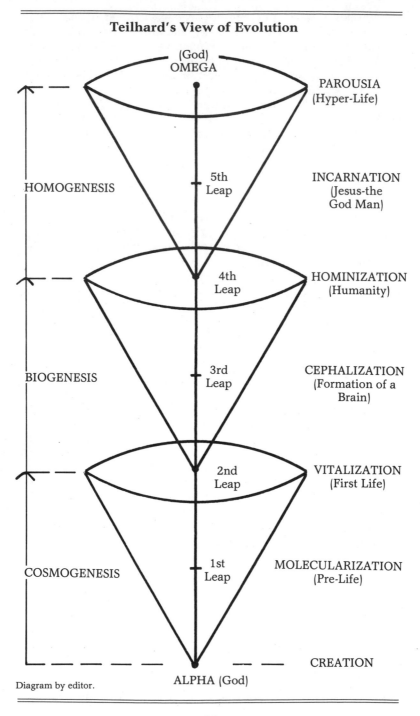

(God)
OMEGA

PAROUSIA
(Hyper-Life)

5th
Leap

INCARNATION
(Jesus-the
God Man)

HOMOGENESIS

4th
Leap

HOMINIZATION
(Humanity)

BIOGENESIS

3rd
Leap

CEPHALIZATION
(Formation of a
Brain)

2nd
Leap

VITALIZATION
(First Life)

1st
Leap

MOLECULARIZATION
(Pre-Life)

COSMOGENESIS

CREATION

Diagram by editor.

ALPHA (God)

eventually disintegrates. Physicists reckon that the sun, for example, will consume all its available hydrogen atoms in about 15 billion years, then cool off and die. "A rocket rising in the wake of time's arrow that bursts only to be extingished," Teilhard reflected poetically, "an eddy rushing on the bosom of a descending current—such then must be our picture of the descending current—such then must be our picture of the world. So says science, and I believe in science, but up to now has science ever troubled to look at the world except from without?"

Teilhard rejected the prospect of the universe thus reduced to a cold, black void, of evolution vanquished. God, he believed could not have intended such an end of his creation. There must exist some other kind of energy capable of producing higher forms ad infinitum and thereby preventing universal decay. Teilhard looked for such an energy on the Inside of Things, by which he meant consciousness to even the lowest forms of inorganic matter. Operating on the Inside, on consciousness, he concluded, was a "radial" or spiritual energy, separate from but related to tangential energy. Reversing the laws of thermodynamics, he formulated the Law of Complexity-Consciousness.

According to this law, complexity increases on the Outside until stopped by the loss of tangential energy. But on the Inside, radial energy, which is inexhaustible, drives the organism toward higher levels of both complexity and consciousness. In the evolution of animals, complexity-consciousness reached the level of instinct and awareness, in man, the level of thought, moral judgment, freedom of choice, spiritually. "Animals merely know," said Teilhard, "but man knows he knows." Since radial energy is a tremendous reservoir, it will go on producing more and more complex forms and so outdistance the rate of atomic disintegration.

Reinterpreting Evolution

Through this interplay of the Outside and the Inside, Teilhard reinterpreted evolution, the universe and God. Geologists describing the successive layers of the earth speak of the barysphere, composed of metals; the lithosphere, of rocks; the hydrosphere, of water. Teilhard invented a new layer, the noosphere (from the Greek noos: mind). Thought, he explained, generated the noosphere. "The idea is that of the earth not only becoming covered by myriads of grains of thought but becoming enclosed in a single thinking envelope so as to form, functionally, no more than a single vast grain of thought...."

But the noosphere is not the apex of evolution. Beyond it, Teilhard believed, beckons a further series of syntheses converging toward the Omega Point. The prerequisite to this final ascent is man's social consciousness. Just as aggregates of cells form an individual, so the aggregate of individuals will form a super-

Improving the Human Condition

HEAVEN	Most religions promise a reward after death for a life well spent.
EVOLUTION	Some scientists, skeptical of a divine presence in history, claim that humanity's hope for the future lies in improving its surroundings, and more importantly, humanity itself.
TEILHARD	There is a source of energy in humanity, divinely implanted, that propels it forward and upward, physically, mentally and spiritually.

Diagram by editor.

organism, a collective, combining the sum total of human consciousness. But how can personality and collectivity combine without damage to either? Teilhard finds the answer in a special property of radial energy—love. And the power that moves the universe through love toward the zenith is Christianity. In the culminating synthesis of evolution a universal consciousness, forever freed from material shackles, will fuse with Omega.

"Man should live for loving, for understanding, and for creating."

Love, Creation, and Understanding Give Life Meaning

Arnold Toynbee

From 1925 until his retirement in 1955, Arnold Toynbee (1889-1975) was director of studies in the Royal Institute of International Affairs and professor of history at London University. Although he became internationally famous for his multi-volume series, *Study of History*, that traced the rise and fall of civilizations, his main interest in the latter part of his life was religion as the means to world unity. In the following viewpoint, Toynbee answers the question "What should one live for?" In answering the question, he draws on his considerable knowledge of diverse civilizations and cultures.

As you read, consider the following questions:

1. Why does the author claim that self-denial is the only true form of fulfillment?
2. What does Toynbee mean when he says "We should live for being creative"?
3. What conclusion does the author come to in asking the question "What should man live for?"

From Arnold Toynbee, *Surviving the Future*. Copyright © 1971 by Oxford University Press. Reprinted with permission.

The confusion, strain, pressures, complications, and rapid changes in contemporary life are having their effect all over the world, and they are particularly disturbing for the young. The young want to find their way, to understand the meaning of life, to cope with the circumstances with which they are confronted. What should man live for? This question is particularly acute for the young, but it haunts everyone at every stage of life.

Three Aims of Life

I would say that man should live for loving, for understanding, and for creating. I think man should spend all his ability and all his strength on pursuing all these three aims, and he should sacrifice himself, if necessary, for the sake of achieving them. Anything worthwhile may demand self-sacrifice, and, if you think it worthwhile, you will be prepared to make the sacrifice.

Live for Loving

I myself believe that love does have an absolute value, that it is what gives value to human life, and also to the life of some other species of mammals and birds. I can think of some birds and mammals, besides ourselves, that live for love. I also believe (I know that this cannot be demonstrated) that love, as we know it by direct experience in living creatures on this planet, is also present as a spiritual presence behind the universe. Love can and does sometimes bring out responsive love, as we know in our own human experience, and, when that happens, love spreads and expands itself. But love may also meet with hostility, and then it will call for self-sacrifice, which may seem sometimes to be in vain. All the same, love, if it is strong enough, will move us to sacrifice ourselves, even if we see no prospect that this self-sacrifice will win a victory by transforming hostility into love. The only way in which love can conquer is by changing the state of feeling, the state of mind, of some other person from hostility to an answering love. I believe, though it is hard of course for any of us to live up to this belief, that the lead given by love ought to be followed at all costs, whatever the consequences. I think that love is the only spiritual power that can overcome the self-centeredness that is inherent in being alive. Love is the only thing that makes life possible, or, indeed, tolerable.

I had better say, before I go on, a few words about what I mean by love. This is so important, as I see it, that I want to make the meaning of the word love, as I use the word, clear, because, at any rate in English, this word 'love' is ambiguous. I can say 'I love whisky', or 'I love sexual relations', or 'I love chocolate'; that is not the kind of love that I mean. Or I can say 'I love my wife', or 'I love my children', or 'I love my fellow human beings', or 'I love God'. . . .

True love is an emotion which discharges itself in an activity that overcomes self-centeredness by expending the self on people and on purposes beyond the self. It is an outward-going spiritual movement from the self toward the universe and toward the ultimate spiritual reality behind the universe.

Love Is the Key

Love is the key to a fulfilling life: love yourselves; love others; love truth, goodness, and beauty; love nature—the trees, the flowers, the sky, the stars. If you feel love, then you will be able to be compassionate with yourselves and with others. Being compassionate, you will be tolerant and respectful. Being tolerant and respectful, you will be nonviolent. This attitude will elicit love, compassion, tolerance, and respect from others. Then you will feel a special happiness, together with a sense of peace and well-being.

Al-Abdin in *Letters to Young People*, 1989.

There is a paradox here. This love that is a form of self-denial is the only true self-fulfillment, as has been pointed out by the founders of all the great historic religions. It is self-fulfillment because this outward-going love reintegrates the self into the ultimate spiritual reality of which the self is a kind of splinter that has been temporarily separated and alienated. The self seeks to fulfill itself, and it seeks blindly to fulfill itself by exploiting the universe. But the only way in which it can fulfill itself truly is to unite itself with the spiritual reality behind the universe, so this outgoing love, which is a form of reunion, a union with other people and with ultimate spiritual reality, is the true form of fulfillment. . . .

Man is a social being, and therefore, among all the objects for his love that there are in the universe and beyond it, he ought, I suppose, to love his fellow human beings first and foremost. But he should also love all non-human living creatures, animals, and plants, as well, because they are akin to man; they too are branches of the great tree of life. This tree has a common root; we do not know where the root comes from, but we do know that we all spring from it. Man should also love inanimate nature, because this, too, is part of the universe which is mankind's habitat.

I think people in India and Eastern Asia have a greater wish, and a greater sense of the need, to love non-human living creatures, and also inanimate nature, than people in the Western world have. This wish to expand the field of human love is not

73

so strong in the Western tradition. By Western I do not mean just Christian: I mean Christian and Jewish and Muslim, because Christianity and Islam are derivatives, offshoots, of Judaism. However, in the Western tradition, too, there are traces of this feeling for nature. For instance, Saint Francis of Assisi, one of the greatest religious figures in Western history so far, has written, in the earliest surviving piece of Italian poetry, a hymn in which he praises God for our brothers the Sun, Wind, Air, Clouds, Fire, and for our sisters the Moon, the Stars, the Waters, the Earth, and every mortal human body. Saint Francis is very conscious of this brotherhood and sisterhood of all living creatures. . . .

If you travel in India, and if you are a Westerner, you are at once struck by the fact that wild animals and birds are not afraid of you, as they are, for the most part, in the Western world. In India they are on familiar terms with human beings. This is because Indians have a reverent consideration for the life of non-human living creatures. This is particularly strong in one Indian sect, the Jains. This Indian attitude toward living creatures does give the Westerner reason to think. Is not the Western attitude toward non-human living creatures too possessive, too exploiting an attitude?

Live for Understanding

I have said that we should live in order to love, and I do think that love should be the first call on every human being, but I have mentioned other things to live for. One of them was understanding and another was creating. Man seems to be unique among living creatures on this planet in having consciousness and reason, and therefore having the power of making deliberate choices, and we need to use these specifically human faculties in order to direct our love right. It is so difficult to know how to apportion our love, and to decide what objects should have priority, that conscious reasoned thought is needed for this. I think, also, that using, cultivating, and developing our human reason is all the more important because even our human nature is only very partially rational. We human beings, like non-human living creatures, are governed partly by emotions and by unconscious motives. Our human reason is only on the surface of the psyche. The subconscious depths below it are unfathomable. Our unconscious motives may be good or evil. We need to bring them up to consciousness, so far as we can, and to look at them closely, in order to see whether they are good or bad and to choose and follow the good and reject the bad. There again, we need to keep our reason and our consciousness at work. A human being's life is a constant struggle between the rational and the irrational side of human nature. We are always

74

trying to conquer a bit more of our nature for reason from blind emotion, and we are often losing ground, and then the irrational gains on the rational. As I see it, the whole of human life is a struggle to keep the reason uppermost.

Two Impressions

I am an old man, already past the allotted three score and ten and, as the old do, I quite often wake up in the night, half out of my body, so that I see between the sheets the old battered carcass I shall soon be leaving for good, and in the distance a glow in the sky, the lights of Augustine's City of God. Let me, in conclusion, pass on to you two extraordinarily sharp impressions which accompany this condition. The first is of the incredible beauty of our earth, its colors and shapes and smells and creatures; of the enchantment of human love and companionship, of human work and the fulfillment of human procreation. The second, a certainty surpassing all words and thought, that as an infinitesimal particle of God's creation I am a participant in his purposes which are loving, not malign, creative, not destructive, orderly, not chaotic and in that certainty a great peace and a great joy.

Malcolm Muggeridge, *Vital Speeches of the Day*, December 1, 1975.

Finally, we should live for being creative. What do I mean by creative? I mean trying to change this universe in which we find ourselves placed—trying to add good things to it, if possible. The universe, in the state in which we find it when we wake up to consciousness, is obviously imperfect and unsatisfactory. Many living creatures prey on each other. All animals live either on other animals which they kill in order to eat, or on vegetation, and, apart from living creatures, inanimate nature, when it is unmodified and uncontrolled, can be extremely inimical, not only to human life, but to all kinds of life. I am thinking of the earthquakes, the floods, the droughts, the storms, and the tornadoes that may destroy hundreds of thousands of lives and wreck the works of man. This, too, is an imperfection in the universe. So we should strive to add to the universe by supplementing the natural environment in which we find ourselves and partially replacing it by a man-made environment. Here, however, we have to be cautious. Since our ancestors became human, since we awoke to consciousness, we have been working on the natural environment and changing it. We have been domesticating plants and animals, instead of gathering wild plants and hunting wild animals for food. We have been constructing buildings which are not part of the non-human natural environment;

we have been building great engineering works. In the non-material spiritual side of life, we have been creating works of science and of architecture and of art which have a value for us in themselves. We do this creative work from disinterested motives, not from immediate utilitarian motives, yet this kind of work often turns out to have undesigned and unexpected practical uses.

I have now answered the question: 'What should man live for?' In my belief, love, creation, and understanding are the purposes for which man should live, for which he should give his life, and for which he should sacrifice himself if, in pursuit of these objects, sacrifice turns out to be demanded of him.

a critical thinking activity

Identifying Your Beliefs

MISS PEACH by Mell Lazarus. Reprinted by special permission of North America Syndicate.

It is probably fair to say that most people, like Arthur in the cartoon above, rarely reflect on their basic beliefs in a systematic way. They do not methodically catalog those things that make up their belief systems. For those interested in self-awareness, such an exercise is essential. Below are a number of statements that can help you begin to identify your basic beliefs. Read each one carefully and decide if you agree, disagree, or are undecided.

I BELIEVE

1. God exists.
2. I agree with humanism, as described in Viewpoint Two of Chapter Three.
3. After death good will be rewarded and evil punished.
4. There is no afterlife of any kind.
5. The Devil exists.
6. Original sin is the cause of human evil and suffering.
7. Love of self and others is life's most important goal.
8. As Sarvepalli Radhakrishnan claims in Viewpoint Three of Chapter Three, no single religious tradition can reveal the mystery of God or the meaning of life.
9. The Bible is inspired by God.
10. Atheism is the way of common sense.
11. When wronged you should forgive the offender.
12. Material comfort and financial security are life's most important goals.

Periodical Bibliography

The following articles have been selected to supplement the diverse views in this chapter. Because the subject matter of all chapters in this book is closely related, it may be helpful to examine the other chapter bibliographies when doing further study.

Mortimer Adler — "God Exists: No Doubt About It," *U.S. Catholic*, October 1980.

Rochelle Albin and Donald D. Montagna — "Mystical Aspects of Science," *The Humanist*, March/April 1971.

H.O. Brown — "Only God Satisfies the Complexities of the Cosmos," *Christianity Today*, December 12, 1980.

Stanley Brown — "Science, Scientism, Scientists," *American Atheist*, November 1983.

Luther Burbank — "Our Savior Science," *The Humanist*, November/December 1976.

Christianity Today — "I Believe: A 1,600-Year-Old Confession of Faith," December 11, 1981.

Perry G. Downs — "Is Faith Staged?" *Christianity Today*, October 17, 1986.

W. Ward Gasque — "Is Man's Purpose an Enigma?" *Christianity Today*, July 29, 1977.

S. Guernsey Jones — "A Layman's Liberal Theology," *Vital Speeches of the Day*, February 1, 1989.

Konstantin Kolenda — "To Be a Person: An Essay on the Meaning of Life," *The Humanist*, January/February 1985.

Brian Lanker — "The Meaning of Life," *Life*, December 1988.

Norman Lear — "Nurturing Our Spiritual Imagination in an Age of Science and Technology," *Creation Spirituality*, January/February 1992. Available from Holy Name College, 3500 Mountain Blvd., Oakland, CA 94169.

Malcolm Muggeridge — "Albion Agnostics: Man's Relationship with His Creator," *Vital Speeches of the Day*, December 1, 1975.

Bertrand Russell — "Bertrand Russell Speaks: The BBC Interviews," *The Humanist*, November/December 1982.

Carl Sagan — "Science and Religion: 'Similar Objective, Different Methods'," *U.S. News & World Report*, December 1, 1980.

Joyce Terry — "Finding Meaning in Life," *The Humanist*, January/February 1982.

How Do Religions Give Life Meaning?

Constructing a Life
PHILOSOPHY

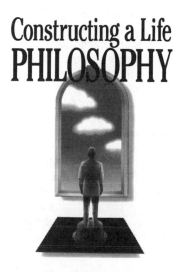

Chapter Preface

Viktor Frankl was an Austrian psychiatrist who spent part of World War II in Nazi concentration camps, including the infamous Auschwitz. Most of those who entered these death camps died there. Frankl, who wrote about his death camp experiences in his book *Man's Search for Meaning*, puzzled over why some inmates died more easily than others. He observed that frail individuals often survived while more robust fellow prisoners died. His experiences led to the development of a theory called logotherapy (meaning therapy).

Logotherapy helps mentally or spiritually disturbed people find meaning and purpose in their lives. Frankl's theory has become known as the Third School of Viennese Psychiatry—the school of logotherapy. As a result of his death camp observations, Frankl concluded that those frail individuals who survived often did so because they had meaning and purpose in their lives, which gave them the will to survive, while their stronger fellow inmates perished because of a lack of meaning.

Since the beginning of human history religions have offered belief systems that give adherents meaning and purpose. In addition to providing meaning to live by, many religious followers have gone willingly to their deaths for their religious beliefs. For centuries Christians have honored saints and martyrs who have died for their faith. During the war between Iraq and Iran, soldiers from both sides went to their deaths, confident that they were doing the will of the same god, Allah. Belief systems that can make the sting of death a positive experience can provide even more powerful motivation and guidelines for living.

The viewpoints in this chapter present some of the belief systems constructed by religious believers. In addition to presenting a sampling of major religions, the chapter also looks at two belief systems that would not ordinarily be considered religious: atheism and mythology. The chapter concludes with a viewpoint that offers a new interpretation of Christianity, creation-centered spirituality. While reading these viewpoints, the reader might wonder how each advocate would have fared in Frankl's camps. Would any of these viewpoints have sustained you and aided your survival if you had been an inmate? Would one help you now?

"Judaism is a way of life that endeavors to transform virtually every human action into a means of communion with God."

Judaism Is a Way to Commune with God

Louis Finkelstein

Louis Finkelstein was the chancellor of Jewish Theological Seminary of America from 1951 to 1972 and chancellor emeritus until his death in 1991. He was thought by many to be the dominant leader of conservative Judaism in the twentieth century and was the author and editor of many scholarly works, including the two-volume work *The Jews: Their History, Culture, and Religion*, from which the following viewpoint is taken. Finkelstein argued that Judaism is a way of life rather than the acceptance of a creed or a confession of faith. The central doctrine of Judaism, in his opinion, is the belief in the "One God the Father of all." For Jews, Finkelstein explained, life's meaning revolves around God's covenant with Moses on Mt. Sinai. Every Jew is "a child of the covenant."

As you read, consider the following questions:

1. What is the Torah, and how important is it to Judaism?
2. How does one become a Jew?
3. What is the Talmud?
4. Why is study so important to Judaism?
5. How do Reform, Orthodox, and Conservative Jews differ?

From Louis Finkelstein, "The Jewish Religion: Its Beliefs and Practices," in *The Jews: Their History, Culture, and Religion*. Vol. 2. Louis Finkelstein, ed. Copyright © 1949, 1955 by Louis Finkelstein. Reprinted by permission of HarperCollins Publishers.

Judaism is a way of life that endeavors to transform virtually every human action into a means of communion with God. Through this communion with God, the Jew is enabled to make his contribution to the establishment of the Kingdom of God and the brotherhood of men on earth. So far as its adherents are concerned, Judaism seeks to extend the concept of right and wrong to every aspect of their behavior. Jewish rules of conduct apply not merely to worship, ceremonial, and justice between man and man, but also to such matters as philanthropy, personal friendships and kindnesses, intellectual pursuits, artistic creation, courtesy, the preservation of health, and the care of diet.[1]

Jewish Law

So rigorous is this discipline, as ideally conceived in Jewish writings, that it may be compared to those specified for members of religious orders in other faiths. A casual conversation or a thoughtless remark may, for instance, be considered a grave violation of Jewish Law. It is forbidden, as a matter not merely of good form but of religious law, to use obscene language, to rouse a person to anger, or to display unusual ability in the presence of the handicapped. The ceremonial observances are equally detailed. The ceremonial Law expects each Jew to pray thrice every day, if possible at the synagogue; to recite a blessing before and after each meal; to thank God for any special pleasure, such as a curious sight, the perfume of a flower, or the receipt of good news; to wear a fringed garment about his body; to recite certain passages from Scripture each day; and to don *tephillin* (cubical receptacles containing certain biblical passages) during the morning prayers.

Decisions regarding right and wrong under given conditions are not left for the moment, but are formulated with great care in the vast literature created by the Jewish religious teachers. At the heart of this literature are the Hebrew Scriptures, usually described as the Old Testament, consisting of the Five Books of Moses (usually called the *Torah*), the Prophets and the Hagiographa. These works, particularly the Five Books of Moses, contain the prescriptions for human conduct composed under Divine inspiration. The ultimate purpose of Jewish religious study is the application of the principles enunciated in the Scriptures, to cases and circumstances the principles do not explicitly cover.

Because Judaism is a way of life, no confession of faith can by itself make one a Jew. Belief in the dogmas of Judaism must be expressed in the acceptance of its discipline rather than in the repetition of a verbal formula. But no failure either to accept the beliefs of Judaism or to follow its prescriptions is sufficient to exclude from the fold a member of the Jewish faith. According to Jewish tradition, the covenant between God and Moses on Mt. Sinai included all those who were present and also all their descendants. . . . There

The above picture shows a **Bar Mitzvah,** a two part ceremony, religious and social, that initiates male Jews into adult membership of the Jewish community. **Bat Mitzvah** is a similar ceremony for girls.

is therefore no need for any ceremony to admit a Jewish child into the faith of Judaism. Born in a Jewish household, he becomes at once "a child of the covenant." The fact that the child has Jewish parents involves the assumption of the obligations that God has placed on these parents and their descendants. . . .

Judaism and Government

Like other religions, Judaism can be, and indeed has been, practiced under various forms of civil government: monarchical, semi-monarchical, feudal, democratic, and totalitarian. Adherents of the Jewish faith, like those of other religions, regard themselves as citizens or subjects of their respective states. In every synagogue prayers are offered for the safety of the government of the country of its location; and in the ancient Temple of Jerusalem daily sacrifices were offered on behalf of the imperial Roman government, as long as Palestine remained under its dominion. This patriotic loyalty to the state has often persisted in the face of cruel persecution. The principle followed has been that formulated by the ancient teacher, Rabbi Haninah: "Pray for the welfare of the government; for without fear of the government, men would have swallowed each other up alive."

Despite this ability to adjust itself to the exigencies of any form of temporal government, Judaism, like other faiths derived from the Prophets, has always upheld the principles of the Fatherhood of God and the dignity and worth of man as the child and creature of God; and its ideals are more consistent with those of democracy than any other system of government.

The most vigorous and consistent effort to formulate the discipline of Judaism in terms of daily life was that made in ancient Palestine and Babylonia. The Palestinian schools devoted to this purpose were founded in the second or third century before the Common Era, and flourished in their original form for six centuries and in a somewhat altered form until the Crusades. The Babylonian schools were founded in the third century of the Common Era and ended the first and most significant phase of their activity about three hundred years later.[2]

The rules of conduct worked out in the discussion of these academies form the substance of Jewish Law. In arriving at these precepts, the ancient teachers were guided by their desire to know the Will of God. So far as possible they sought to discover His will through an intensive study of the Scriptures. Where Scripture offered no clear guidance, they tried to ascertain His will by applying its general principles of moral right. In addition, they had a number of oral traditions, going back to antiquity, which they regarded as supplementary to the written Law, and equal to it in authority and inspiration.

The high purpose of the discussions made them of monumental importance to Judaism. As a result, they were committed to memory by eager and faithful disciples, until the memorized materials grew to such proportions that it had to be reduced to writing. The work in which the discussions were thus preserved is known as the Talmud. . . .

The Place of Study in Judaism

It is impossible to understand Judaism without an appreciation of the place it assigns to the study and practice of the talmudic Law. Doing the Will of God is the primary spiritual concern of the Jew. Therefore, to this day, he must devote considerable time not merely to the mastery of the content of the Talmud, but also to training in its method of reasoning. The study of the Bible and the Talmud is thus far more than a pleasing intellectual exercise, and is itself a means of communication with God. According to some teachers, this study is the highest form of such communion imaginable.[3]

Because the preservation of the Divine will regarding human conduct is basic to all civilization, none of the commandments is more important than that of studying and teaching the Law. The most sacred object in Judaism is the Scroll containing the Five Books of Moses. Every synagogue must contain at least one copy of it. The Scroll must be placed in a separate Ark, before which burns an eternal light. The position of this Ark in the synagogue is in the direction of Jerusalem; everyone turns toward the Ark in prayer. When the Scroll is taken from the Ark for the purpose of reading, all those present must rise. No irreverent or profane action may be performed in a room which contains a Scroll, nor may a Scroll be moved from place to place except for the performance of religious rites. From time to time the Scroll must be examined to ascertain that its writing is intact. . . .

No less important than this homage paid to the Scroll as symbol of the Law, is that paid to the living Law itself. Fully three-fourths of the Hebrew literature produced within the first nineteen cen-

The **Western Wall**, also known as the **Wailing Wall**, pictured above, is the last remnant of the ancient Jerusalem Temple Court and is an object of Jewish pilgrimages. Whenever circumstances have permitted, Jews have gathered at the Wall for prayer.

turies of the Common Era, is devoted to the elucidation of the Law. Many of the best minds in Judaism have been devoted to its study. Every parent is required to teach his child its basic elements. Its study is considered vital not only for the guidance it offers in the practice of Judaism, but for liberation from the burden of secular ambition and anxieties. The study of the Law is believed to be a foretaste of the immortal life, for the Sages of the Talmud believed that Paradise itself could offer men no nearer communion with God than the opportunity of discovering His will in the study of the Law.

The Talmud derives its authority from the position held by the ancient academies. The teachers of those academies, both of Babylonia and of Palestine, were considered the rightful successors of the older Sanhedrin, or Supreme Court, which before the destruction of Jerusalem (in the year 70 of the Common Era) was the arbiter of Jewish Law and custom. The Sanhedrin derived its authority from the statement in Deut. 17:8-13, that whenever a question of interpretation of the Law arises, it is to be finally decided by the Sages and priests in Jerusalem.

The Role of Rabbis

At the present time, the Jewish people have no living central authority comparable in status to the ancient Sanhedrin or the later academies. Therefore any decision regarding the Jewish religion must be based on the Talmud, as the final resume of the teachings of those authorities when they existed. The right of an individual to decide questions of religious Law depends entirely on his knowledge of the Bible, the Talmud, and the later manuals based on them, and upon his fidelity to their teachings. Those who have acquired this knowledge are called rabbis. There is no sharp distinction in religious status between the rabbi and the layman in Judaism. The rabbi is simply a layman especially learned in Scripture and Talmud. Nor is there any hierarchical organization or government among the rabbis of the world. Yet some rabbis, by virtue of their special distinction in learning, by common consent come to be regarded as superior authorities on questions of Jewish Law. Difficult and complicated issues are referred to them for clarification.

To be recognized as a rabbi, a talmudic student customarily is ordained. Traditionally, the authority to act as rabbi may be conferred by any other rabbi. It is usual, however, for students at various theological schools to receive this authority from their teachers. In America, there are several rabbinical schools, each of which ordains its graduates in the manner in which degrees are conferred on graduates of other institutions of learning.... There is considerable variation among the interpretations of Judaism taught at these seminaries, and consequently there is a considerable difference in emphasis on the subjects included in their respective curricula. This has resulted from the fact that during the second half of the nineteenth century various groups of rabbis, primarily in Germany and America, claimed authority not merely to interpret but also to amend talmudic, and even biblical Law. These rabbis are known as Reform rabbis, and their congregations as Reform congregations. Of the rabbis who adhere to traditional Judaism, some reject any significant innovations from customary practice; these rabbis are called Orthodox. Others maintain that Jewish law is a living tradition, subject to change, but they insist that such changes must be made in accordance with traditional canons for the interpretation and development of Rabbinic law. These rabbis are usually called Conservative.[4]

The difference between the various groups of American rabbis have not led to any sectarian schism. Although the difference in practice between the traditional and Reform groups is considerable, each accepts the other as being within the fold of Judaism. It is possible for them to do so, because of the principle that even an unobservant or a heretical Jew does not cease to be a member of the covenant made between God and Israel at the time of the Revelation. Only actual rejection of Judaism, by affiliation with another faith, is recognized as separating one from the Jewish community. So long as a follower of the Jewish faith has not by overt act or word and of his own free will declared himself a member of another religion, other Jews are bound to regard him as one of their own faith, and to seek his return to its practice and beliefs. . . .

The Basic Concepts of Judaism

The central doctrine of Judaism is the belief in the One God, the Father of all mankind. The first Hebrew words a Jewish child learns are the confession of faith contained in the verse "Hear, O Israel, the Lord is our God, the Lord is One," and every believing Jew hopes that as he approaches his end in the fullness of time he will be sufficiently conscious to repeat this same confession. This monotheistic belief is subject to no qualification or compromise. . . .

There is a wide variety of interpretation among Rabbinical scholars, both ancient and modern, with regard to the concepts of Judaism. In some instances, the differences of interpretation are so great that it is difficult to speak of a concept as being basically or universally Jewish or Rabbinic. There are thus a number of concepts, each having its own limited authority and following.

This applies also to a degree to the fundamental beliefs which have been brought together in the best known Jewish creed, that of Maimonides. According to this creed, there are thirteen basic dogmas in Judaism. They are as follows:

1. The belief in God's existence.
2. The belief in His unity.

3. The belief in His incorporeality.
4. The belief in His timelessness.
5. The belief that He is approachable through prayer.
6. The belief in prophecy.
7. The belief in the superiority of Moses to all other prophets.
8. The belief in the revelation of the Law, and that the Law as contained in the Pentateuch is that revealed to Moses.
9. The belief in the immutability of the Law.
10. The belief in Divine providence.
11. The belief in Divine justice.
12. The belief in the coming of the Messiah.
13. The belief in the resurrection and human immortality.

1. Without desiring to ascribe to them any responsibility for this statement, the author records with deep gratitude the assistance in its preparation given by colleagues from different schools of Jewish thought. These include Rabbis Max Arzt, Ben Zion Bokser, Samuel S. Cohon, Judah Goldin, Israel M. Goldman, Simon Greenberg, David de Sola Pool, Samuel Schulman, and Aaron J. Tofield.
2. Cf. Judah Goldin, "The Period of the Talmud (135 B.C.E.-1035 C.E.)," this work, Vol. I, Chap. 3, *passim.*
3. Cf. the essay on "Study as a Mode of Worship," by Professor Nathan Isaacs, in *The Jewish Library*, edited by Rabbi Leo Jung, 1928, pp. 51-70.
4. For a survey of the Orthodox, Conservative, and Reform movements in the United States, see Moshe Davis, *Jewish Religious Life and Institutions in America (A Historical Study)*, pp. 310 f., 326 f.

"Humanism in a nutshell . . . rejects all forms of supernaturalism, pantheism, and metaphysical idealism, and considers man's supreme ethical aim as working for the welfare of all humanity in this one and only life."

Humanism Is a Way to Commune with People

Corliss Lamont

Corliss Lamont, honorary president of the American Humanist Association, is author of *The Philosophy of Humanism.* The following viewpoint is excerpted from an article in the *Humanist,* a bimonthly magazine of the association to which Lamont frequently contributes. In this viewpoint Lamont presents a concise overview of humanism. He uses the phrase "naturalistic humanism" in labeling humanism and refers to it as a "way of life" rather than a religion. He believes humanism focuses on people and improving the human situation rather than on supernatural beliefs and manufactured theistic constraints.

As you read, consider the following questions:

1. What is the position of naturalistic humanism on the subject of God or the supernatural?
2. Why could humanists be called rationalists?
3. What is the author's position on ethics and sex?

From Corliss Lamont, "Naturalistic Humanism," *The Humanist,* September/October 1971, pp. 9-10. The original article has been revised for inclusion in this book. Reprinted with permission.

Humanism is such a warm and attractive word that in the 20th century it has been adopted by various groups, often diametrically opposed in ideology, whose use of it is most questionable. Even the Catholics, who still adhere to every outworn myth of Christian supernaturalism, promote what they call *Catholic Humanism;* while the Marxists, who reject in practice political democracy and civil liberties, continually talk of *Socialist Humanism.*

But the Humanism that has become increasingly influential in this century, in English-speaking countries and throughout the non-Communist world, is *naturalistic Humanism.* This is the Humanism that I have supported through the written and spoken word for some 50 years.

To define naturalistic Humanism in a nutshell, it rejects all forms of supernaturalism, pantheism, and metaphysical idealism, and considers man's supreme ethical aim as working for the welfare of all humanity in this one and only life, using the methods of reason, science, and democracy for the solution of problems.

To become more specific, Humanism believes, **first,** that Nature or the universe makes up the totality of existence and is completely self-operating according to natural law, with no need for a God or gods to keep it functioning. This cosmos, unbounded in space and infinite in time, consists fundamentally of a constantly changing system of matter and energy, and is neutral in regard to man's well-being and values.

Second, Humanism holds that the race of man is the present culmination of a time-defying evolutionary process on this planet that has lasted billions of years; that each human being exists as an inseparable unity of mind and body, and that therefore after death there can be no personal immortality or survival of consciousness.

Third, in working out its basic views on man and the universe, Humanism relies on reason, and especially on the established facts, laws, and methods of modern experimental science. In general, people's best hope for solving their problems is through the use of intelligence and scientific method applied with vision and determination. Such qualities as courage, love, and perseverance provide emotional drive for successfully coping with difficulties, but it is reason that finds the actual solution.

Fourth, Humanism is opposed to all theories of universal determinism, fatalism, or predestination and believes that human beings possess genuine freedom of choice (free will) in making decisions both important and unimportant. Free choice is conditioned by inheritance, education, the external environment (including economic conditions), and other factors. Nonetheless, it remains real and substantial. Humanism rejects both Marxist economic determinism and Christian theistic determinism.

Fifth, Humanism advocates an ethics or morality that grounds all human values in this-earthly experiences and relationships, and

90

that views man as a functioning unity of physical, emotional, and intellectual faculties. The Humanist holds as his highest ethical goal the this-worldly happiness, freedom, and progress—economic, cultural, and material—of all mankind, irrespective of nation, race, religion, sex, or economic status. Reserving the word *love* for their families and friends, he has an attitude of *compassionate concern* toward his fellow men in general.

What Is Humanism?

Humanism is the belief that people shape their own destiny. It is a constructive philosophy, a non-theistic religion, a way of life.

Open-ended, without dogma, humanism is a world-view geared to our times. By focusing on the quality of each individual's life and stressing the need to work for social ideals, it fuses emotion and intellect.

Modern humanism has developed out of a growing respect for human dignity, for individual rights, and for the ideas of human equality, enthusiasm for life and for nature, recognition that ethical values grow out of experience, and feeling for humanity beyond one's national boundaries.

There are special challenges for the humanistic approach in the 1980's. We must try to lessen the widening gap between technology and everyday experience, between current emphasis on living in the present and the need for foresight and planning. We must help recognize how everything has become interconnected. Ecological problems have become value problems. Regional problems are now world problems.

Humanists rely upon themselves and their fellow humans rather than upon any supernatural power. They believe they can make headway in meeting difficulties by using intelligence and good will. They endeavor to become more tolerant and compassionate.

"I use the word 'Humanist' to mean someone who believes that man is just as much a natural phenomenon as an animal or plant; that his body, mind and soul were not supernaturally created but are products of evolution, and that he is not under the control or guidance of any supernatural being or beings, but has to rely on himself and his own powers."—*Julian Huxley*

American Humanist Association

Sixth, in the controversial realm of sex relations, Humanism rejects entirely dualistic theories that separate soul from body and claim that the highest morality is to keep the soul pure and undefiled from physical pleasure and desire. The Humanist regards sexual emotions and their fulfillment as healthy, beautiful, and

Nature's wonderful way of making possible the continued reproduction of the human race. While Humanism advocates high standards of conduct between the sexes, it rejects the puritanism of
the past and looks upon sex love and sex pleasure as among the
greatest of human experiences and values.

Seventh, Humanism believes that every individual must exercise a considerable amount of self-interest, if only to keep alive and
healthy, but that altruistic endeavors on behalf of the community
can be harmoniously combined with normal self-interest. Thus the
good life is best attained by uniting the more personal satisfactions
with important work and other activities that contribute to the welfare of one's city, nation, or other social unit. Significant work
usually deepens a person's happiness.

HUMANIST

"HAPPY PERSON"

SYMBOL

Source: American Humanist Association.

Eighth, Humanism supports the widest possible development
of the arts and the awareness of beauty, so that the aesthetic experience may become a pervasive reality in people's lives. The Humanist eschews the artificial distinction between the fine arts and
the useful arts and asserts that the common objects of daily use
should embody a fusion of utility and grace. The mass production
of industrial goods by machinery need not necessarily defeat this
aim. Among other things, Humanism calls for the planned architec-
tural reconstruction of towns and cities throughout America, so
that beauty may prevail in our urban life.

Ninth, Humanism gives special emphasis to appreciation of the
beauty and splendor of Nature. There is no heavenly Father in or
behind Nature, but Nature is truly our fatherland. The Humanists
energetically back the widespread efforts for conservation, the pro-
tection of wild life, and the campaigns to maintain and extend ecological values. Their keen responsiveness to every sort of natural
beauty evokes in them a feeling of profound kinship with Nature
and its myriad forms of life.

Tenth, for the actualization of human happiness and freedom
everywhere on earth, Humanism advocates the establishment of
international peace, democracy, and a high standard of living
throughout the world. Humanists, in their concern for the welfare
of all nations, peoples, and races, adopt William Lloyd Garrison's
aphorism, "Our country is the world; our countrymen are all

mankind." It follows that Humanists are strongly opposed to all forms of nationalist and racial prejudice.

Eleventh, Humanism believes that the best type of government is some form of political democracy, including civil liberties and full freedom of expression throughout all areas of economic, political, and cultural life. Reason and science are crippled unless they remain unfettered in the pursuit of truth. In the United States, the Humanist militantly supports the fundamental guarantees in the Bill of Rights.

Twelfth, Humanism, in accordance with scientific method, encourages the unending questioning of basic assumptions and convictions in every field of thought. This includes, of course, philosophy, naturalistic Humanism, and the 12 points I have outlined in this attempt at definition. Humanism is not a new dogma, but is a developing philosophy ever open to experimental testing, newly discovered facts, and more rigorous reasoning.

I do not claim that every Humanist will accept all of the 12 points I have suggested. There will be particular disagreement, I imagine, on the fourth point; that is, the one concerning free choice.

Not every Humanist wants to use the phrase *naturalistic* Humanism. Some prefer the term *scientific* Humanism, *secular* Humanism, or *democratic* Humanism. There is also a large group who consider Humanism a *religion* and who find an institutional home in the Fellowship of Religious Humanists, with its quarterly journal, *Religious Humanism.* For my own part, I prefer to call naturalistic Humanism a philosophy or way of life.

"Hinduism does not distinguish ideas of God as true and false, adopting one particular idea as the standard for the whole human race."

Hinduism Supports All Ways to God

Sarvepalli Radhakrishnan

Sir Sarvepalli Radhakrishnan, an Indian (1888-1975), had a long and amazingly productive career. In addition to being a philosopher and the author of numerous books, many dealing with religion, he taught religion and ethics at Oxford. He also represented India as its ambassador to the USSR, acted as chancellor of Delhi University, and served as vice-president of his country. In the following viewpoint, Radhakrishnan stresses the universality of Hinduism and its acceptance of all ways to God. He claims that what is important is not creed but conduct. Hinduism, he points out, is not concerned with "correct belief but righteous living."

As you read, consider the following questions:

1. How does Hinduism differ from Western religions?
2. How does Hinduism attempt to define God?
3. Some claim that more than most religions, Hinduism exemplifies the virtue of an open mind. How does this viewpoint help justify this observation?

The Hindu attitude to religion is interesting. While fixed intellectual beliefs mark off one religion from another, Hinduism sets itself no such limits. Intellect is subordinated to intuition, dogma to experience, outer expression to inward realization. Religion is not the acceptance of academic abstractions or the celebration of ceremonies, but a kind of life or experience. It is insight into the nature of reality (darsana), or experience of reality (anubhava). This experience is not an emotional thrill, or a subjective fancy, but is the response of the whole personality, the integrated self to the central reality. Religion is a specific attitude of the self, itself and no other, though it is mixed up generally with intellectual views, aesthetic forms, and moral valuations. . . .

The Vedas

The chief sacred scriptures of the Hindus, the Vedas, register the intuitions of the perfected souls.[1] They are not so much dogmatic dicta as transcripts from life. They record the spiritual experiences of souls strongly endowed with the sense for reality. They are held to be authoritative on the ground that they express the experiences of the experts in the field of religion. If the utterances of the Vedas were uninformed by spiritual insight, they would have no claim to our belief. The truths revealed in the Vedas are capable of being re-experienced on compliance with ascertained conditions. . . .

The Hindu philosophy of religion starts from and returns to an experimental basis. Only this basis is as wide as human nature itself. Other religious systems start with this or that particular experimental datum. Christian theology, for example, takes its stand on the immediate certitude of Jesus as one whose absolute authority over conscience is self-certifying and whose ability and willingness to save the soul it is impossible not to trust. Christian theology becomes relevant only for those who share or accept a particular kind of spiritual experience, and these are tempted to dismiss other experiences as illusory and other scriptures as imperfect. Hinduism was not betrayed into this situation on account of its adherence to fact. The Hindu thinker readily admits other points of view than his own and considers them to be just as worthy of attention. If the whole race of man, in every land of every colour, and every stage of culture is the offspring of God, then we must admit that, in the vast compass of his providence, all are being trained by his wisdom and supported by his love to reach within the limits of their powers a knowledge of the Supreme. When the Hindu found that different people aimed at and achieved God-realization in different ways, he generously recognized them all and justified their place in the course of history. He used the distinctive scriptures of the different groups for their uplift since they remain the source, almost the only source, for the development of their tastes and talents for the enrichment of their thought and life, for the appeal to their emotions and the inspiration of their efforts. . . .

It is sometimes urged that the descriptions of God conflict with one another. It only shows that our notions are not true. To say that our ideas of God are not true is not to deny the reality of God to which our ideas refer. Refined definitions of God as moral personality, and holy love may contradict cruder ones which look upon Him as a primitive despot, a sort of sultan in the sky, but they all intend the same reality. . . .

Religious Truth Unifies

The unity of religions is to be found in that which is divine or universal in them and not in what is temporary and local. Where there is the spirit of truth there is unity. As in other matters, so in the sphere of religion there is room for diversity and no need for discord. To claim that any one religious tradition bears unique witness to the truth and reveals the presence of the true God is inconsistent with belief in a living God who has spoken to men "by diverse portions and in diverse manners." God is essentially self-communicative and is of ungrudging goodness, as Plato taught. There is no such thing as a faith once for all delivered to the saints. Revelation is divine-human. As God does not reveal His Being to a stone or a tree, but only to men, His revelation is attuned to the state of the human mind. The Creative Spirit is ever ready to reveal Himself to the seeking soul provided the search is genuine and the effort intense. The authority for revelation is not an Infallible Book or an Infallible Church but the witness of the inner light. What is needed is not submission to an external authority but inward illumination which, of course, is tested by tradition and logic. If we reflect on the matter deeply we will perceive the unity of spiritual aspiration and endeavor underlying the varied upward paths indicated in the different world faiths. The diversity in the traditional formulations tends to diminish as we climb up the scale of spiritual perfection. All the paths of ascent lead to the mountaintop.

Sarvepalli Radhakrishnan, *This Is My Philosophy*, edited by Whit Burnett, 1957.

When asked to define the nature of God, the seer of the Upanisad sat silent, and when pressed to answer exclaimed that the Absolute is silence, santa 'yam atma. The mystery of the divine reality eludes the machinery of speech and symbol. The "Divine Darkness," "That of which nothing can be said," and such other expressions are used by the devout when they attempt to describe their consciousness of direct communion with God.

The Hindu thinkers bring out the sense of the otherness of the divine by the use of negatives, "There the eye goes not, speech goes not, nor mind, we know not, we understand not how one would teach it."[2] . . .

Hindu thought believes in the evolution of our knowledge of God. We have to vary continually our notions of God until we pass beyond all notions into the heart of the reality itself, which our ideas endeavour to report. Hinduism does not distinguish ideas of God as true and false, adopting one particular idea as the standard for the whole human race. It accepts the obvious fact that mankind seeks its goal of God at various levels and in various directions, and feels sympathy with every stage of the search. The same God expresses itself at one stage as power, at another as personality, at a third as all-comprehensive spirit, just as the same forces which put forth the green leaves also cause the crimson flower to grow. We do not say that the crimson flowers are all the truth and the green leaves are all false. Hinduism accepts all religious notions as facts and arranges them in the order of their more or less intrinsic significance. The bewildering polytheism of the masses and the uncompromising monotheism of the classes are for the Hindu the expressions of one and the same force at different levels. Hinduism insists on our working steadily upwards and improving our knowledge of God.

> "The worshippers of the Absolute are the highest in rank; second to them are the worshippers of the personal God; then come the worshippers of the incarnations like Rama, Krsna, Buddha; below them are those who worship ancestors, deities and sages, and lowest of all are the worshippers of the petty forces and spirits."[3] Again, "The deities of some men are in water (i.e., bathing places), those of the child (in religion) are in images of wood and stone, but the sage finds his God in his deeper self."[4] "The man of action finds his God in fire, the man of feeling in the heart, and the feeble-minded in the idol, but the strong in spirit find God everywhere."[5] The seers see the Supreme in the self, and not in images. . . .

Hinduism developed an attitude of comprehensive charity instead of a fanatic faith in an inflexible creed. It accepted the multiplicity of aboriginal gods and others which originated, most of them outside the Aryan tradition, and justified them all. It brought together into one whole all believers in God. Many sects professing many different beliefs live within the Hindu fold. Heresy-hunting, the favourite game of many religions, is singularly absent from Hinduism.

Acceptance of Other Faiths

Hinduism is wholly free from the strange obsession of the Semitic faiths that the acceptance of a particular religious metaphysic is necessary for salvation, and nonacceptance thereof is a heinous sin meriting eternal punishment in hell. . . .

After all, what counts is not creed but conduct. By their fruits ye shall know them and not by their beliefs. Religion is not correct belief but righteous living.[6] The truly religious never worry about other people's beliefs. Look at the great saying of Jesus: Other sheep I have which are not of this fold." Jesus was born a Jew and died a Jew. He did not tell the Jewish people among whom he found himself, "It is wicked to be Jews. Become Christians." He did his best to rid the Jewish religion of its impurities. He would have done the same with Hinduism were he born a Hindu. The true reformer purifies and enlarges the heritage of mankind and does not belittle, still less deny it.

Those who love their sects more than truth end by loving themselves more than their sects. We start by claiming that Christianity is the only true religion and then affirm that Protestantism is the only true sect of Christianity, Episcopalianism the only true Protestantism, the High Church the only true Episcopal Protestant Christian religion, and our particular standpoint the only true representation of the High Church View.

The Hindu theory that every human being, every group and every nation has an individuality worthy of reverence is slowly gaining ground. Such a view requires that we should allow absolute freedom to every group to cultivate what is most distinctive and characteristic of it. All peculiarity is unique and incommunicable, and it will be to disregard the nature of reality to assume that what is useful to one will be useful to everyone else to the same extent. The world is wide enough to hold men whose natures are different.

1. Taittiriya Aranyaka, i.2.
2. Kena Up., 3.
3. upasana brahmanah prak, dvitiya sagunasya ca trtiya smaryate lilavigrahopasana budhaih upantya pitrdevarsigananam astyupasana antima ksudradevanam pretadinam vidhiyate.
4. apsu deva manusyanam divi deva manisinam balanam kasthalosthesu buddhasy atmani devata.
5. agnau kriyavato devo hrdi devo manisinam pratimasv alpabuddhinam jnaminam sarvatah sivah.
6. Cp. Spinoza: "Religion is universal to the human race; wherever justice and charity have the force of law and ordinance, there is God's kingdom."

> *"The only happiness, the only fulfillment, the only total living you will ever have is right here and right now."*

Atheism Is the Way of Common Sense

Madalyn O'Hair

Madalyn O'Hair is the founder of the Society of Separationists and the American Atheist Library and Archives in Austin, Texas. America's most famous atheist is currently editor emeritus of *American Atheist*, a magazine she originated in 1965. The author of numerous publications on atheism, O'Hair argues that atheism is not just a negative attack on theism but has its own positive agenda. She believes that atheists love their fellow humans, not a nonexistent God. Heaven, she argues, "is something for which we should work now—here on earth."

As you read, consider the following questions:

1. According to the author, what do atheists believe?
2. How does O'Hair distinguish the atheist's philosophy of materialism from hedonism?
3. What three rules of conduct does the author suggest should guide one's life?

From Madalyn O'Hair, *Why I Am an Atheist*, a pamphlet published in 1966 and revised in 1976 by the Society of Separationists, Inc. Reprinted with permission.

I am neither afraid nor ashamed to say what I believe or what I think. I am an Atheist and this means at least that I do not believe there is a *god* or *any* god, personal or in nature or manifesting himself, herself, or itself in any way. I do not believe there is such thing as heaven or hell or perdition or any of the stages in between. I do not believe there is any life after death. I do not believe in miracles, I do not believe in angels. I do not believe in Prophets and I do not accept any holy book of any kind be they the Bible, the Torah, the Veda, the Koran, the Upanishads, the Oahspe, the Urantia, or anything else in any age in the history of man, written by Moses, Mary Baker Eddy, Joseph Smith, Mohammed, Gautama Buddha, or even the finger of fate.

I do not believe in saviors and this includes any so called saviors from Moses to Jesus Christ, Mohammed, or his daughter Fatima, the angel Moroni, or the popes or any oracles, self appointed or appointed by other persons. I do not believe in the efficacy of prayers said either by myself or a priest, a rabbi, a minister, or guru.

Please, as adults we must face that this is silly. These ancient fables and ideas are silly and we no longer need to cling to them. Do you really believe any woman can have a child without a sexual relationship? This is an insult to you and to me. It is an insult to our intelligence and to our common sense and to our own experience which we have gained from living.

What Atheists Believe

Well, that is what I don't believe. A charge against any Atheist is that we are negative, that we do *not* believe and that we should have a positive program. And so, many people ask us, "What is your positive approach to the problems of man, of man living in human relationships, in a hard, cruel world?"

Now this isn't corny because it is a hard and cruel world. The most difficult thing in the world to do is to live and to get along with other people, to earn a living, to meet our basic needs. It is very difficult to do this. You have a hard time doing it and so do I and we need a decent modern, sophisticated and workable set of standards by which we can get along with ourselves and with others. We can toss out all this old garbage of rules laid down by god. No god ever gave *any* man *anything and never will. We solve our problems ourselves or they are not going to get solved and you know it and I know it.*

When we got involved in this suit to take bible and prayer out of schools we did a very unique thing. We went to a court of this land and for the first time in the history of the United States we said in court and in our legal brief that we objected to bible reading and prayer recitation *because* we were Atheists.

We did not say that we were Jews and did not, therefore, accept the New Testament. We did not say that we were Catholics and did not, therefore, accept the King James version of the Bible. We did not say that we were Buddhists or Mohammedans and therefore, could not accept the Christian practice. We said that we were Atheists, living in a modern world and that we did not accept any of these fairy tales of any kind. Our attorney said to me "O.K. Madalyn, if you want to base your suit on this and this alone, then you can write up a little blurb about what an Atheist is and I'll put it into the suit." So, I did and he did and this is it.

Atheists Believe in the Truth

We Atheists replace god with the truth. Truth has no enemy except the people who live in deadly fear of it. Truth boldly confronts mysteries and probes them. Truth has no temple, no priests nor altars, and does not demand human sacrifices; no heart will be pulled, still palpitating, from young men's chests; no maidens will be thrown alive into dark, deep wells; no horrible tortures nor burnings-alive in public places will take place, to impose truth. No war will be declared requiring the extermination of any infidels. . . .

We do not believe in eternal life, but we consider the life of each person sacred because of its uniqueness—and because each of us has only one brief span to live! When we encounter something we do not fully comprehend, we frankly acknowledge the fact; and we do not try to replace that "something" with something even less comprehensible, giving it a name and trembling with fear in front of it. We have rejected the immense pretension of being a special creation of some deity; but we believe we can make a reasonable human claim of having surpassed the creativeness and intelligence of any known deity on this tiny planet—and we didn't have eternity in our favor.

We believe in the sane and edifying power of the truth!

We believe in the supreme healing power of love!

We believe in the arts and the cultivation of the beautiful.

Atheism is the product of comprehension and reflection, not compulsion.

We believe in a philosophy of life, not in a philosophy of death!

Louis Parle, "Apologia for Atheism," *The American Atheist*, October 1982.

For the first time in any law books, in any history books, you can go and read it for yourself. It is in the records of the Baltimore, Maryland, Superior Court in the case of *William J. Mur-*

ray III vs John N. Curlett. William Murray III is my oldest son and John N. Curlett is the President of the Board of School Commissioners of Baltimore City. The case was field in December 1960 and it reached the United States Supreme Court for argument in February 1963. The statement to which I refer says, and you'll understand this despite the legal terminology here and there:

> Your petitioners are Atheists and they define their beliefs as follows. An Atheist loves his fellow man instead of god. An Atheist believes that heaven is something for which we should work now—here on earth for all men together to enjoy. An Atheist believes that he can get no help through prayer but that he must find in himself the inner conviction and strength to meet life, to grapple with it, to subdue it and enjoy it. An Atheist believes that only in a knowledge of himself and a knowledge of his fellow man can he find the understanding that will help to [live] a life of fulfillment.
>
> He seeks to know himself and his fellow man rather than to know a god. An Atheist believes that a hospital should be built instead of a church. An Atheist believes that a deed must be done instead of a prayer said. An Atheist strives for involvement in life and not to escape death. He wants disease conquered, poverty vanished, war eliminated. He wants man to understand and love man. He wants an ethical way of life. He believes that we cannot rely on a god or channel action into prayer nor hope for an end of troubles in a hereafter. He believes that we are our brother's keepers; and are keepers of our own lives; that we are responsible persons and the job is here and the time is now.

Doesn't that sound awfully serious and intense? Well, we really are persons who subscribe to the "do it yourself fad." Do you know that we could knock tuberculosis completely off the map within two years if we gave a concentrated national effort to it. We won't ever do it by praying. The churches are never going to bother themselves with it. They are much too interested in seeing that everyone gets to heaven when they die than to prevent anyone from dying.

The Philosophy of Materialism

Getting to heaven: We Atheists are not charlatans who promise "pie in the sky." We tell you frankly, that the only happiness, the only fulfillment, the only total living you will ever have is right here and right now. You will get somewhere only with well thought out planning and hard work that you do. No one is involved in helping you but you.

Well, you say, that statement which you put into your suit sounds like everything that everybody really wants, so you are no different than we are. Well, you're right in a way. We are knowledgeable, we Atheists. We try to find some basis of ratio-

102

Reprinted with permission from *The American Atheist*, January 1985.

nal thinking in which we can base our actions and our beliefs and we have it. It has existed for thousands of years and it anti-dates Christianity which is only about 1600 years old.

We accepted the technical philosophy of materialism. Aha you think—materialism, that is a dirty word, you are communists! We are like hell! Materialism has been around for over 6000 years and Marxist communism is not even a hundred years old. Materialism is a valid philosophy of living and it cannot be discredited.

In a nutshell, oversimplified perhaps, but absolutely accurate, let me try to explain to you what materialism is. It's technical in a way, but in another way it isn't and I think you will understand.

Materialism's philosophy holds that nothing exists but natural phenomena—that there are no supernatural forces, no supernatural entities such as gods or heaven or hell or anything else. *There are no supernatural forces* nor can there be.

Nature simply exists—matter is, material is. There are those who would deny this—really this is an important point. There are those who would deny nature exists. *Really, they deny that nature or material exists and they assert that only the mind exists,* (the mind or idea or spirit or whatever they want to call it) and they claim that this is primary or first. The question of the relationship of the mind to material being is the root of the issue between religion, which is a way of death, and materialism, which is a way of life.

Those who regard nature as primary and thought as a property of nature (or a function of nature) belong to the camp of materialism. Those who maintain that idea, or spirit, or mind, existed before nature and that it created nature belong to the camp of idealism. All conventional religions are based on idealism. Incidentally, I think that religionists should not call this "idealism," for people like you and I get confused and we think idealism is the pursuit of ideals. But, maybe our religious brothers want people to be confused about it. I think they should call their philosophy *idea-ism* since it asserts that only "ideas" exist.

The Brain

Let's take an example that isn't too technical. Your brain. The materialists say that you think, and you have ideas, because you have a brain in your head and that this is made up of gray matter. It is so long, so wide, so high, and it weighs so much, and has so much volume, etc. But the religionists say that ideas come first, and that your ideas and thoughts don't really come from your brain but that the brain really came from the ideas. Well, could you possibly think of anything more confused than that? Really this is not a joke. This is the basis of the argument between materialists and religionists and you can check it in your library or in any elementary book of philosophy. The argument is not academic. It isn't an argument just to be an argument—it is a real living thing. For, the church then proceeds to teach a contempt for earthly life, and they claim that the goal of your life is to die, *the goal of life is death*, so that you can reunite with ideas once again in heaven and that heaven is really a big pool of ideas floating around out there somewhere.

But the goal of life, which is actually death, significantly can be achieved only as reward for obedience and meekness and bowing to the authority of the church. Hellfire and the very wrath of god is threatened to those who think otherwise.

Human Life Is an Accident

The human species has inhabited this planet for only 250,000 years or so—roughly .0015 percent of the history of life, the last inch of the cosmic mile. The world fared perfectly well without us for all but the last moment of earthly time—and this fact makes our appearance look more like an accidental afterthought than the culmination of a prefigured plan. Moreover, the pathways that have led to our evolution are quirky, improbable, unrepeatable and utterly unpredictable. Human evolution is not random; it makes sense and can be explained after the fact. But wind back life's tape to the dawn of time and let it play again—and you will never get humans a second time.

We are here because one odd group of fishes had a peculiar fin anatomy that could transform into legs for terrestrial creatures; because the earth never froze entirely during an ice age; because a small and tenuous species, arising in Africa a quarter of a million years ago, has managed, so far, to survive by hook and by crook. We may yearn for a "higher" answer—but none exists. This explanation, though superficially troubling, if not terrifying, is ultimately liberating and exhilarating. We cannot read the meaning of life passively in the facts of nature. We must construct these answers ourselves—from our own wisdom and ethical sense. There is no other way.

Stephen Jay Gould in *The Meaning of Life*, 1991.

But let's go back to materialism now. Materialism liberates us by teaching us not to hope for heaven beyond the grave, not to hope for happiness in death, but rather to prize life on earth and strive always to improve it. Materialism restores to man his dignity and his intellectual integrity. Man is capable of mastering the forces of nature. Man is capable of creating a social system based on reason and justice. Materialism's faith is in man and man's ability to transform the world by its own efforts. This is a philosophy in every essence life asserting. It considers the struggle for progress as a moral obligation and impossible without noble ideals that inspire man to struggle and bold creative work.

Ah, but then you say to us, we thought that materialism was the accumulation of material goods and the practice of hedonism, that is, just getting pleasure out of life, and that this was the sole objective of life of a materialist. I hate to be the one to tell you this, but it just is *not true*. . . .

Materialists, and we call ourselves Atheists, do not believe in

105

the divinity of man. And because of this we shy away from systems of thought which exalt the human animal. We are embarrassingly aware that we are most insignificant. We are more insignificant than the sea or the wind or just our planet alone. Man must share the earth with all other animals. *And, we are animals.* We must share the earth also with the earth's resources. Naturally, therefore, a materialist is not an exploiter of man or nature. A materialist is not an accumulator nor a wasteful user nor a conspicuous consumer, and least of all does he revel in the glorification of man.

Well, you say how does this fit in with living day by day. Do you live by the golden rule? No, I don't like the golden rule and you know what the golden rule is these days. It is "Do unto others, what they would do unto you, but do it first." Personally I try to live by what is called the categorical imperative. The *what? What's that you say?* Well, we have the writings of Immanuel Kant, a philosopher who lived in the eighteenth century. He struggled with ideas of rules of conduct and ideas of morality. He came up with three suggestions. One was that we should treat every other person and ourselves as "ends" and not as "means." *That we should treat ourselves and others as ends in themselves and not as means to an end.* You just try that one. I've tried to keep this rule for 30 years and I break it all the time. It is a terrible exacting idea by which to try to live.

Kant's second suggestion was to so act that any of your actions could be made into universal laws. That's something. Cheat that poor Joe out of a nickel and then have a universal law that everyone always cheats everybody else out of a nickel, including you.

His third suggestion was to search for truth. Well I just gave up on that one. I don't know if we'll ever find out what truth is or what it isn't. Hitler said that truth was to kill six million Jews. The Roman Catholic Church said that truth was to exterminate thousands and thousands, maybe hundreds of thousands, of persons in the Inquisition. So I have amended his third suggestion to "seek knowledge," keep on a quest, find out as much as you can about everything. Don't take anyone's word. Go find out for yourself.

"The Bible is the only *written revelation which God has given to man."*

The Bible Is God's Way to Humanity

Emmaus Bible College

The Emmaus Bible College, located in Dubuque, Iowa, follows an evangelical interpretation of the Bible. It is founded on the principle that "the Bible is inspired of God, inerrant in the original documents and of final authority in all matters of faith and practice." The College's purpose is to provide a place "where young men and women come to have Scriptures opened to them." The following viewpoint, excerpted from a book written by staff members of the College, presents a conservative perspective of Christianity based on the assumptions described above.

As you read, consider the following questions:

1. In the authors' opinion, what role did God have in writing the Bible?
2. What do the authors claim the Bible tells us about the nature of God?
3. The authors state that "if we want to know the truth about man we must turn to the Bible." What do they claim the Bible says about human nature and life's purpose?
4. What does the Bible say about the time of death, in the authors' opinion?

From *What Christians Believe* by Emmaus Bible College. Copyright © 1949, 1951 by Emmaus Bible College. Reprinted by permission of Moody Bible Institute, Chicago.

Someone has called the Holy Bible "the divine library," and this is a true statement. . . .

Who Wrote the Bible

From the human standpoint the Bible was written by not less than thirty-six authors over a period of about sixteen hundred years. But the important thing to remember is that these men wrote under the direct control of God. God guided them in writing the very words. This is what we mean by inspiration. The following Scriptures clearly teach that the Bible is inspired by God.

> For the prophecy came not in old time by the will of man, but holy men of God spake as they were moved by the Holy Ghost. 2 Peter 1:21.
>
> All Scripture is given by inspiration of God and is profitable for doctrine, for reproof, for correction, for instruction in righteousness; that the man of God may be perfect, thoroughly furnished unto all good works. 2 Timothy 3:16-17.

Thus the Bible *is* the word of God. It is not enough to say that the Bible *contains* the Word of God. This might imply that parts of it are inspired and parts are not. *Every part of the Bible is inspired.* "All Scripture is given by inspiration of God."

Another important point to remember is that the Bible is the *only* written revelation which God has given to man. In the last chapter of the Bible, God warns men against adding to the Bible or taking away from it. Revelation 22:18-19. . . .

The Bible is the record of the world from the beginning of time until the future when there will be a new heaven and a new earth.

Genesis tells of the creation of the world, the entrance of sin, the flood, and the beginning of the nation of Israel. From Exodus to Esther we have the history of Israel up to about 400 years before the birth of Christ. The books from Job to the Song of Solomon contain wonderful poetry and wisdom. The rest of the Old Testament, from Isaiah to Malachi, is prophetic,—that is, these books contain messages from God to Israel concerning its present condition and its future destiny.

The New Testament opens with four Gospels, each of which present the life of the Lord Jesus Christ. Acts tells the story of the Christian movement in its infancy and the life of the great apostle Paul. From Romans to Jude, we find letters to churches and individuals, concerning the great truths of the Christian faith, and practical instruction concerning the Christian life. Revelation gives us a glimpse into the future,—to events that will yet take place in heaven, on earth, and in hell. . . .

The Existence of God

1. The Bible does not seek to prove the existence of God. The fact that there is a God is assumed throughout the Scriptures. The first verse of the Bible is an example. "In the beginning God created the

heaven and the earth." God's existence is presented as a statement of fact that needs no proof. The man who says that there is no God is called a fool in Psalm 14:1.

2. However, even apart from the Bible, there are certain evidences for the existence of God. (1) Mankind has always believed in a universal being. (2) Creation must have a creator. The universe could not originate without a cause. (3) The wonderful design which we see in creation demands an infinite designer. (4) Since man is an intelligent, moral being, his creator must have been of a much higher order in order to create him.

The Nature of God

1. God is a spirit. John 4:24. This means that God does not have a body. He is invisible. However, He can reveal Himself to man in visible form. In the person of Jesus Christ, God came into the world in a body of flesh. John 1:14, 18; Colossians 1:15; Hebrews 1:3.

Read It and Decide

The best way to prove the truth of the Bible is to read it. It has overcome the doubts of many. General Lew Wallace had this experience. He was a friend of Bob Ingersoll, the notorious atheist, and like Ingersoll he had no confidence in the Bible. Wallace decided to write a book against the Bible, but thought it only fair to read the Bible first. However, in doing this he came to believe it completely! The book he finally wrote was *Ben Hur*, a powerful best-seller; a beautiful story centered around Christ.

Clyde M. Narramore, *Why a Psychologist Believes the Bible*, pamphlet by The Narramore Christian Foundation dated 1969.

---

2. God is a person. Personal names are used in reference to Him. Exodus 3:14. Matthew 11:25. Personal characteristics are ascribed to Him, such as (1) knowledge, Isaiah 55:9-10; (2) emotions, Genesis 6:6; and (3) will, Joshua 3:10.

3. The Unity of God. Scripture clearly teaches that there is one God. I Timothy 2:5. The false teaching that there are many gods is contrary to reason. There can be only one Supreme Being.

4. The Trinity. The Bible teaches not only that there is one God, but also that there are three persons in the Godhead,—Father, Son and Holy Spirit. This is a mystery to the human mind, but although it cannot be understood, it can be believed because God's Word says it is so. . . .

The Attributes of God

It is difficult to define God. One of the best ways is to describe certain of His qualities or characteristics. These are known as His attributes.

1. God is omnipresent. This means that God is present everywhere at the same time. Jeremiah 23:24.

2. God is omniscient. In other words, He knows all things. He knows every thought and deed of man. Proverbs 15:3. He knows everything that takes place in nature, including even the death of a sparrow, Matthew 10:29.

"Though limitless the universe, and gloriously grand, He knows the eternal story of every grain of sand."

3. God is omnipotent. He has all power. He created the universe, and now controls it by His power. There is nothing that He cannot do. Matthew 19:26.

4. God is eternal. He never had a beginning, and He will never cease to exist. Psalm 90:2.

5. God is unchangeable. "I am the Lord, I change not." Malachi 3:6.

6. God is holy. He is absolutely pure and sinless. He hates sin and loves goodness. Proverbs 15:9, 26. He must separate Himself from sinners, and must punish sin. Isaiah 59:1,2.

7. God is just. Everything He does is right and fair. He fulfills all His promises. Psalm 119:137.

8. God is love. Although God hates sin, yet He loves sinners. John 3:16....

Man's Origin

If we want to know the truth about man, we must turn to the Bible. "Truth is what God says about a thing." The Bible tells about man's creation, nature, relation to other beings, his fall and destiny....

The Bible tells us: In the beginning God created the heavens and the earth...God created man. Gen. 1:1,27.

God says concerning His creature man, "I have created him for my glory, I have formed him: yea, I have made him." Isaiah 43:7. So the old question, "What is the chief end of man?" is properly answered, "The chief end of man is to glorify God."

Man's Nature

Anyone who has witnessed a deathbed understands vividly that man has a physical body and also a soul or spirit. At one moment the person is alive...the next he is gone. Yet his body is still there. But the life principle has departed; a dead body remains. Man is not merely a body, but also is or has a soul and spirit.

The Bible teaches us that man exists as a three-fold being: body, soul and spirit. I Thessalonians 5:23. While it is hard for us to distinguish between soul and spirit, since both are in contrast with the physical body, the Bible shows that there is a difference. Animals have a body and soul, but no spirit. A man has a body, soul and spirit.

110

The soul distinguishes a living being from a dead one, but the spirit distinguishes a man from an animal. The spirit of man makes it possible for him to have communion or fellowship with God. The soul is the seat of the emotions and passions, while the term spirit includes our ability to know and reason. Man is responsible to God and it is his greatest duty to find out what God wants him to do, then do it. . . .

Man's Future

Just as the Bible tells us of man's origin, as coming from the hand of God; and of man's shameful fall and the consequent separation from God; so it faithfully tells us that every man, woman and child will some day stand before God as his Judge. The fact of death is so common that everyone understands the inevitable end of every man. But the Bible adds, "After this the judgment." God has created man and revealed to him His will. God will absolutely hold every person responsible for everything he has done. This life is primarily a preparation for the next one. Man does not die like the animal. His spirit must go to God, his Creator and Judge.

What Is Sin?

No one can read the Bible very much without realizing that a great deal of attention is given to the subject of sin, its cause and cure. We often think of sin in connection with crime and murder. But sin in the Bible refers to anything short of God's perfection. In Romans 3:23, we read, "All have sinned and come short of the glory of God." The "glory of God" includes the thought of absolute perfection. Sin is therefore falling short of the mark. All men are guilty of this. . . .

The Origin of Sin

The first recorded instance of sin took place in heaven. The angel Lucifer became ambitious to be equal with God. Isaiah 14:12-14. For this sin of pride, he was cast out of heaven, and became the one whom the Bible elsewhere describes as the devil or Satan.

The first instance of sin on earth is described in the Third Chapter of Genesis. It took place in the Garden of Eden. God forbade Adam and Eve to eat the fruit of the tree of knowledge of good and evil. They disobeyed God and ate the forbidden fruit. They thus became sinners.

The Results of Sin

1. As soon as the parents of the human race sinned, they became conscious of the fact that they were naked, and they tried to hide from God. Genesis 3:10.

2. The penalty of sin is death. Adam became spiritually dead the moment he sinned. By this we mean that he became separated from

God, and banished from God's presence. He also became subject to physical death. Although he did not die immediately, his body was doomed to die eventually.

3. Adam's sinful nature was passed on to all the human race. Every child born of sinful parents is a sinner by birth. Thus Adam's oldest son, Cain, was a murderer. Because all men are born sinners, they are all dead spiritually, and are all doomed to die physically some day. Romans 5:12-18.

4. Man's sin brought God's curse upon all creation. Thorns and thistles, for instance, are an evidence of this. Other evidences are mentioned in Genesis 3:14-19. Sin needs no proof as long as we have prisons, hospitals, and funeral parlors. Tears, sickness, sorrow, pain and death are some of the results of sin. . . .

The Remedy for Sin

God has provided a remedy so that men do not need to suffer everlasting punishment for their sins. He sent His Son into the world to provide a way of escape for man. The Lord Jesus Christ was born of the Virgin Mary. He did not inherit Adam's sinful nature. He was the only sinless man who ever lived. On the Cross of Calvary He willingly suffered the penalty of sin, and satisifed all God's holy demands. Since the penalty of sin has been met, God can now give eternal life to every sinner who confesses the fact that he is a sinner and receives the Lord Jesus Christ as his Lord and Savior.

When a person trusts in Christ, he is saved from the penalty and power of sin. This does not mean that he no longer commits sin. But it does mean that all his sins, past, present and future, have been forgiven, that he will never be judged for them, and that he has power to live for God instead of for the pleasures of sin.

What Happens to a Man at the Time of Death?

At the outset, we need to remember that man is a tripartite being, that is, he is composed of three parts—body, soul, and spirit. I Thessalonians 5:23. The first part is material being, the other two are non-material. With a spirit, man is capable of God-consciousness; with a soul, he is capable of self-consciousness; with a body, he is capable of world-consciousness. Only God's Word can divide between the soul and the spirit. Hebrews 4:12.

Now, at the time of death, the soul and spirit leave the body. The body is put into the grave. In the case of believers, the body is described as sleeping, Acts 7:59, 60; 8:2, while the unsaved person's body is spoken of as dead. The soul and spirit never sleep. If the person who died was saved, the soul and the spirit go to a place of joy and happiness—heaven, II Cor. 5:8; Phil. 1:21, 23. If the person was unsaved, the spirit and soul go to a place of sorrow and punishment—hades. In Luke 16:19-31, our Lord clearly teaches that those who have died are conscious. . . .

What Do We Know About Heaven?

The Scriptures clearly teach that there is a place of bliss for all who know and love our Lord Jesus Christ. Heaven is a place. The word is used in the Bible in three different ways. First of all, the region of the clouds is called heaven. Genesis 1:8. Then the area where the stars are located is known as heaven. Genesis 1:17. Finally, the word is used to describe God's dwelling place. Paul calls this the "third heaven" and "Paradise." II Corinthians 12:2-4. Heaven is always mentioned as being "up." Satan said, in Isaiah 14:13-14, "I will ascend into heaven."

We know that our Lord is in heaven today. After He was raised from the dead, He ascended in a body of flesh and bones. He carried glorified humanity into heaven. Luke 24:38, 39, 51; I Peter 3:22; Hebrews 1:3.

There is a great host of believers in heaven for when the true Christian dies, he is "absent from the body—present with the Lord." II Corinthians 5:8. These believers are enjoying the presence of Christ "which is very far better." Philippians 1:23.

What is heaven like? The writers of the Scriptures could not find language that would describe it. In Revelation 21:10-27, John describes the foundations, wall, gates, and street of the heavenly city. Our hearts are attracted by its beauty. We know that there will be no sickness, sorrow, tears, pain or death in that fair place. Revelation 21:4. But best of all, the Lord Jesus Christ will be there, and He will be the supreme delight of every believer's heart.

"Although Scripture and tradition are important, the basepoint of liberal morality has been reason."

Liberal Christianity Is Humanity's Way to God

Donald E. Miller

Donald E. Miller is associate professor in the School of Religion of the University of Southern California, where he specializes in the sociology of religion and the relationship between ethical analysis and the social sciences. In the following viewpoint, excerpted from *The Case for Liberal Christianity*, Miller presents a viable alternative to conservative Christianity for Christians who do not believe all the tenets of traditional Christianity. He argues for a resurgence of the "liberal spirit" and presents a case for the liberal Christian in contemporary society.

As you read, consider the following questions:

1. In the author's opinion, why do liberal Christians consider the arts and education important aspects of life?
2. Why does Miller believe liberal Christians view the Social Gospel differently than conservative Christians?
3. How does the author think a liberal Christian theologian would view Scripture differently than a conservative Christian theologian?

Excerpts from *The Case for Liberal Christianity* by Donald E. Miller, © 1981 by Donald E. Miller. Reprinted by permission of HarperCollins Publishers.

One of the central facts of contemporary existence is the diversity of meaning systems that individuals follow. Liberal Christianity is one framework of meaning and values. In addition to being unique as a religious framework of meaning—as opposed to a strictly secular framework, which makes no reference to things sacred, or to a transcendent reference point for evaluating the meaningfulness of human existence—liberal Christianity is distinctive insofar as it is one of several perspectives within the Christian religious framework. . . .

Defining Liberal Christianity

Liberal Christians differ from their more conservative counterparts at a number of points, but let me begin with their *view toward culture*. Rather than perceiving culture, particularly science and the arts, as a potential threat to religious faith, liberal Christians have understood that Christianity must evolve and adapt itself—or at least its expression—from age to age. They have believed that the application of the gospel must be reinterpreted from each new cultural context. Although there may be a core essence to Christianity, liberal Christians view accommodation to culture as necessary and positive, if what one means by "accommodation" is that they should seek to understand God and their moral responsibility in terms of the best available scientific knowledge and social analysis.

The Arts and Education

Liberal Christians look upon the arts as important expressions of the problems and tensions of their culture. Liberal Christians also recognize the invaluable moral critiques found in many artistic expressions. Whereas film, theater, and dance may be shunned by many conservative Christians, liberal Christians look to these artistic productions as important occasions for not only self-reflection, but also a potential uplifting and enlivening of the human spirit. Liberal Christians have long recognized that things ultimate and real can be portrayed through a variety of mediums. Thus, an evening spent reading a novel, viewing a theatrical production, or seeing a movie may be as illuminating as a comparable period of time spent reading the Bible. Liberal Christians believe that revelations may come in many forms.

Liberals have long been champions of education. They find that nothing is to be feared in knowledge. To discover the relativity of cultures is not a new insight so much as it is a foundation stone on which liberalism rests. Liberal clergy have usually been highly educated. The task implicit in sermon preparation by liberal clergy has been to blend creatively the "old gospel" with the personal, social, and political problems felt by those in the pew. As a result, psychological, sociological, and philosophical insights often have found their way into the text of sermons

115

given by the liberal clergy. Book discussion groups have been at least as common in liberal churches as Bible study groups and prayer meetings.

MISS PEACH by Mell Lazarus. Reprinted by special permission of North America Syndicate.

The danger in liberalism is that the Christian message may become a mirror reflection of the spirit of the age. This is an ever-present problem for liberal Christians to confront. On the other hand, liberals have protested that one cannot possibly critique culture without understanding it. . . .

Morality

Liberal Christians have always placed considerable emphasis upon the moral witness of their faith. Rooted in the Social Gospel Movement of the last several decades of the nineteenth century and the first three decades of the twentieth century, liberal Christianity has always sought to apply its Gospel to the social betterment of the human community. Political rallies and social action committee meetings have often taken the place of more traditionally pious activities. In its earlier period, liberalism was married to the spirit of socialism. As political winds changed, so did the social ethic of liberal Christianity. Under the pressure of the Neo-orthodox Movement, many liberals were forced into a greater acknowledgment of the reality of sin and of the necessity of a new found political realism. Whatever the ideology, however, liberal Christians have always found themselves in the streets, politicking city councils, writing letters to congressmen, and busying themselves with social welfare concerns. Their approach stands in contrast to that of many conservative Christians who have sought to change the world by changing hearts (through conversion).

Although Scripture and tradition are important, the basepoint of liberal morality has been reason. This emphasis, of course, has coincided nicely with the commitment of liberal Christians to education. In contrast to the scriptural "proof-texting" of

116

many conservative Christians, liberals have often appealed to the broader principles of justice and love as explicated in the Bible. Reason has always been the mediating force in applying these biblical insights to particular situations. Not infrequently liberals have endorsed a contextual or situational ethic. They have been relatively inhospitable, on the other hand, to moral legalisms. Always reason is to be used in weighing the authority of Scripture and tradition. . . .

Another identifying mark of the moral commitment of liberal Christians is that they have characteristically given at least as much attention to social morality as personal morality. Matters of sexual practice and personal vice have been of interest to liberal Christians, but programmatic emphases have more typically been related to issues of war, poverty, racial discrimination, employment practices, and so forth. Systemic and social-structural problems have been understood to be at the root of much of the suffering and misery in the world. For this reason, the prophets of the Old Testament have often been appealed to as frequently as the teachings of Jesus.

Scripture

Liberal Christians differ from conservative Christians in that they generally approach Scripture nondogmatically. Liberal biblical scholars tend to apply historical, sociological, and even psychological tools and insights to their interpretations of Scripture. The hermeneutical principle often applied is that everything— Scripture included—is written within a cultural context. Therefore, to understand the meaning of a document, one must understand how and why it was written. One must also understand the world view of the writer. For example, one of the most famous biblical scholars, Rudolf Bultmann, believed that the New Testament was written from the perspective of a pre-scientific cosmology of a three-tiered universe (with heaven above, hell or the underworld below, and the earth, on which men and women dwell, as a mediating structure between the two). His task of demythologization was an effort to get at the kerygma (message) which lay behind this first century world view.

When the Scriptures are understood as human documents, they then are susceptible to all the canons of modern historical and literary analysis. To the liberal theologian, there is a considerable difference between viewing the Bible primarily through the eyes of faith and being equally open to a cultural and historical perspective. Historically, the resurrection of Jesus and the virgin birth are at best ambiguous as concrete occurrences. From the perspective of faith, however, they may have quite a different significance. But one should never conclude that the

Scriptures are unimportant for the liberal Christian. Quite the contrary, they are central to the Christian faith. The fact that more attention is given to them as symbolic documents than as historical documents does not distort their importance.

The Bible Is Not God

Biblical literalists are always first-rate candidates for atheism. For their God, of course, is actually the Bible. And although the Bible is holy and good, it is not God. Therefore, when faith in their god, the Bible, is in any way shaken, then, like the "intelligent young man named Jitterly," they may "reject the whole thing bitterly." In the meantime, their narrow and shallow interpretation of the Bible may also cause a lot of other folks to reject it as well.

Robert Short, *Something to Believe In*, 1978.

After all, liberal Christianity (as well as fundamentalist Christianity) is based upon a message whose inspiration is taken from the life and teachings of Jesus. Whatever accommodations are to be made in applying Christianity to the contemporary setting, the liberal Christian is nevertheless compelled to go back to the rather radical teachings of Jesus concerning the kingdom. Any compromises to be made with the Sermon on the Mount, for example, are self-consciously made by understanding the setting in which Jesus was teaching and living. Likewise, any alterations of Paul's teachings on women are made, again, from the basis of an interpretation of Paul's social setting. Liberal Christians, by their very approach to Scripture, are spared the agony experienced by many conservatives who are forced, when they disagree with some biblical dictum on the grounds of social conscience, to go through what has been aptly described as a sort of "hermeneutical ventriloquism."

A basic distinction to be drawn between liberal and conservative Christians concerns the issue of God's self-declaration to man. Most conservative Christians begin with the assumption that man exists as the creation of God, a supernatural being who is personal and therefore interested in communicating with his creation. Following on this assumption, conservative Christians postulate that God has revealed himself in time and space at a number of historical junctures, the most important being his decision to give earthly form to his son, Jesus. Jesus, then, is viewed as God's clearest self-declaration of who he is. Furthermore, conservative Christians postulate that God safeguarded his self-declaration by inspiring the writers of the Bible, giving them the very words to say (or, some would argue, only the thoughts were given—while others more liberal, but still within the conservative camp, would argue that God gave official sanction to what was penned by the biblical writers).

Liberal Christians, on the other hand, tend to see the above progression as much too anthropomorphic. Even the father-son imagery seems like a projection. Rather than starting with God, postulating divine initiative, many liberal Christians begin with the human predicament and emphasize *man's search* for God. According to this approach, from the standpoint of a functional definition, God is synonymous with the search for human wholeness, for confidence in the ultimate meaningfulness of human existence. Paul Tillich's definition of faith as the *state* of Ultimate Concern is representative of the liberal perspective because the emphasis is placed upon man's search for God.

Tillich's definition of God, too, is representative of the liberal position. God is the "God above God"—meaning that man's finite limitations forever leave man short of defining in any absolute way who God is. Nevertheless, to the extent that one dares to venture a definition, it is an expansive one: God is the very "Ground of Being"; God is "Being Itself." These definitions are nonreductive. If liberals have a central objection to the view many conservative Christians pose of God, it is that the conservative view reduces God to understandable, human terms—or human projections. Tillich's view of God as the "Ground of Being" is in reaction to that first century cosmological perspective which put God up in the sky, sitting on a throne, looking down on his creation.

Liberal Christians have viewed God in a much more immanentistic fashion. God is within creation. He is the lifeforce. He is at the center of all change, all innovation, all creativity. He is the source of life and is experienced in those profound moments of joy, communion, celebration. God is the "Thou" of the I-Thou encounter. He is the Ground of Being. God is present in all those activities which unite people rather than divide them, which call upon persons to transcend self-interest through brotherhood and sisterhood. God is personal as we discover our own humanity and act in his name to realize community: that state in which we relate to others as "ends" and not "means" to self-centered purposes.

The finer expressions about God in the liberal tradition have not, however, made God totally immanent. While many liberal Christians may have moved toward a healthy mysticism in both their experience and their speech about God, they have maintained the tension between God as transcendant and God as immanent. In other words, they have recognized, above all, that it is idolatrous to reduce God to human standards. He is present within his creation, he is the source of all meaning, he is at the center of all ethical structures, and yet he stands above and outside that which is purely human as the judge of all human projects. He is the "I am" of the Old Testament. He is one to both fear and worship. . . .

Symbolic Realism

Sociologist Robert Bellah has identified an important distinction between two types of "realism" that separate conservatives from liberals. Conservatives tend to be "historical realists" to the extent that they believe the truth of Christianity is found in the historical acts witnessed to in the New Testament—such as literal miracles, a literal bodily resurrection, and so forth. Historical realists are interested in understanding history "as it was." They take a nonmetaphorical and nonfigurative approach to interpreting Scripture. . . . Hence, one is "saved" if one believes that the Bible is the inspired word of God, that Jesus is the literal son of God sent down to earth to atone for mankind's sins, that he died on the cross and three days later was miraculously raised from the dead, and that he presently lives with God, sitting at his right hand.

Today's Liberal Christian

Now I hold, as do many liberal Christians today, that a Christian does not have to accept those philosophical and theological theories of the third and fourth centuries. I think that we can base our Christianity upon Jesus' teachings concerning the reality and love and claim of God, and upon the love ethic that has developed out of it. This provides a framework for life regardless of how much or how little detail we know for sure about Jesus' life.

John Hick, *Free Inquiry*, Fall 1985.

The liberal "symbolic realists," in contrast, emphasize that "meaning" is always a product of the interaction between subject and object. Meaning is *granted* to events—it is not considered inherent in them. According to this view, the Scriptures contain the record of men's and women's reflections regarding the *meaning* which Christ had *for them*. It is not primarily an historical account. The resurrection, the miracles, the virgin birth are valued as symbols that point beyond the historical event to a larger and more ultimate truth. But the truth does not lie in the symbols (as historical events). Symbols are irreducible. They are not identical with actual events, although they may derive from them. To take symbols literally is to engage in idolatry. Symbolic realists have given up hope of discovering what "really happened"; indeed, most of them are not even convinced that such knowledge would make much difference.

The symbols that surround the life of Christ—parables, stories, sayings, etc.—are understood by liberal Christians to be vitally important. It is through the symbol of Christ (which is a complex symbol, indeed) that men and women may come to know God. The symbolic form of Christ, as presented in the Gospel accounts, however, points beyond any purely historical events to a transcendent Truth or Reality (which we symbolize as God)—this is the hope and faith of liberal Christians. . . .

Conclusion

It is my opinion that what is needed in the churches today is a widescale recovery of the liberal spirit. . . .

Our social situation is ripe for a rebirth of Christian liberalism. But the ethical perspective of liberalism is only one reason for the return. Even more persuasive, in my view, is the fact that Christendom has become polarized. With a burgeoning population of evangelicals on one side and radical secularists on the other, the *mediating position. I would say, the temperate alternative*—of liberalism is being lost. Many young people today are unaware that there even is an option to the left of evangelicalism. And for many secularists, particularly young people, the only alternative to evangelicalism—if one wants to be religious—is membership with the "Moonies" or the Hare Krishna cult. . . .

In my view, liberalism is the most viable mode for reasserting the value of the Christian perspective to contemporary culture.

"Myth helps you to put your mind in touch with this experience of being alive. It tells you what the experience is."

Mythology Is a Way to Experience Life

Joseph Campbell

Joseph Campbell, who died in Hawaii in 1987, taught a course at Sarah Lawrence College for almost forty years titled "Folklore and Mythology." His many books, including *The Hero with a Thousand Faces* and *The Masks of God*, have become classics in the field of mythology. Campbell became widely known in America when he appeared on public television with journalist Bill Moyers in a series of interviews dealing with mythology. *Newsweek* magazine described Campbell as "the rarest of intellectuals in American life: a serious thinker who has been embraced by the popular culture." These interviews were published in a book entitled *The Power of Myth*, from which the following viewpoint is excerpted.

As you read, consider the following questions:

1. How does the author describe myths and why does he think they are important in individual lives?
2. What four functions do myths have in Campbell's opinion?
3. What kind of myth does Campbell hope will develop in the future?

Moyers: I came to understand from reading your books—*The Masks of God* or *The Hero with a Thousand Faces*, for example—that what human beings have in common is revealed in myths. Myths are stories of our search through the ages for truth, for meaning, for significance. We all need to tell our story and to understand our story. We all need to understand death and to cope with death, and we all need help in our passages from birth to life and then to death. We need for life to signify, to touch the eternal, to understand the mysterious, to find out who we are.

Campbell: People say that what we're all seeking is a meaning for life. I don't think that's what we're really seeking. I think that what we're seeking is an experience of being alive, so that our life experiences on the purely physical plane will have resonances within our own innermost being and reality, so that we actually feel the rapture of being alive. That's what it's all finally about, and that's what these clues help us to find within ourselves.

Moyers: Myths are clues?

Campbell: Myths are clues to the spiritual potentialities of the human life.

Moyers: What we're capable of knowing and experiencing within?

Campbell: Yes.

Life as an Experience

Moyers: You changed the definition of a myth from the *search* for meaning to the *experience* of meaning.

Campbell: Experience of *life*. The mind has to do with meaning. What's the meaning of a flower? There's a Zen story about a sermon of the Buddha in which he simply lifted a flower. There was only one man who gave him a sign with his eyes that he understood what was said. Now, the Buddha himself is called "the one thus come." There's no meaning. What's the meaning of the universe? What's the meaning of a flea? It's just there. That's it. And your own meaning is that you're there. We're so engaged in doing things to achieve purposes of outer value that we forget that the inner value, the rapture that is associated with being alive, is what it's all about.

Moyers: How do you get that experience?

Campbell: Read myths. They teach you that you can turn inward, and you begin to get the message of the symbols. Read other people's myths, not those of your own religion, because you tend to interpret your own religion in terms of facts—but if you read the other ones, you begin to get the message. Myth helps you to put your mind in touch with this experience of being alive. It tells you what the experience is. . . .

Moyers: What happens when a society no longer embraces a powerful mythology?

Campbell: What we've got on our hands. If you want to find out what it means to have a society without any rituals, read the New York *Times*.

Moyers: And you'd find?

Campbell: The news of the day, including destructive and violent acts by young people who don't know how to behave in a civilized society.

The Meaning of Life Is Living

I would say the meaning of life is living and all the rest is commentary. But I have to amplify that. What I mean by that is that life is filled with paradox. Life is joy and sorrow, pain and pleasure, success and failure, life and death. Somehow we have to live through all that in order to live.

Herbert Ravetch, *Los Angeles Times*, May 22, 1985.

Moyers: Society has provided them no rituals by which they become members of the tribe, of the community. All children need to be twice born, to learn to function rationally in the present world, leaving childhood behind. I think of that passage in the first book of Corinthians: "When I was a child, I spake as a child, I understood as a child, I thought as a child: but when I became a man, I put away childish things."

Campbell: That's exactly it. That's the significance of the puberty rites. In primal societies, there are teeth knocked out, there are scarifications, there are circumcisions, there are all kinds of things done. So you don't have your little baby body anymore, you're something else entirely.

When I was a kid, we wore short trousers, you know, knee pants. And then there was a great moment when you put on long pants. Boys now don't get that. I see even five-year-olds walking around with long trousers. When are they going to know that they're now men and must put aside childish things?

Moyers: Where do the kids growing up in the city—on 125th and Broadway, for example—where do these kids get their myths today?

Campbell: They make them up themselves. This is why we have graffiti all over the city. These kids have their own gangs and their own initiations and their own morality, and they're doing the best they can. But they're dangerous because their own laws are not those of the city. They have not been initiated into our society. . . .

Moyers: Do you remember the first time you discovered myth? The first time the story came alive in you?

Campbell: I was brought up as a Roman Catholic. Now, one of the great advantages of being brought up a Roman Catholic is that you're taught to take myth seriously and to let it operate on your life and to live in terms of these mythic motifs. I was brought up in terms of the seasonal relationships to the cycle of Christ's coming into the world, teaching in the world, dying, resurrecting, and returning to heaven. The ceremonies all through the year keep you in mind of the eternal core of all that changes in time. Sin is simply getting out of touch with that harmony.

And then I fell in love with American Indians because Buffalo Bill used to come to Madison Square Garden every year with his marvelous Wild West Show. And I wanted to know more about Indians. My father and mother were very generous parents and found what books were being written for boys about Indians at that time. So I began to read American Indian myths, and it wasn't long before I found the same motifs in the American Indian stories that I was being taught by the nuns at school.

Moyers: Creation—

Campbell:—creation, death and resurrection, ascension to heaven, virgin births—I didn't know what it was, but I recognized the vocabulary. One after another.

Moyers: And what happened?

Campbell: I was excited. That was the beginning of my interest in comparative mythology.

Moyers: Did you begin by asking, "Why does it say it this way while the Bible says it that way?"

Campbell: No, I didn't start the comparative analysis until many years later.

A Rich Mythology

Moyers: What appealed to you about the Indian stories?

Campbell: In those days there was still American Indian lore in the air. Indians were still around. Even now, when I deal with myths from all parts of the world, I find the American Indian tales and narratives to be very rich, very well developed.

And then my parents had a place out in the woods where the Delaware Indians had lived, and the Iroquois had come down and fought them. There was a big ledge where we could dig for Indian arrowheads and things like that. And the very animals that play the role in the Indian stories were there in the woods around me. It was a grand introduction to this material.

Moyers: Did these stories begin to collide with your Catholic faith?

Campbell: No, there was no collision. The collision with my

religion came much later in relation to scientific studies and things of that kind. Later I became interested in Hinduism, and there were the same stories again. And in my graduate work I was dealing with the Arthurian medieval material, and there were the same stories again. So you can't tell me that they're not the same stories. I've been with them all my life.

Religious Traditions Are Strengthened by Mythology

In a study of comparative mythology, we compare the images in one system with the images in another, and both become illuminated because one will accent and give clear expression to one aspect of the meaning, and another to another. They clarify each other.

When I started teaching comparative mythology, I was afraid I might destroy my students' religious beliefs, but what I found was just the opposite. Religious traditions, which didn't mean very much to them, but which were the ones their parents had given them, suddenly became illuminated in a new way when we compared them with other traditions, where similar images had been given a more inward or spiritual interpretation.

I had Christian students, Jewish students, Buddhist students, a couple of Zoroastrian students—they all had this experience. There's no danger in interpreting the symbols of a religious system and calling them metaphors instead of facts. What that does is to turn them into messages for your own inward experience and life. The system suddenly becomes a personal experience.

Joseph Campbell, *The Power of Myth*, 1988.

Moyers: They come from every culture but with timeless themes.

Campbell: The themes are timeless, and the inflection is to the culture.

Moyers: So the stories may take the same universal theme but apply it slightly differently, depending upon the accent of the people who are speaking?

Campbell: Oh, yes. If you were not alert to the parallel themes, you perhaps would think they were quite different stories, but they're not. . . .

Moyers: Where are we now in our mythology for the way of man?

Campbell: We can't have a mythology for a long, long time to come. Things are changing too fast to become mythologized.

Moyers: How do we live without myths then?

Campbell: The individual has to find an aspect of myth that relates to his own life. Myth basically serves four functions. The first is the mystical function—that is the one I've been speaking about, realizing what a wonder the universe is, and what a wonder you are, and experiencing awe before this mystery. Myth opens the world to the dimension of mystery, to the realization of the mystery that underlies all forms. If you lose that, you don't have a mythology. If mystery is manifest through all things, the universe becomes, as it were, a holy picture. You are always addressing the transcendent mystery through the conditions of your actual world.

The second is a cosmological dimension, the dimension with which science is concerned—showing you what the shape of the universe is, but showing it in such a way that the mystery again comes through. Today we tend to think that scientists have all the answers. But the great ones tell us, "No, we haven't got all the answers. We're telling you how it works—but what is it?" You strike a match, what's fire? You can tell me about oxidation, but that doesn't tell me a thing.

The third function is the sociological one—supporting and validating a certain social order. And here's where the myths vary enormously from place to place. You can have a whole mythology for polygamy, a whole mythology for monogamy. Either one's okay. It depends on where you are. It is this sociological function of myth that has taken over in our world—and it is out of date.

Moyers: What do you mean?

Campbell: Ethical laws. The laws of life as it should be in the good society. All of Yahweh's pages and pages and pages of what kind of clothes to wear, how to behave to each other, and so forth, in the first millenium B.C.

But there is a fourth function of myth, and this is the one that I think everyone must try today to relate to—and that is the pedagogical function, of how to live a human lifetime under any circumstances. Myths can teach you that.

Time for a New Myth

Moyers: So the old story, so long known and transmitted through the generations, isn't functioning, and we have not yet learned a new one?

Campbell: The story that we have in the West, so far as it is based on the Bible, is based on a view of the universe that belongs to the first millennium B.C. It does not accord with our concept either of the universe or of the dignity of man. It belongs entirely somewhere else.

We have today to learn to get back into accord with the wisdom of nature and realize again our brotherhood with the animals and with the water and the sea. To say that the divinity informs the world and all things is condemned as pantheism. But

127

pan*theism* is a misleading word. It suggests that a personal god is supposed to inhabit the world, but that is not the idea at all. The idea is trans-theological. It is of an undefinable, inconceivable mystery, thought of as a power, that is the source and end and supporting ground of all life and being.

Moyers: Don't you think modern Americans have rejected the ancient idea of nature as a divinity because it would have kept us from achieving dominance over nature? How can you cut down trees and uproot the land and turn the rivers into real estate without killing God?

Campbell: Yes, but that's not simply a characteristic of modern Americans, that is the biblical condemnation of nature which they inherited from their own religion and brought with them, mainly from England. God is separate from nature, and nature is condemned of God. It's right there in Genesis: we are to be the masters of the world.

You Must Determine Your Own Meaning

You really can't follow a guru. You can't ask somebody to give The Reason, but you can find one for yourself; you decide what the meaning of your life is to be. People talk about the meaning of life; there is no meaning of life—there are lots of meanings of different lives, and you must decide what you want your own to be.

Joseph Campbell, *An Open Life*, 1989.

But if you will think of ourselves as coming out of the earth, rather than having been thrown in here from somewhere else, you see that we are the earth, we are the consciousness of the earth. These are the eyes of the earth. And this is the voice of the earth.

The Gaia Principle

Moyers: Scientists are beginning to talk quite openly about the Gaia principle.

Campbell: There you are, the whole planet as an organism.

Moyers: Mother Earth. Will new myths come from this image?

Campbell: Well, something might. You can't predict what a myth is going to be any more than you can predict what you're going to dream tonight. Myths and dreams come from the same place. They come from realizations of some kind that have then to find expression in symbolic form. And the only myth that is going to be worth thinking about in the immediate future is one that is talking about the planet, not the city, not these people, but the planet, and everybody on it. That's my main thought for what the future myth is going to be.

And what it will have to deal with will be exactly what all myths have dealt with—the maturation of the individual, from dependency through adulthood, through maturity, and then to the exit; and then how to relate to this society and how to relate this society to the world of nature and the cosmos. That's what the myths have all talked about, and what this one's got to talk about. But the society that it's got to talk about is the society of the planet. And until that gets going, you don't have anything.

"Spirit is not something far off that you need to seek or . . . go to Tibet to find. Spirit lives in you, . . . in every cell."

The Way to the Spirit Is to Go Within Oneself

Brooke Medicine Eagle

Brooke Medicine Eagle, a member of the Crow Indian tribe, is a grandniece of Chief Joseph, the Nez Percé leader. She was given her sacred name Medicine Eagle to "fly high and see far" as visionaries and prophets do. Her goal is to bring the ancient wisdom of her ancestors, who learned from Mother Earth and Father Spirit, to today's secular culture. A licensed counselor, she conducts training camps, retreats, and ceremonies across the country. In the following viewpoint, Medicine Eagle explains her belief that one can only find true meaning in life by knowing and understanding the spirit within oneself.

As you read, consider the following questions:

1. What point is the author making when she advocates expanding one's attention span?
2. How does Medicine Eagle use the hologram to explain one's relationship with God?

Brooke Medicine Eagle, "Open to the Great Mystery," excerpted from *For the Love of God*, Benjamin Shields and Richard Carlson, eds., © 1990. Reprinted with permission of New World Library, San Rafael, CA 94903.

My relationship with God developed at an early age. I was raised on a remote little ranch, where I had for company and for the fullness of my life three other humans and an enormous amount of animals and land and sky and wind. As a child, my experience of God included everything—a love of the whole beauty around me. And the country was so beautiful: mountains that ended in aspen groves and streams, thick with wild animals and game of all kinds. One time I said to my mother, "You know, I think heaven is just like this, only the animals would speak to us, they wouldn't be afraid of us."

In developing a personal relationship with the Great Spirit, you first pay attention to the fact that you already have a relationship with Spirit. Spirit is not something far off that you need to seek or call or grab or go to Tibet to find. Spirit lives in you; it lives within your body, in every cell. You can touch the Great Spirit by touching into your own aliveness. All you need is a different attitude about how big you are, how deep you are, how high you are. You must be willing to own that you are God; even though you are a minute part of the All That Is, you are connected and one with it.

You Must Expand Your Attention Span

It is also good for you to develop another kind of attention and ability: to hold more and more of life, more and more of the holiness, the whole circle. An elder once asked me, "How long has it been since we sang in celebration of the life of the great whale? How long has it been since we danced in celebration of the life of the flowers? How long has it been since we danced in celebration of each and every part of life?" It's been much too long.

When we are newborns, we have attention only for our mothers. Our little faces look into their faces and that's all we see. Then perhaps father gets connected in; then the other siblings. Our ability to love or pay attention to or be connected with things begins to expand. We may belong to a clan or a group, and we can expand our arms and hold all its members inside our circle. Sometimes we become big enough to hold more, perhaps big enough to be called a Mother of the City. This person loves all the people, the whole city; loves and holds them in a good way and does good things in honor of them. Some people are Mothers of Nations. As we expand our attention we have the kind of love that can hold something that big. Mother Earth is enormous compared to that kind of love. She is big enough and loving enough to hold all of us in her arms all the time. When we expand our attention to the Great Mystery, to the All That Is—which is in and attentive to everything, because every cell, every tiny bit of matter, has consciousness in it—then we have an omniscient, omnipresent, powerful experience. We must build the ability to do that. When we talk about moving toward God realization, that's where we're moving.

Related to Nature

When I speak about attention, I mean literally, "How much attention can we pay to ourselves?" As children, sometimes we cannot hold our attention for more than a couple of seconds. Over the years we are able to attend to more and more. Yet, we're seldom schooled to hold life in respect, to enlarge our ability to love, take care of, and be respectfully connected with all things around us. In the old days, the primary job of the native Lakota mother was to teach the new child that he or she was connected with every thing in the circle of life. She would take the child walking and say, "See the squirrel? That's your brother. See the tree? We are related. This is your family; these are all your family." Because they were all brought up that way, they knew deeply that they were all interconnected, they were all family, they were all conscious. Lakota children had an opportunity to begin early in life to attend to the whole or the holiness, the spiritual side of things, and then to expand this ability powerfully as they grew.

The Words of Jesus

The kingdom of God is within you.

The Bible, Luke 17:21.

We, too, can acknowledge that Spirit lives within us, that we are a part of God. The more we can love ourselves and attend to all of life around us with a loving, open, connected heart and good relationship, the more we can be in a very beautiful place. All it takes is practice.

Dialogue with the Great Spirit Within You

Dialogue also is important in relating to the Great Spirit. It's not just my talking to the enormous All That Is. The All That Is also talks to me—gives me information, support, nurturance, food. It's a totally open connection. In the Sacred Pipe of our Lakota people, the bowl represents the earth and all of life. The open wooden stem represents our eternal connection to the Great Spirit. The pipe has an open channel that our breath or vibration or energy or thought can go through. Not only can it go out, but it can also come in. When we breathe through the pipe, it's like drawing Spirit into us. We can draw in information, and we can send out whatever we want across the bridge to everything else by blowing out the smoke or by praying with just our breath, energy, thoughts, and gratitude.

The channel is open in everyone. No one, whether priest or medicine man, needs to intercede or interpret or make that bridge any better, more open, more clear, more truthful, more sacred, or more holy. We have an open channel to the deepest, most beautiful part of ourselves, which is the same as our connection with everything. You don't need someone to put a hand on your head and say, "Yes, you're okay, and now you can talk to God." This priestly attitude assumes that you are not already in touch with Spirit and capable in that realm, although perhaps you may not be so practiced as some. That bridge to Spirit is always there, always open. You never need to stand at a toll gate on that bridge.

It's wonderful to be in the energy of elders and others who are practiced in that relationship with God. When that connection is humming, it's like a song going on. The elders give you suggestions and pray with you and hold you in their energy and light and wisdom as you go upon the mountain and have your own unique and powerful connection with Spirit.

It is very hard on people to assume that they don't have the ability to make that spiritual contact directly. It is sad that in the wider culture—and even now in native cultures, because of the breakup of old ways—there are very few who have the breadth and depth of attention to be holy people. Think how powerful it would be if our mothers really acknowledged, and were grateful for, our connection to everything. We would have turned out very differently.

The Hologram Example

Hologram theory offers a powerful example about who we are and who God is. A holographic picture is three dimensional. If you tear the picture in half, each half retains the same image and is still three dimensional. If you tear one of those halves in half, you still have the same dimensional image. No matter how many times you tear the fragments in half, the same image is still there. The tinier you tear it and the more times you tear it the dimmer it gets, the less distinct and real it becomes to your eyes.

I am and you are and we all are individual tiny pieces—all individuated or torn up out of the sheet that is God, that is All That Is. The whole picture is connected in us. It's all here. My little scrap may be torn to look a little different, but the whole picture is, in fact, within me. The exciting thing is that I can make that picture more distinct by joining my piece with your piece, and then with my family's piece, and then with my friend's piece, and on and on. The more I can attend to or connect myself with everything else around me, the more distinct the pictures become for us all. And we can reach out to others in the same way. Together we can acknowledge and enlarge our attentions so that we stand in a holy place—in a place that takes in the whole circle, a place that is healed in this wholeness, this holiness, a world that is healed and complete.

"Zen holds that there is no god outside the universe who has created it. . . . The universe and man are one indissoluble existence, one total whole."

Buddhism Is the Way to Ultimate Reality

Ruth Fuller Sasaki

The following viewpoint is taken from a speech Ruth Fuller Sasaki made in 1958. At the time, Sasaki was director of the First Zen Institute of America in Japan. In the following viewpoint, Sasaki explains that Buddhism is not a doctrinaire faith. Its teachings do not require the blind acceptance of articles of faith or dogma. Rather, it emphasizes direct involvement, personal experience, and a spiritual awakening that can only come from within.

As you read, consider the following questions:

1. What does the term Dharma signify, according to Sasaki?
2. What is a koan, according to the author?
3. In Sasaki's opinion, how does Zen Buddhism deal with doctrines?

From Ruth Fuller Sasaki, "Zen: A Method for Religious Awakening," in *The World of Zen,* Nancy Wilson Ross, ed. Copyright © 1964 by Nancy Wilson Ross. Reprinted by permission of Vintage Books, a division of Random House, Inc.

I am a Zen Buddhist and have been one for over twenty-five years. So I speak from within Zen, not as one who observes it from the outside. Though brought up in a strict Presbyterian family, I became a Buddhist in my twenties. The study of early Buddhism, into which I soon plunged, brought me to the conclusion that the pivot of that religion was Awakening and the Buddhist life a life lived in accordance with Awakening. Meditation was the means through which Sakyamuni, the historical Buddha, had come to his enlightenment. The forty-nine years of his life after his great experience were spent in trying to show other men how they, by following the path he had pursued, might attain this awakening for themselves. . . .

Perhaps for westerners the primary hindrance in understanding Zen, even intellectually, lies in the fact that the great verities that Zen, with Buddhism, takes as basic are diametrically opposed to those the Hebraic-Christian religions have always assumed to be absolute. It is difficult to put aside one's way of looking at even an inconsequential matter and to observe it from a totally new and different standpoint. How much more difficult to do so with religious concepts and beliefs with which we have been inculcated from earliest childhood. But unless you can put aside your usual viewpoint, you will never be able to understand what Zen is concerned with, and why, and who. Try, now, for a few minutes to clear your minds of all your previously held notions and read what I am going to say with what, in Buddhism, is called a "mirror mind."

The Buddhist Concept of God

Zen does not hold that there is a god apart from the universe who first created this universe and then created man to enjoy, or even master it—and these days it seems not to be enough to master the planet Earth; we must now master the universe as well. Rather, Zen holds that there is no god outside the universe who has created it and created man. God—if I may borrow that word for a moment—the universe, and man are one indissoluble existence, one total whole. Only THIS—capital THIS—is. Anything and everything that appears to us as an individual entity or phenomenon, whether it be a planet or an atom, a mouse or a man, is but a temporary manifestation of THIS in form; every activity that takes place, whether it be birth or death, loving or eating breakfast, is but a temporary manifestation of THIS in activity. When we look at things this way, naturally we cannot believe that each individual person has been endowed with a special and individual soul or self. Each one of us is but a cell, as it were, in the body of the Great Self, a cell that comes into being, performs its functions, and passes away, transformed into another manifestation. Though we have temporary individuality,

The Buddha

The Buddha, whose personal name was Siddhattha (Siddhartha in Sanskrit), and family name Gotama (Skt. Gautama), lived in North India in the 6th century B.C. His father, Suddhodana, was the ruler of the kingdom of the Sākyas (in modern Nepal). His mother was queen Māyā. According to the custom of the time, he was married quite young, at the age of sixteen, to a beautiful and devoted young princess named Yasodharā. The young prince lived in his palace with every luxury at his command. But all of a sudden, confronted with the reality of life and the suffering of mankind, he decided to find the solution—the way out of this universal suffering. At the age of 29, soon after the birth of his only child, Rāhula, he left his kingdom and became an ascetic in search of this solution.

For six years the ascetic Gotama wandered about the valley of the Ganges, meeting famous religious teachers, studying and following their systems and methods, and submitting himself to rigorous ascetic practices. They did not satisfy him. So he abandoned all traditional religions and their methods and went his own way. It was thus that one evening, seated under a tree (since then known as the Bodhi- or Bo-tree, 'the Tree of Wisdom') on the bank of the river Neranjara at Buddha-Gaya (near Gaya in modern Bihar), at the age of 35, Gotama attained Enlightenment, after which he was known as the Buddha, 'The Enlightened One'.

Walpola Rahula, *What the Buddha Taught*, 1959

---

that temporary, limited individuality is not either a true self or our true self. Our true self is the Great Self; our true body is the Body of Reality, or the Dharmakāya, to give it its technical Buddhist name.

Reality Can Only Be Experienced by Awakening

Buddhism, and Zen, grant that this view is not one that can be reasoned about intellectually. Nor, on the other hand, do they ask us to take this doctrine on faith. They tell us it must be experienced, it must be realized. Such realization can be brought about through the awakening of that intuitive wisdom which is intrinsic to all men. The method for awakening this intuitive wisdom is meditation. Zen, among the various schools of Buddhism, is the one which has emphasized over everything else the attainment of this realization in this very body, here and now, and provided a method, tested through the centuries, for accomplishing it.

It is the generally accepted view today that, as far as doctrines are concerned—and, as you see, Zen does have them, contrary to what you may have heard—Zen is developed Mahayana Buddhism as the Chinese mind, steeped in the Chinese world view and classical Taoism, realized it. In fewer words, we might say that Zen is Indian Buddhism dyed with the dye of Chinese Taoism. Japanese Zennists, however, while conceding this, consider Zen to be rather a return to the Buddha's Buddhism. By that they do not mean a return to Hinayana or Theravada Buddhism, the Buddhism of the monkish schools that arose after the Buddah's death, but rather a return to Sākyamuni's basic teaching that every man can and should attain this transforming religious experience of awakening for himself. Sākyamuni, as the embodiment of his total teaching, is the central figure for Japanese Rinzai Zen, and Sākyamuni's image is always the main image in its temples.

From the very beginning of its history the first aim of the followers of the Zen Sect has been the attainment of awakening. The founders of the sect left to other schools the writing of dissertations on methods, descriptions of progressive stages along the way, discussions and treatises on the doctrinal implications of the experience. The old Zen masters said: "Get Awakening yourself! Then you'll know what it is." In other words, if you want to know the taste of water, drink it. . . .

The Importance of Teachers

Now who are these Zen masters or teachers and what is the role they have played throughout the long history of Zen and continue to play today? From the very beginning, as strongly as it has emphasized meditation as the basic practice, Zen has emphasized the necessity for the direct transmission from teacher to disciple of the intuitive understanding of THIS. Traditionally it is said that Sākyamuni Buddha transmitted his Dharma—his understanding THIS or of Ultimate Truth, to use the technical Buddhist term—to his disciple Kāsyapa; Kāsyapa, in his turn, transmitted his understanding to Ananda, and so on down through a long line of Indian teachers and disciples until, through Bodhidharma, it was eventually transmitted to Hui-nêng (Eno), known as the Sixth Patriarch of Zen in China. Hui-nêng had a number of immediate disciples to whom he transmitted his Dharma. To two of Hui-nêng's Dharmaheirs can be traced back all the major lines of Zen teaching and Zen teachers throughout the history of Chinese and Japanese Zen up to the present day.

What is this transmission? When the disciple has reached the same profound depth of intuitive understanding and realized completely the same deepest truth as his master, when both see inner eye to inner eye, or when they "lock eyebrows together," as the old texts put it, then only does the master put his seal on the disciple's attainment, guarantee it, as it were. And only when the disciple has had his attainment "sealed" is he properly prepared to teach others and may he, in turn, transmit the Dharma to another, "transmit" meaning, of course, "acknowledge the attainment of his disciple.". . .

The Focus of Buddhism

Buddhism does not take its starting-point on grand metaphysical questions like *Who made the world?; What is the meaning of Life?;* and *What happens to us after death?* It is not concerned with proving the existence of a God or gods. Rather its root focus is on the down-to-earth fact that all existence, including human existence, is imperfect in a very deep way. "Suffering I teach—and the way out of suffering," the Buddha declared.

John Snelling, *The Buddhist Handbook*, 1991.

Now how does one go about studying and practicing Zen today? A would-be student goes to a Zen roshi, one for whom he has deep respect, in whom he has faith, and with whom he has a distinct feeling of relationship. In a polite and humble manner the student requests to be accepted as a disciple. If the roshi consents, he will turn the student over to his head monk or senior disciple to be instructed in zazen, or meditation practice. The student will be told how to sit and how to breathe; he will be given certain concentration exercises to practice. For a considerable period the student pursues these elementary practices at home several hours a day, or sits with a group of other students who meet for zazen practice at certain specified times. When the head monk or senior disciple decides that the student has acquired a "good seat," that is, can sit in the correct posture for a considerable length of time and is proficient in concentration, he will inform the roshi that the student is now prepared to begin his koan study. . . .

The word "koan" was originally a Chinese legal term meaning "case," that is, a legal case that had been decided and thereafter was used as a precedent for decisions in cases of the same kind. In Zen, koans are used both as a means of opening up the student's intuitive mind and as tests of the depth to which it has been opened. Koans are not solvable by the rational mind or intellect. To solve a koan the student, through meditation upon it, particular kind of meditation we call in Japanese *kufu*, must reach the same level of intuitive understanding as that from which the master spoke the words of the koan. When the student has reached this level of understanding, his understanding and, therefore, his answer to the koan will be approximately the

139

same as that of all the Zen students who have solved it in the past. Each koan has what may be called a "classic" answer. Against this classic answer the master tests the student's answer. When the two agree, the student may be said to have "solved" or "passed" the koan. . . .

The student then goes to the roshi and, during the private interview known as *sanzen*, an interview conducted in a formal and specifically prescribed manner, the master gives the student a koan which he is now to meditate upon. At definite times from then on the student is expected to go to the roshi for a like interview, and during each interview to express to the master his view at the moment of the inner meaning or content of the koan on which he has been continuously meditating. When the student attains correct insight into the koan, the master, to test his understanding still further, will ask him to bring a word or phrase, preferably from some old Chinese proverb, pithy saying, or poem, that conveys in secular words the inner meaning of the koan. These words or phrases are known in Japanese as *jakugo*. I have yet to find a suitable English word for this expression, though perhaps "capping verse" might do. When the student has brought the correct jakugo—and almost every koan has a fixed jakugo—the master will give him another koan to meditate upon. And thus the student's Zen study will continue—hours and hours of meditation upon koan after koan for years and years. The constant supervision of the master throughout the course of this study assures that the student's own personal views and his mistaken and deluded notions are discarded one by one, for, in order to pass a koan, he must reach the traditionally correct understanding of it. No other understanding is acceptable or accepted. It is undoubtedly due to this teaching method that Rinzai Zen has continued to flow in so pure a stream in spite of the many hands it has passed through in the course of so many centuries.

Zen Doctrines

Since each koan deals with some aspect of Truth as it is held in Zen Buddhism, little by little the student is brought to realize the total of Zen doctrine which is wholly concerned with the THIS, of which I have spoken earlier, and its relative, or manifested, aspects. The doctrines of Zen are not stated specifically either in written or spoken words, but, through long-continued meditation upon the succession of koans, deeper and deeper levels of the student's intuitive mind are opened, levels where these unspoken doctrines are realized as truths. For the Zen master teaches his student nothing. He guides him in such a way that the student finds everything he would learn within his own mind. As an old Chinese saying has it, "The treasures of the house do not come in through the gate." The treasure of Truth lies deep within the mind of each one of us; it is to be awakened or revealed or attained only through our own efforts. . . .

In the course of studying and practicing Zen for a long, long time . . . the small personal self gradually dissolves and one knows no self but the Great Self, no personal will, only the Great Will. One comes to understand the true meaning of the term *wu-wêi*, or in Japanese *mui*, "non-action," for one knows that, as a separate individual, there is nothing further to do. One does not cease to act, but one's actions arise spontaneously out of the eternal flow of the activity of THIS, which one is not only in accord with, but Is. The man of Zen is clearly aware that he is abiding in and will eternally abide in, THIS AS IT IS; that the world in which he is living his everyday life is indeed THIS in its myriads of manifestations, forever changing, forever transforming, but forever THIS. In the words of the sutras: "Nirvāna is none other than Saṁsāra; Saṁsāra is none other than Nirvāna."

[*Saṁsāra* is a Sanskrit word meaning "faring on" or coming-to-be, *i.e.*, the world of becoming or existence here on earth as contrasted to *Nirvāna*, the annihilation of the personal as we understand it.]

Kindness Is My True Religion

The essence of all religions is love, compassion, and tolerance. Kindness is my true religion. No matter whether you are learned or not, whether you believe in the next life or not, whether you believe in God or Buddha or some other religion or not, in day-to-day life you must be a kind person. When you are motivated by kindness, it doesn't matter whether you are a practitioner, a lawyer, a politician, an administrator, a worker, or an engineer: whatever your profession or field, deep down you are a kind person.

Love, compassion, and tolerance are necessities, not luxuries. Without them, humanity cannot survive. If you have a particular faith or religion, that is good. But you can survive without it if you have love, compassion, and tolerance.

Dalai Lama in *For the Love of God*, 1990.

But in Zen, when we must speak, everyday words are preferred to quotations from the scriptures. So, in conclusion, let me put more simply what I have just said. The aim of Zen is first of all awakening, awakening to our true self. With this awakening to our true self comes emancipation from our small self or personal ego. When this emancipation from the personal

141

ego is finally complete, then we know the freedom spoken of in Zen and so widely misconstrued by those who take the name for the experience. Of course, as long as this human frame hangs together and we exist as one manifested form in the world of forms, we carry on what appears to be an individual existence as an individual ego. But no longer is that ego in control with its likes and dislikes, its characteristics and its foibles. The True Self, which from the beginning we have always been, has at last become the master. Freely the True Self uses this individual form and this individual ego as it will. With no resistance and no hindrance it uses them in all the activities of everyday life, whatever they are and wherever they may be.

"I believe that the creation-centered spiritual tradition represents the appropriate spiritual paradigm for our time. "

Creation-Centered Spirituality Offers a New Religious Paradigm

Matthew Fox

Matthew Fox, a Catholic priest, is the director of the Institute in Culture and Creation Spirituality at Holy Names College in Oakland, California. The institute combines the tenets of Catholicism with those of the New Age movement. In addition, Fox is the editor-in-chief of the magazine *Creation Spirituality*, which strives to awaken mysticism, revitalize Western religion and culture, and promote justice by mining the wisdom of ancient spiritual traditions and the insights of contemporary science. Its proponents believe that creation spirituality honors the wisdom of women and the philosophies of native cultures. In the following viewpoint, Fox advocates creation spirituality as the best philosophy for humankind. Fox is author of numerous books, including *Sheer Joy! Conversations with Thomas Aquinas on Creation Spirituality.*

As you read, consider the following questions:

1. How does the author distinguish between fall/redemption spirituality and creation-centered spirituality?
2. From where does the author trace the roots of creation spirituality?
3. Why does Fox claim creation-centered spirituality is the new religious paradigm the human race requires?

Reprinted from *Original Blessing* by Matthew Fox, © 1983, Bear & Co. Inc., PO Drawer 2860, Santa Fe, NM 87504.

I wish to pose two questions:

1. In our quest for wisdom and survival, does the human race require a new religious paradigm?

2. Does the creation-centered spiritual tradition offer such a paradigm?

As the reader may guess, my answer to both these questions is: *yes*. When I use the word "wisdom," I think of the definition that the Native American tradition gives us: that the people may live. I am very at home with this understanding of wisdom. I believe it encompasses the breadth and depth of cosmic and human living and I believe it names what God the Creator wants for all of her children: that the people of this precious earth, all global peoples, may live. Bangladesh people, old people, hungry children people, robust adolescent people, people in socialist countries, people in capitalist countries—that the people may live. But wisdom wants the people *to live*. What does that mean? Obviously, that they not die before their time. But what else does it mean? To live is not merely to survive. Living implies beauty, freedom of choice, giving birth, discipline, celebration. Living is not the same as going shopping or buying, nor is it the same as making a nest in which to escape the sufferings of one another. Living has something to do with Eros, love of life, and with the love of others' lives, others' right to Eros and dignity. Here lies wisdom: that the people may live. But where do we find it?

There Are Two Places to Find Wisdom

The late E.F. Schumacher believed that there are two places to find wisdom: in nature and in religious traditions. To seek wisdom in nature we should obviously go to those who have loved nature enough to study it. Because science explores nature it can be a powerful source of wisdom. It often has been. For in just about every culture imaginable, religion and science were teammates who offered to the people a cosmic myth that allowed them to understand their universe, to find meaning in it, and to live out their lives with meaning. In the West, however, religion and science have been at odds ever since the seventeenth century. This split has been disastrous for the people: religion has become privatized and science a violent employee of technology, with the result that the people have become alternately bored, violent, lonely, sad, and pessimistic. Above all, the people have become victims—victims of world wars, massive military taxes, needless unemployment, dire conflict between haves and have-nots.

The seventeenth century, that era of such great scientific genius and discovery, actually began with the burning of Giordano Bruno at the stake in 1600 by Church authorities. Bruno, in spite of whatever errors he may have made in his lifetime, was a religious person (he had been a Dominican friar) who sought to discover the cosmos anew according to the scientific work of his contemporaries. His murder by religious and political authorities did not go unnoticed by scientists, who at that time held little power in the political establishment.

What Is Creation Spirituality?

For starters, let's say that it's liberation theology for the First World, for the overdeveloped peoples. Unlike that of Third World peoples, our poverty is not so much material as it is spiritual and psychological. Our addictions to alcohol, drugs, sports, entertainment and work spring from our alienation from the earth and God and our effort to cover up both our pain and our joy. The mystical tradition that I am seeking to revive has a lot to say about freeing ourselves from addiction, getting high on the beauty of the created world and recreating our society.

Matthew Fox, *Psychology Today*, June 1989.

In our century the tide has turned so that scientists, now sharing power with the military, corporate, and political chiefs of our nation-states, are not without sin: they are implicated in the innocent lives sacrificed in a Hiroshima or Nagasaki, or at Love Canal or in the rain forests of Brazil or the ovens of Auschwitz. Clearly, there has been enough sin on both the religious and the scientific fronts in Western cultural history. We seek now a truce—and more than a truce, a common exploration for wisdom among scientists and spiritual seekers alike: the wisdom that nature can teach us and the wisdom that religious traditions can teach us. It is evident that the Einsteinian and post-Einsteinian models of the universe are opening up such avenues of wisdom from nature to the scientist, and to the rest of the culture via the scientists.

Fall/Redemption Versus Creation-Centered Spirituality

But how about religion? Is it in touch with its sources of wisdom? Is it willing to let go of outdated, dualistic paradigms with the courage with which science lets go? Alfred North Whitehead writes, "Religion is tending to degenerate into a decent formula wherewith to embellish a comfortable life. . . . Religion will not regain its old power until it can face change in the same spirit as does science." To recover the wisdom that is lurking in religious traditions we have to let go of more recent religious traditions—"Only those who dare to let go can dare to reenter," advises Meister Eckhart. Specifically, what religion must let go of in the West is an exclusively fall/redemption model of spirituality—a model that has dominated theology, Bible studies, seminary and novitiate training, hagiography, psychology for centuries. It is a dualistic model and a patriarchal one; it begins its theology with sin and original sin, and it generally ends with redemption. Fall/redemption spirituality does not teach believers about the New Creation or creativity, about justice-making and social transformation, or about Eros, play, pleasure, and the God of delight. It fails to teach love of the earth or care for the cosmos, and it is so frightened of passion that it fails to listen to the impassioned pleas of the *anawim*, the little ones, of human history. This same fear of passion prevents it from helping lovers to celebrate their experiences as spiritual and mystical. This tradition has not proven friendly to artists or prophets or Native American peoples or women.

The fall/redemption spiritual tradition is not nearly as ancient as is the creation-centered one. The former goes back principally to St. Augustine (354-430 A.D.); to Thomas à Kempis, who said, "Every time I go into creation, I withdraw from God"; to Cardinal Bossuet; Cotton Mather; and Father Tanquerry. The creation-centered tradition traces its roots to the ninth century B.C., with the very first author of the Bible, the Yahwist or J source, to the psalms, to wisdom books of the Bible, to much of the prophets, to Jesus and much of the New Testament, and to the very first Christian theologian in the West, St. Irenaeus (c. 130-200 A.D.). . . .

The New Religious Paradigm

To consider this ancient tradition as a paradigm for religion would prove a whole new starting point not only for religion in the West and in the world but for the relationship of religion and science. Because the fall/redemption tradition considers all nature "fallen" and does not seek God in nature but inside the individual soul, it is not only silent toward science but hostile to it. Professor Michael Polanyi has written that Augustine "destroyed interest in science all over Europe for a thousand years" because for him science "contributed nothing to the pursuit of salvation." To recover a spiritual tradition in which creation and the study of creation matters would be to inaugurate new possibilities between spirituality and science that would shape the paradigms for culture, its institutions, and its people. These paradigms would be powerful in their capacity to transform. For if wisdom comes from nature and religious traditions, as Schumacher teaches, then what might happen if science and religious traditions agreed to birth together instead of ignoring, fighting, or rejecting one another? Is not recovering a creation-centered spirituality recovering two sources of wisdom at once, that of nature via science and that of nature via religious traditions? The creation-centered tradition seems to combine the best of both worlds in our search for wisdom today.

We Must Start with Original Blessing

I don't deny original sin, but I insist that we start with original blessing. We have to begin thinking about our condition with the fact that we inherited an earth that is hospitable toward us, with the right levels of ozone, oxygen and water, and healthy DNA in our bodies and reproductive systems. There were 19 billion years or so of history and God's creative activity before human beings appeared on the scene and invented sin.

I also object to original sin as the starting point of religion because of the tremendous psychic damage it has done. People are already terribly vulnerable to self-doubt and guilt, especially members of minority groups—women, blacks, Native Americans, homosexuals. The whole ideology of original sin increases one's alienation and feeds the sado-masochistic energies in the culture—the sense that one is not worthy.

If you start with the notion that you were born a blotch on existence, you will never be empowered to do something about the brokenness of life. In creation spirituality, we begin with the idea that each of us is born a unique expression of divinity, an image of God. Teaching our children is the only way to build the pride and security our culture needs so desperately.

Matthew Fox, *Psychology Today*, June 1989

When I use the word "new," as in "new paradigm," I do not mean we are to birth a religious vision off of the tops of our heads, brand new. . . . By "new" I mean that in the past three centuries of Western culture and religion, the creation tradition has been forgotten almost entirely as religion. It has been kept alive by artists, poets, scientists, feminists, and political prophets, but not by theologians. Creation spirituality is a tradition: it has a past; it has historical and biblical roots; it boasts a communion of saints. But it is for the most part new to religious believers of our time. And it is utterly new to our culture, which, if it has been touched by religion at all, has been touched by fall/redemption and not creation-centered spirituality. When I talk of tradition I do not mean that all we have to do is to study the past, much less that all we need do is to imitate it. There is indeed a newness to what our generation will do with this tradition, to what forms and expressions we will create along with current scientists, mystics, artists, peace and jus-

147

tice workers, feminists, and Third World peoples. But in the great task of recreating a culture, which in our times means creating the first global culture, one needs all the help one can get. And it comes as very good news indeed that wisdom comes from this tradition, from the past, and, for Westerners, even from our religious traditions. . . .

The Mystical Journey

At least since the fifth century, under the influence of Neoplatonism, we have identified the mystical journey as a process that begins with an acute awareness of sin, the necessity for redemption, repentance and purgation. Supposedly it is only after this plunge that we experience something like illumination, light and a vision of the divine. Then, finally we move toward some kind of union with the divine or betrothal to God. I deliberately reject this tradition. It is patriarchal pessimism. And it leaves out delight, creativity and justice.

We should begin with a positive accent, the spirit of wonder, awe or radical amazement we have when we first attend to the original blessing, to the beauty that is around and within us. Only then do we enter into the darkness, what the mystics called the nothingness and Jung called the shadow—the awareness of evil, suffering and death. We must confront our wounds, but not without the empowerment that comes from the awe and wonder of the universe. You don't go into a mine without a lantern.

Matthew Fox, *Psychology Today*, June 1989.

I believe that the creation-centered spiritual tradition represents the appropriate spiritual paradigm for our time. I also believe that this tradition and the living of it represents a Copernican revolution in religion. Copernicus moved people from believing that Earth was the center around which the universe revolved to believing that Earth moved about the sun. In religion we have been operating under the model that humanity, and especially sinful humanity, was the center of the spiritual universe. This is not so. The universe itself, blessed and graced, is the proper starting point for spirituality. Original blessing is prior to any sin, original or less than original. I do not consider this book to be a polemic against Augustine or the fall/redemption model for religion. Maybe it was necessary that humanity concentrate during a certain period on its fallenness. But the time has come to let anthropocentrism go, and with it to let the preoccupation with human sinfulness give way to attention to divine grace. In the process sin itself will be more fully understood and more successfully dealt with. . . .

148

"Fall/Redemption and Creation-Centered Spiritualities Compared at a Glance," allows the reader to recognize some differences between the two spiritual traditions. Some people will object that to contrast fall/redemption and creation spirituality is to create a dualism of either/or instead of living out a dialectic of both/and. But when it comes to human concepts, there are either/or choices that we must make—a psychology that says, "The soul makes war with the body," (fall/redemption, Augustine) and one that says, "The soul loves the body," (creation spirituality, Eckhart) are not saying the same thing. Only a mushy and basically sentimental mind would say they are of equal value. We must choose. A spirituality is a way, a path. We do not come to two paths in a road and say, out of timidity and fear to make a decision, "I will go down both roads at once." The West has been traveling the fall/redemption path for centuries. We all know it; we all have it ingrained in our souls; we have given it 95 percent of our energies in churches both Catholic and Protestant. And look where it has gotten us. Into sexism, militarism, racism, genocide against native peoples, biocide, consumerist capitalism, and violent communism. I believe it is time we chose another path. The path that is the most ancient, the most healing, the most feminist of the paths, even in the biblical tradition itself. If we throw ourselves into this path, who can predict what the happy results might be? After all, since the fourth century the followers of Jesus have rarely as a body explored this path.

Recognizing Ethnocentrism

Ethnocentrism is the attitude or tendency of people to view their own race, religion, culture, group, or nation as superior to others, and to judge others on that basis. An American, whose custom is to eat with a fork or spoon, would be making an ethnocentric statement when saying, "The Chinese custom of eating with chopsticks is stupid."

Ethnocentrism has promoted much misunderstanding and conflict. It emphasizes cultural and religious differences and the notion that one's national institutions or group customs are superior.

Ethnocentrism limits people's ability to be objective and to learn from others. Education in the truest sense stresses the similarities of the human condition throughout the world and the basic equality and dignity of all people.

Some of the following statements are taken from the viewpoints in this book. Others have other sources. Consider each statement carefully. *Mark E for any statement you think is ethnocentric. Mark N for any statement you think is not ethnocentric. Mark U if you are undecided about any statement.*

If you are doing this activity as a member of a class or group, compare your answers with those of other class or group members. Be able to defend your answers. You may discover that others will come to different conclusions than you. Listening to the reasons others present for their answers may give you valuable insights in recognizing ethnocentric statements.

If you are reading this book alone, ask others if they agree with your answers. You too will find this interaction very valuable.

1. Asian peoples do not have the intellectual capacity to understand the message of Jesus.

2. The message of Jesus (Christianity) is superior to the message of Mohammed (Islam).

3. My religion is that of one scientist. It is wholly secular. It contains no supernatural elements. Nature is enough for me.

4. Looking out for Number One is important because it leads to a simple, uncomplicated life in which you spend more time doing those things which give you the greatest amount of pleasure.

5. Jews are God's "chosen people."

6. The Absolute Moralist is the creature—looking deceptively like any ordinary human being—who spends his life deciding what is right for you.

7. Christianity is the dominant religion in America.

8. Humanism considers man's supreme ethical aim as working for the welfare of humanity in this one and only life.

9. All people should look to the stars and astrology to guide their lives.

10. The Bible is the only written revelation which God has given to man.

11. Western religions are more advanced than Eastern religions.

12. Atheists do not believe in God.

Periodical Bibliography

The following articles have been selected to supplement the diverse views in this chapter. Because the subject matter of all chapters in this book is closely related, it may be helpful to examine the other chapter bibliographies when doing further study.

Morris Adler	"What Is a Jew?" *Harper's*, January 1964.
America	April 12, 1975. Entire issue on Teilhard de Chardin.
Ian G. Barbour	"The Significance of Teilhard," *The Christian Century*, August 30, 1967.
Nancy Barcus and Dick Bohrer	"The Humanist Builds His House upon the Sand," *Moody*, September 1980.
Browne Barr	"Hang Tough: The Thinking Person's Guide to the Bible as the Book of Faith," *The Christian Century*, April 11, 1979.
David L. Bartlett	"The Historical Jesus and the Life of Faith," *The Christian Century*, May 6, 1992.
Burnham Beckwith	"The Refutation of 'Liberal' Religion," *American Atheist*, March 1986.
Wayne G. Boulton	"The Thoroughly Modern Mysticism of Matthew Fox," *The Christian Century*, April 25, 1990.
Clarence Darrow	"Absurdities of the Bible," *The Humanist*, September/October 1975.
Bruce A. Demarest	"Six Modern Christologies: Doing Away with the God-Man," *Christianity Today*, April 20, 1979.
Joseph C. Dillow	"The Bible as a Scientific Text," *Moody*, January 1982. Available from 820 N. La Salle Dr., Chicago, IL 60610.
Eternity	"Secular vs. Christian Humanism," January 1982.
W.W. Finslator	"Why I Am a Secular Humanist," *The Churchman*, January 1985. Available from 1074 23rd Ave. N, St. Petersburg, FL 33704.

Matthew Fox — "Original Blessing, Not Original Sin," *Psychology Today*, June 1989.

Free Inquiry — "A Call for the Critical Examination of the Bible and Religion," Spring 1982.

Free Inquiry — "Personal Paths to Humanism," Spring 1987.

Emma Goldman — "The Failure of Christianity," *American Atheist*, November 1983.

Adolf Grunbaum — "The Place of Secular Humanism," *Vital Speeches of the Day*, November 1, 1987.

John Hick — "A Liberal Christian View," *Free Inquiry*, Fall 1985.

Gerald A. Larue — "The Way of Ethical Humanism," *The Humanist*, September/October 1984.

John Macquarrie — "The Aims of Christianity," *USA Today*, November 1979.

Donald E. Miller — "The Future of Liberal Christianity," *The Christian Century*, March 10, 1982.

Cullen Murphy — "Who Do Men Say That I Am?" *The Atlantic*, December 1986.

Richard Ostling — "Who Was Jesus?" *Time*, August 15, 1988.

John Phillips — "Jesus Forever," *Moody*, December 1980.

Kerry Temple — "Who Do Men Say That I Am?" *The Humanist*, May/June 1991.

Paul Tirmenstein — "This Is Atheism," *American Atheist*, January 1984.

Dan Wakefield — "Returning to Church," *The New York Times Magazine*, December 11, 1985.

How Do Others Make Moral Decisions?

Constructing a Life
PHILOSOPHY

Chapter Preface

Many contemporary books on the state of ethics in America start with a description of the sad condition of the society's ethical climate. One need not read books written by experts to become discouraged about the country's falling ethical temperature. Newspapers daily record the crimes and unethical escapades of Americans from every part of the country. From the latest serial murderer with a new record body count to a white collar criminal who managed to bleed a bank or company and its investors dry of a previously unheard of amount, in addition to the millions of ethical and criminal offenses in between, the reading public has probably decided that these are indeed the worst of times. From the halls of government to the streets of every small town, Americans may wonder what happened to traditional values like honesty, integrity, accountability, and concern for others.

In a society that seems to have lost its ethical rudder, citizens will find it more difficult to steer their individual ships straight. In America the problem is compounded by cultural diversity. Although pluralism brings the strength of many talents to the melting pot, it also presents the difficult choice of whose ethical system individuals should adopt. In a more monolithic or homogeneous society, the choice is made for you. You simply do what the majority does. Peer pressure forces you to accept and follow the dominant ethical standard of the society. In contemporary America, the dominant ethical standard has become blurred. We are each the captain of our own ship, adrift in a sea of confusing choices. We must chart our own course with little or no help from our culture and family.

This chapter presents the charts of seven ships' captains. Each has suggestions for those who are charting ethical courses. Each uses a slightly different method although they all have the same destination in mind. It is not surprising that such a diversity of voyages is suggested. Each captain is an American and his course exemplifies pluralism at work. It is time for you to take the helm. Your ship is in the water and has been caught in the current. Which way will you steer? Is there a course in this chapter you would follow? Will a viewpoint from a previous chapter help you plan your voyage?

"The situationist follows a moral law or violates it according to love's need."

Love Is Life's Best Guide

Joseph Fletcher

Joseph Fletcher was visiting professor of biomedical ethics at the University of Virginia in Charlottesville. He has been called the father of biomedical ethics by his admirers. His major work, *Morals and Medicine*, was a pioneering effort in the field of medicine and ethics. However, he is best known for his book, *Situation Ethics*, which has sold more than a million copies and from which the following viewpoint is taken. In addition to coining the expression "situation ethics," the book ignited a debate that is still active almost three decades after its publication. Fletcher states that there is only one moral absolute—to do whatever increases love in a particular situation.

As you read, consider the following questions:

1. According to the author there are three ways to make a moral decision. What are they and how do they differ?
2. What is the one commandment that the Christian situationist observes?
3. What distinction does the situationist make between principles and rules?

There are at bottom only three alternative routes or approaches to follow in making moral decisions. They are: (1) the legalistic; (2) the antinomian, the opposite extreme—i.e., a lawless or unprincipled approach; and (3) the situational. All three have played their part in the history of Western morals, legalism being by far the most common and persistent. Just as legalism triumphed among the Jews after the exile, so, in spite of Jesus' and Paul's revolt against it, it has managed to dominate Christianity constantly from very early days. As we shall be seeing, in many real-life situations legalism demonstrates what Henry Miller, in a shrewd phrase, calls "the immorality of morality."[1]. . .

Approaches to Decision Making

1. Legalism

With this approach one enters into every decision-making situation encumbered with a whole apparatus of prefabricated rules and regulations. Not just the spirit but the letter of the law reigns. Its principles, codified in rules, are not merely guidelines or maxims to illuminate the situation; they are *directives* to be followed. Solutions are preset, and you can "look them up" in a book—a Bible or a confessor's manual.

Judaism, Catholicism, Protestantism—all major Western religious traditions have been legalistic. In morals as in doctrine they have kept to a spelled-out, "systematic" orthodoxy. . . .

2. Antinomianism

Over against legalism, as a sort of polar opposite, we can put antinomianism. This is the approach with which one enters into the decision-making situation armed with no principles or maxims whatsoever, to say nothing of rules. In every "existential moment" or "unique" situation, it declares, one must rely upon the situation of itself, *there and then*, to provide its ethical solution. . . .

3. Situationism

A third approach, in between legalism and antinomian unprincipledness, is situation ethics. (To jump from one polarity to the other would be only to go from the frying pan to the fire.) The situationist enters into every decision-making situation fully armed with the ethical maxims of his community and its heritage, and he treats them with respect as illuminators of his problems. Just the same he is prepared in any situation to compromise them or set them aside *in the situation* if love seems better served by doing so.

Situation ethics goes part of the way with natural law, by accepting reason as the instrument of moral judgment, while rejecting the notion that the good is "given" in the nature of things, objectively. It goes part of the way with Scriptural law by accepting revelation as the source of the norm, while rejecting all "revealed" norms or laws but the one command—to love God in the neighbor. The situationist follows a moral law or violates it according to love's need. For example, "almsgiving is a good thing if. . . ." The situationist never says, "Almsgiving is a good thing. Period!" His decisions are hypothetical, not categorical. Only the commandment to love is categorically good. "Owe no one anything, except to love one another." (Rom. 13:8.) If help to an indigent only pauperizes and degrades him, the situationist refuses a handout and finds some other way. He makes no law out of Jesus' "Give to every one who begs from you.". . .

There Is Only One Principle

Christian situation ethics has only one norm or principle or law (call it what you will) that is binding and unexceptionable, always good and right regardless of the circumstances. That is "love"— the agape of the summary commandment to love God and the neighbor.

Joseph Fletcher, *Situation Ethics*, 1966.

Christian situation ethics has only one norm or principle or law (call it what you will) that is binding and unexceptionable, always good and right regardless of the circumstances. That is "love"—the agape of the summary commandment to love God and the neighbor.[2] Everything else without exception, all laws and rules and principles and ideals and norms, are only *contingent*, only valid *if they happen* to serve love in any situation. Christian situation ethics is not a system or program of living according to a code, but an effort to relate love to a world of relativities through a casuistry obedient to love. It is the strategy of love. This strategy denies that there are, as Sophocles thought, any unwritten immutable laws of heaven, agreeing with Bultmann that all such notions are idolatrous and a demonic pretension.[3] . . .

Principles, Yes, but Not Rules

It is necessary to insist that situation ethics is willing to make full and respectful use of principles, to be treated as maxims but not as laws or precepts. We might call it "principled relativism." To repeat the term used above, principles of maxims or general rules are *illuminators*. But they are not directors. The classic rule of moral theology has been to follow laws but do it as much as possible according to love and according to reason *(secundum caritatem et secundum rationem]*. Situation ethics, on the other hand, calls upon us to keep law in a subservient place, so that only love and reason really count when the chips are down! . . .

The Golden Rule

Confucianism
What you don't want done to yourself, don't do to others.
—SIXTH CENTURY, B.C.

Buddhism
Hurt not others with that which pains thyself.
—FIFTH CENTURY, B.C.

Jainism
In happiness and suffering, in joy and grief, we should regard all creatures as we regard our own self, and should therefore refrain from inflicting upon others such injury as would appear undesirable to us if inflicted upon ourselves.
—FIFTH CENTURY, B.C.

Zoroastrianism
Do not do unto others all that which is not well for oneself.
—FIFTH CENTURY, B.C.

Classical Paganism
May I do to others as I would that they should do unto me.
Plato—FOURTH CENTURY, B.C.

Hinduism
Do naught to others which if done to thee would cause thee pain.
Mahabharata—THIRD CENTURY, B.C.

Judaism
What is hateful to yourself, don't do to your fellow man.
Rabbi Hillel—FIRST CENTURY, B.C.

Christianity
Whatsoever ye would that men should do to you, do ye even so to them.
Jesus of Nazareth—FIRST CENTURY, A.D.

Sikhism
Treat others as thou wouldst be treated thyself.
—SIXTEENTH CENTURY, A.D.

In 1962 a patient in a state mental hospital raped a fellow patient, an unmarried girl ill with a radical schizophrenic psychosis. The victim's father, learning what had happened, charged the hospital with culpable negligence and requested that an abortion to end the unwanted pregnancy be performed at once, in an early stage of the embryo. The staff and administrators of the hospital refused to do so, on the ground that the criminal law forbids all abortion except "therapeutic" ones when the mother's life is at stake—because the moral law, it is supposed, holds that any interference with an embryo after fertilization is murder, i.e., the taking of an innocent human being's life.

Morality Is Humanistic Not Theistic

For the past thirty years I have seen a lot of what goes on in the secular professions, the "helping professions" of social workers, people in public services, and physicians, and I have always been impressed by how nonreligious their decision-making is and how consistently they ignore and bypass religious beliefs and theological doctrines. They consistently and for the most part constructively disregard "commandment ethics" and choose instead whatever courses of action rationally promise the most humanly beneficial consequences. It is human benefit, not "revealed" or "divine" norms, that provides the moral values of serious decision-makers. In other words, their morality is humanistic, not theistic.

Joseph Fletcher, *Free Inquiry*, 1987.

Let's relate the three ethical approaches to this situation. The rape has occurred and the decisional question is: May we rightly (licitly) terminate this pregnancy, begun in an act of force and violence by a mentally unbalanced rapist upon a frightened, mentally sick girl? Mother and embryo are apparently healthy on all the usual counts.

The legalists would say *NO*. Their position is that killing is absolutely wrong, inherently evil. It is permissible only as self-defense and in military service, which is held to be presumptive self-defense or justifiable homicide. If the mother's life is threatened, abortion is therefore justified, but for no other reasons. (Many doctors take an elastic view of "life" and thereby justify abortions to save a patient's *mental* life as well as physical.) Even in cases where they justify it, it is only excused—it is still held to be inherently evil. Many Protestants hold this view, and some humanists.

Catholic moral theology goes far beyond even the rigid legalism of the criminal law, absolutizing their prohibition of abortion *absolutely*, by denying all exceptions and calling even therapeutic abortion wrong. (They allow killing in self-defense against malicious, i.e., deliberate, aggressors but not in self-defense against innocent, i.e., unintentional, aggressors.) Thus if it is a tragic choice of the mother's life or the baby's, as can happen in rare cases, neither can be saved.

To this ethical nightmare legalism replies: "It is here that the Church appears merciless, but she is not. It is her logic which is merciless; and she promises that if the logic is followed the woman will receive a reward far greater than a number of years of life."[4] Inexplicably, shockingly, Dietrich Bonhoeffer says the same thing: "The life of the mother is in the hand of God, but the life of the child is arbitrarily extinguished. The question whether the life of the mother or the life of the child is of greater value can hardly be a matter for a human decision."[5]

The antinomians—but who can predict what they would say? Their ethic is by its nature and definition outside the reach of even generalities. We can only guess, not unreasonably, that if the antinomian lives by a love norm, he will be apt to favor abortion in this case.

The situationists, if their norm is the Christian commandment to love the neighbor, would almost certainly, *in this case*, favor abortion and support the girl's father's request. (Many purely humanistic decision makers are of the same mind about abortion following rape, and after incest, too.) They would in all likelihood favor abortion for the sake of the patient's physical and mental health, not only if it were needed to save her life. It is even likely they would favor abortion for the sake of the victim's self-respect or reputation or happiness or simply on the ground that no *unwanted and unintended* baby should ever be born.

They would, one hopes, reason that it is *not* killing because there is no person or human life in an embryo at an early stage of pregnancy (Aristotle and St. Thomas held that opinion), or even if it *were* killing, it would not be murder because it is self-defense against, in this case, not one but two aggressors. First there is the rapist, who being insane was morally and legally innocent, and then there is the "innocent" embryo which is continuing the ravisher's original aggression! Even self-defense legalism would have allowed the girl to kill her attacker, no matter that he was innocent in the forum of conscience because of his madness. The embryo is no more innocent, no less an aggressor or unwelcome invader! Is not the most loving thing possible (the right thing) in this case a responsible decision to terminate the pregnancy?

What think ye?

1. *Stand Still Like the Hummingbird* (New Directions, 1962), pp. 92-96.
2. Matt. 5:43-48 and 22:34-40; Luke 6:67-28; 10:25-28 and vss. 29-37; Mark 12:28-34, Gal., 5:14, Rom. 13:8-10; etc.
3. Rudolf Bultmann, *Essays Philosophical and Theological* (The Macmillan Company, 1955), pp. 22, 154.
4. Alan Keenan, O.F.M., and John Ryan, M.D., *Marriage: A Medical and Sacramental Study* (Sheed & Ward, Inc., 1955), p. 53.
5. *Ethics*, p. 131n.

"To understand what we should do or avoid in life, as well as to know what we should believe, we consult the Bible."

Scripture Is Life's Best Guide

Milton L. Rudnick

Milton L. Rudnick is president of Concordia Lutheran Seminary in Edmonton, Canada. The seminary is affiliated with the Lutheran Church-Missouri Synod. The following viewpoint, an evangelical Christian perspective on ethical decision making, is excerpted from Rudnick's book *Christian Ethics for Today*. In this viewpoint, he presents a defense of the moral absolutes which Joseph Fletcher attacks in the chapter's first viewpoint. Rudnick develops a detailed process for making ethical decisions based on biblical guidelines.

As you read, consider the following questions:

1. What does the author mean when he states that evangelical Christian ethics must be Christocentric?
2. What role does Rudnick claim the Bible must have in evangelical Christian ethics?
3. What ten step process does the author recommend when making complex ethical decisions?

From Milton L. Rudnick, *Ethics for Today*. Grand Rapids, MI: Baker Book House, 1979. Reprinted with permission.

An evangelical approach to ethics is a method of determining right and wrong which grows out of a particular understanding and interpretation of the Christian message. Evangelical ethics is, first of all, Christian ethics. Of course, it is possible to develop workable ethics from the assumptions and beliefs of other Christian perspectives, and from non-Christian religions. It is even possible to develop ethics without relation to any religious point of view. Much, in fact, most ethics is built on philosophical rather than religious foundations. However, here we present an approach which is religious rather than philosophical; Christian rather than non-Christian; and evangelical rather than liberal, neo-orthodox, or Roman Catholic, for example.

Christocentricity

In order for ethics to be evangelical, it must reflect the basic emphases of evangelical Christians. First of all, it must be Christocentric. That is to say, evangelical ethics must keep Christ and His redemptive work in the center of the discussion. Christ must be regarded, not only as the source of forgiveness and eternal life, but also as the source of ethical guidance and the source of the power to change. . . .

Scripture-Based

The other basic emphasis that should characterize evangelical ethics is a very high view of biblical authority. The gospel of Jesus Christ is the heart of the message as well as its unifying element. Scripture is its source, the divinely inspired record of God's atoning love for us in Jesus Christ. It is also the revelation of His will for us. To understand what we should do or avoid in life, as well as to know what we should believe, we consult the Bible. Evangelical ethics as well as evangelical theology should be based solidly on Scripture. The Bible is the only source and norm of Christian teaching and practice.

Diversity

The approach to ethics developed in this book seriously attempts to reflect these emphases. To the extent that it succeeds it can properly be called "an evangelical approach to ethics." It is *an* evangelical approach, not *the* evangelical approach to ethics. There is no single, definitive treatment of evangelical ethics, and not all evangelical ethicists agree with one another. . . .

Maintaining Perspective

I point out this diversity in the interest of maintaining a proper perspective. In this book I present directly and unequivocally the approach which to me best seems to express what Scripture and evangelical theology teach about knowing and doing what is right. Then I plug these elements into a problem-solving process which

Forming Biblically Based Convictions

I firmly believe that when it comes to "doubtful" activities, we *should* have convictions—recognizing, of course, that our standards do not necessarily apply to everyone else. When seeking to define your convictions in areas not specifically mentioned in God's Word, carefully consider the following Biblical principles:

1. *Do everything for God's glory, not for man's praise* (I Corinthians 10:31; I Thessalonians 2:4-6). Why do we struggle with "doubtful" activities, anyway? If we are truly following the Lord, we will want to honor Him in everything we say and do. This is of utmost importance.

2. *Recognize that some believers have freedom in areas that others do not* (Romans 14:1-5; I Corinthians 8:1-9:18). In the early church, some could not eat meat that might have been sacrificed to idols. Why? Because they had been converted from pagan religions and wanted to forsake everything that had been associated with their past. . . .

The Apostle Paul addressed this problem on several occasions. Instead of favoring one group over the other, he acknowledged the validity of *both* points of view.

3. *Pursue—*

• *Whatever allows you to give thanks to God* (Romans 14:6; I Thessalonians 5:18). In the Apostle Paul's day, some regarded one day as more special than others. "Fine," he said, "do so with gratitude to the Lord." Others felt free to eat meat. "When you eat, give thanks to God." Still others abstained from certain foods. "Continue to thank the Lord." We should be able to honestly thank God in all we say and do.

• *Whatever promotes the Gospel of Jesus Christ* (I Corinthians 9:19-23). Strange as it may seem, exercising our liberty in Christ can hinder the proclamation of the Gospel. That's why Paul became "weak" to those who were weak, in order to win the weak. If wearing a certain style of clothes would hinder evangelism, Paul wouldn't wear that style. He made cultural adjustments in order to witness to as many people as possible.

4. *Avoid—*

• *Whatever controls or masters you* (I Corinthians 6:12). The Apostle said he would not allow anything to dominate him. Something may not be a sin in itself, but if it dominates (or controls) our thinking, it's wrong. We are not to let anything but God and His Word have such supremacy in our lives.

• *Whatever offends others or prompts them toward going against their consciences* (I Corinthians 8:9-13). As Christians, we are sometimes "stronger" brothers, sometimes "weaker" brothers. We demonstrate maturity when we recognize which position we occupy in a given situation and respond Biblically towards those who don't share our views.

5. *Finally, think of your convictions about "doubtful" activities as personal guidelines, not divine commandments* (Romans 14:22). I have no right to make *my* conscience everyone else's guide.

This is an excerpt from the article *Should Your Conscience Be Your Guide?* by James M. Williams, which appeared in the February 1985 issue of *Psychology for Living.* Copyright © 1984 by Luis Palau Evangelistic Team and reprinted by permission.

facilitates their application to daily life. . . .

At this point we need a process, an orderly and systematic method which puts these things together and makes an operable ethical system. In this chapter such a process is described. It consists of a conventional problem-solving method into which the basic components of Christian ethics have been inserted. The form into which this process has been integrated is a step-by-step operation, concrete and practical in nature, by which the serious Christian can make the kinds of analysis and application that the ethical task requires. . . .

A process of this kind is necessary only for exceptionally complex and ambiguous ethical questions. For the vast majority of our ethical decisions, the detailed or involved process described below is unnecessary. We have a moral standard, this is, clear and confident convictions about right and wrong, in most areas of life. In at least nine out of ten ethical decisions conscience applies the moral standard, and no further thought or research is necessary. . . .

1. Seek the Spirit's Guidance

As has been stated, evangelical ethics is, above all, ethics of the Holy Spirit. In the struggle to arrive at a perception of right and wrong in a confusing situation, we have more to go on than some written guidelines and our own judgment. We have a Person, a living, loving, divine Person—the Holy Spirit. He is present with us in the struggle, communicating, influencing, and encouraging. Jesus refers to Him as the Counselor who will lead us into all truth. . . .

We should admit our weakness and rely confidently on Him to provide the needed strength. Only what we do by His power and guidance can be considered good, in the strictest sense of the word. If we neglect this first step—involving the Spirit—the rest of the process is certain to break down.

2. Analyze and Research the Issue

The second step consists of rational inquiry, in which we gather information about the problem at hand and interpret it to the best of our ability. It includes taking advantage of the study and experience of others by reading what they have written on the subject or by consulting them. . . .

3. Come to Terms with Corruption in Self and Others

The presence and power of sin intrudes prominently into the decision-making process. We need to be aware of this and to have a healthy respect for it. Although the guilt of our sin is completely forgiven through faith in Jesus Christ, the power of sin is still active within us, confusing and misleading. In ways that are often very subtle and difficult to discern, the power of sin tries to make

165

good seem evil and evil good. . . .

One important way to test an idea, view, or value for corruption is to compare it, in presupposition, implication, and substance, with God's revealed will in the law. The problem is that many of the most troublesome issues which we confront are dealt with only indirectly or obliquely in Scripture. However, by careful study and inference we will be able to discover areas of contact and similarity. We will be able to detect or at least to sense deviation from God's will.

Six-point Test for Deciding Right from Wrong

Dear Ann: In this age of conflicting philosophies, shifting standards and the emergence of what some choose to call The New Morality, please tell me how a person can differentiate between right and wrong.

Everyday I am beset by new conflicts. I'm frank to admit that I am utterly confused. Can you give me and others some words of guidance? — **Dark Side of the Moon**

Ann Says: Several weeks ago I heard a sermon by the beloved pastor of The Peoples Church of Chicago, Dr. Preston Bradley. He discussed this very subject and in conclusion quoted Dr. Harry Emerson Fosdick's six-point test for deciding right from wrong. I asked Dr. Bradley if he would send me his distilled version and he did so. Here it is:

Does the course of action you plan to follow seem logical and reasonable? Never mind what anyone else has to say. Does it make sense to you? If it does, it is probably right.

Does it pass the test of sportsmanship? In other words, if everyone followed this same course of action would the results be beneficial for all?

Where will your plan of action lead? How will it affect others? What will it do to you?

Will you think well of yourself when you look back at what you have done?

Try to separate yourself from the problem. Pretend, for one moment, it is the problem of the person you most admire. Ask yourself how that person would handle it.

Hold up the final decision to the glaring light of publicity. Would you want your family and friends to know what you have done? The decisions we make in the hope that no one will find out are usually wrong.

Reprinted from *The Minneapolis Tribune* with permission from Ann Landers and Publishers-Hall Syndicate,

---

In addition to the written Word of Scripture with which to test for corruption, we also have the Holy Spirit within. He illuminates and judges the components of moral decisions as they are forming. As we deal with information and views about moral issues, we should submit them to Him in prayer and contemplation, asking Him to expose and condemn whatever is wrong. Scripture and the Spirit keep us alert to the presence of corruption and thus able to minimize its influence.

4. Identify, Interpret, and Apply Biblical Norms

Discovering biblical norms can be very challenging. In this part of the process we are trying to find guidance in the Bible for issues which are not discussed there directly or in detail. We are working with issues and points of interpretation about which there may be no clear consensus even among sensitive, committed, and informed evangelical Christians. To identify, interpret, and apply biblical norms under these circumstances is a delicate and somewhat tenuous operation. However, it must be undertaken. Otherwise, instead of depending primarily on God for guidance, we will be depending on ourselves or other equally limited and corrupt human beings, and that would be dangerous. . . . We should be wiling to consider the ethical views of those who disagree with us; we should examine the Scriptural and factual bases of their views and compare them with our own. The element of uncertainty makes an attitude of humility and openness on our part most appropriate. Nevertheless, the conclusion to which we have come by our own prayer, study, and reflection is authoritative and binding for us until and unless we are convinced differently from Scripture or other valid sources.

In this connection it may be well to restate some basic guidelines for interpreting biblical ethical norms. . . . (1) New Testament material has precedence over Old Testament material. (2) Clear imperatives have more authority than moral examples. (3) Clear imperatives have more authority than directives inferred from doctrines. (4) Historically and culturally conditioned commands must be distinguished from those which are binding for all times. (5) Ethical norms should be based on at least several clear passages of Scripture.

Here, as in the previous step of the process, the assistance of a knowledgeable and experienced person can be invaluable. . . .

5. Examine, Correct, and Strengthen Motives

Motives can make or break an ethical decision. They profoundly affect the quality of a moral action. As a critical factor in the process, they require close scrutiny, delicate adjustment, and solid support.

To properly investigate and evaluate our own motives we must be not only candid but even downright suspicious. We have to ask

167

some deep and unsettling questions: What is moving me as I make this decision or take this course or action? Are my professed reasons the real reasons? Or are they just a cover for other, less admirable motives which I do not like to admit even to myself? Am I really most concerned to honor God and help people and only secondarily to please or serve myself? To what extent are my motives mixed, that is, permeated with selfish, loveless, godless impulses? To what extent is the devil moving me, rather than God? . . .

6. Establish Suitable Goals

A goal is something we hope to accomplish through a specific course of action. Ordinarily it involves a change which we intend to make in a given situation. Our goal should be consistent with and expressive of the directive we arrive at as we identify, interpret, and apply biblical norms. In fact, the goal is the concrete application of that directive or norm. . . .

To be suitable, a goal must not only be specific and consistent with God's will, it must also be feasible and attainable. It must hold some realistic promise of being accomplished. . . .

A critical factor in goal setting is assessment of probable consequences. As we determine the target or our moral effort, we should try to anticipate both the short- and long-range results of the goals under consideration. . . .

7. Determine and Employ Appropriate Means

Once we have arrived at a suitable goal, we must devise a way to reach it. Usually there are a number of possibilities. In selecting a means, the Christian is concerned that the means itself be moral, consistent with and expressive of God's will. No matter how worthy the goal, it is wrong to attempt to reach it by evil means. *The end does not justify the means. . . .*

This raises the issue of what is sometimes called "the principle of the lesser evil." In this corrupt and complicated world, we do not always have a choice between good and evil alternatives. Sometimes all the alternatives appear to contain clear and serious evil. For example, in order to save someone from a murderous assailant, we may lie about that person's whereabouts. Under such circumstances is the lie good and right?

Some ethicists would say yes. Because it was done to help and protect someone in great danger, the lie in this case was not only permissible but actually good. However, Christians who believe in absolute biblical ethical norms say no. They claim that lying is always a sin, even when done in a desperate situation and in order to avert suffering or death. The person who tells a lie even under these circumstances must humbly bow under the judgment of God's law on account of it and cast himself on God's mercy in Christ.

Faced with a moral dilemma in which we must choose among several evils, we select the alternative which is least evil. However, in so doing we must not assume that we or the action are justified because it was the lesser evil. If we are justified, it is only because we acknowledge it penitently as sin and accept God's pardon for the sake of Jesus' sacrifice.

To be appropriate, a means, like a goal, must also be feasible. It must be workable, sensible, likely to succeed. . . .

8. Draw Upon Spiritual and Moral Resources

In order to make good ethical decisions and then live by them, we need to be spiritually and morally strong. This will happen only if we use the resources that God has provided, the media through which He conveys His guidance and power to us. Especially when working through a difficult moral issue, we need to draw heavily upon His Word and sacrament and make much use of prayer. . . .

In addition to God's Word the Lord's Supper, and prayer, the fellowship of His people is a vital spiritual and moral resource. . . .

9. Conduct Adequate Evaluation

Rarely do we progress or improve in any area without some kind of evaluation. Ideally this will include constructive criticism from others as well as self-evaluation. In order to do better we must become aware of our mistakes so that we can avoid them in the future. We also need to know what we are doing that is correct so that we can reinforce these areas of strength and build upon them. . . .

After we have made a decision and acted upon it, we should review what has happened and reflect upon it. Was it wise, honest, effective? Where were our reasoning and interpretation faulty? Where were they sound? Where were we misinformed? Where were we accurately informed? At what points, if any, were we rationalizing? What aided or interfered with the implementation of the decision? What did we do that was valid and responsibile? What were the consequences. . . .

10. Rely on God's Forgiveness

Whether the evaluation is positive or negative, what we need more than anything else in the world is God's forgiveness. Even when we make correct decisions and act upon them conscientiously, our performance is still inadequate, acceptable to God only because of His mercy in Christ. However, in many cases we make very bad decisions or fail to act upon our good decisions. Because of this we are guilty before God and under His judgments. Only through the forgiveness of sins can we or our ethical performance stand before Him. We can be sure that God accepts us not because we are ethically brilliant or morally successful, but rather because His Son died for us.

"The principle of 'enlightened self-interest' is an excellent first approximation to an ethical principle which is both consistent with what we know of human nature and is relevant to the problems of life in a complex society."

Self-Interest Is Life's Best Guide

Frank R. Zindler

Frank R. Zindler, formerly a professor of biology and geology, is currently a science writer and director of the Central Ohio Chapter of American Atheists. In the following viewpoint, which is taken from *American Atheist*, Zindler states that contrary to popular belief, atheists do have a code of morality that guides their actions. It is not fear of a punishing God that forces them to do good, but enlightened self-interest guided by reason. He contends that it is part of human nature to desire love, to seek beauty, and to thrill at the act of creation. Moral actions are the result of informed minds, not religious "do's and don'ts," in his opinion.

As you read, consider the following questions:

1. How does the author distinguish between instinctual and learned behavior?
2. Why does he believe the Ten Commandments are an inadequate guide to moral decision making in today's society?

Frank R. Zindler, "Ethics Without Gods," *American Atheist*, February 1985. Reprinted with permission.

One of the first questions Atheists are asked by true believers and doubters alike is, "If you don't believe in a god, there's nothing to prevent you from committing crimes, is there? Without the fear of hell-fire and eternal damnation, you can do anything you like, can't you?"

It is hard to believe that even intelligent and educated people could hold such an opinion, but they do. It seems never to have occurred to them that the Greeks and Romans, whose gods and goddesses were something less than paragons of virtue, nevertheless led lives not obviously worse than those of the Baptists of Alabama. Moreover, pagans such as Aristotle and Marcus Aurelius—although their systems are not suitable for us today—managed to produce ethical treatises of great sophistication, a sophistication rarely, if ever, equaled by Christian moralists.

The answer to the question posed above is, of course, "Absolutely not!" The behavior of Atheists is subject to the same rules of sociology, psychology, and neurophysiology that govern the behavior of all members of our species, religionists included. Moreover, despite protestations to the contrary, we may assert as a general rule that when religionists practice ethical behavior, it isn't *really* due to their fear of hell-fire and damnation, or to their hopes of heaven. Ethical behavior—regardless of who the practitioner may be—results always from the same causes and is regulated by the same forces, and has nothing to do with the presence or absence of religious belief. The nature of these causes and forces is the subject of this essay.

Psychobiological Foundations

As human beings, we are social animals. Our sociality is the result of evolution, not choice. Natural selection has equipped us with nervous systems which are peculiarly sensitive to the emotional status of our fellows. Among our kind, emotions are contagious, and it is only the rare psychopathic mutants among us who can be happy in the midst of a sad society. It is in our nature to be happy in the midst of happiness, sad in the midst of sadness. It is in our nature, fortunately, to seek happiness for our fellows at the same time as we seek it for ourselves. Our happiness is greater when it is shared.

Nature also has provided us with nervous systems which are, to a considerable degree, imprintable. To be sure, this phenomenon is not as pronounced or as inelectable as it is, say, in geese—where a newly hatched gosling can be "imprinted" to a toy train and will follow it to exhaustion, as if it were its mother. Nevertheless, some degree of imprinting is exhibited by humans. The human nervous system appears to retain its capacity for imprinting well into old age, and it is highly likely that

171

the phenomenon known as "love-at-first-sight" is a form of imprinting. Imprinting is a form of attachment behavior, and it helps us to form strong interpersonal bonds. It is a major force which helps us to break through the ego barrier to create "significant others" whom we can love as much as ourselves. These two characteristics of our nervous system—emotional suggestibility and attachment imprintability—although they are the foundation of all altruistic behavior and art, are thoroughly compatible with the selfishness characteristic of all behaviors created by the process of natural selection. That is to say, to a large extent behaviors which satisfy ourselves will be found, simultaneously, to satisfy our fellows, and *vice-versa.*

Conscience Is One's Guide

Who can be regarded as morally superior: the one who is honest because it is required by god or the one who does not believe in god but is honest by nature? In this connection an incident comes to mind. Once when I was staying in a Soviet village, an old woman entered the building housing the management of the collective farm. She asked where the chairman was and explained that she wanted to get his permission to take fifty eggs at the poultry farm. Someone remarked jokingly: You're a poultry maid yourself, so you can take the eggs, no one will know. The woman replied: I'm too old for that kind of thing. It'll soon be time for me to die and I don't want to answer for it to god in the next world.

I wondered at the time: If the old woman were not afraid of god, would she have stolen the eggs? Was her honesty worth much if it was sustained by fear? Later on I saw that I had been mistaken. The matter was not in god, of course.

That woman was not a thief by nature. Her words about god were merely an outward form in which, by force of habit, she expressed her moral convictions and feelings. It is our conscience that prompts us to do good, and conscience is a quality intrinsic in both believers and non-believers.

Vladislav Sherdakov, "On What Is Atheists' Morality Based?" *American Atheist*, October 11, 1981.

This should not surprise us when we consider that among the societies of our nearest primate cousins, the great apes, social behavior is not chaotic, even if gorillas do lack the Ten Commandments! The young chimpanzee does not need an oracle to tell it to honor its mother and to refrain from killing its brothers and sisters. Of course, family squabbles and even murder have been observed in ape societies, but such behaviors are exceptions, not the norm. So too it is in human societies, everywhere and at all times.

The African apes—whose genes are ninety-eight to ninety-nine percent identical to ours—go about their lives as social animals, cooperating in the living of life, entirely without the benefit of clergy and without the commandments of Exodus, Leviticus, or Deuteronomy. It is further cheering to learn that sociobiologists have even observed altruistic behavior among troops of baboons! More than once, in troops attacked by leopards, aged, post-reproduction-age males have been observed to linger at the rear of the escaping troop and to engage the leopard in what often amounts to a suicidal fight. As an old male delays the leopard's pursuit by sacrificing his very life, the females and young escape and live to fulfill their several destinies. The heroism which we see acted out, from time to time, by our fellow men and women, is far older than their religions. Long before the gods were created by the fear-filled minds of our less courageous ancestors, heroism and acts of self-sacrificing love existed. They did not require a supernatural excuse then, nor do they require one now.

Given the general fact, then, that evolution has equipped us with nervous systems biased in favor of social, rather than antisocial, behaviors, is it not true, nevertheless, that antisocial behavior *does* exist? And does it not exist in amounts greater than a reasonable ethicist would find tolerable? Alas, this is true. But is true largely because we live in worlds far more complex than the Paleolithic world in which our nervous systems originated. To understand the ethical significance of this fact, we must digress a bit and review the evolutionary history of human behavior.

Instinctual and Learned Behavior

Today, heredity can control our behavior in only the most general of ways; it cannot dictate precise behaviors appropriate for infinitely varied circumstances. In our world, heredity needs help.

In the world of a fruit fly, by contrast, the problems to be solved are few in number and highly predictable in nature. Consequently, a fruit fly's brain is largely "hard-wired" by heredity. That is to say, most behaviors result from environmental activation of nerve circuits which are formed automatically by the time of emergence of the adult fly. This is an extreme example of what is called instinctual behavior. Each behavior is coded for by a gene or genes which predispose the nervous system to develop certain types of circuits and not others, and it is all but impossible to act contrary to the genetically predetermined script.

The world of a mammal—say a fox—is much more complex and unpredictable than that of the fruit fly. Consequently, a fox is born with only a portion of its neuronal circuitry hard-wired. Many of its neurons remain "plastic" throughout life. That is, they may or may not hook up with each other in functional circuits, depending upon environmental circumstances. Learned behavior is behavior which results from activation of these environmentally conditioned circuits. Learning allows the individual mammal to assimilate—by trial and error—greater numbers of adaptive behaviors than could be transmitted by heredity. A fox would be wall-to-wall genes if all its behaviors were specified genetically!

Enlightened Self-Interest

In my own life, I've found what moralists and philosophers have called "enlightened self-interest" to be a useful guide in thrashing through some of the more common ethical dilemmas. The phrase "self-interest" has a cold-blooded sound, as if it might lead you to foreclose mortgages on penniless old ladies, but it needn't work that way. Self-interest does not, as some people believe, necessarily imply ruthless manipulation of people or trampling over them and their needs . . . those are unprincipled ways of acting. Just as you can behave barbarously in the service of others (family, country, a "cause"), so, too, can you pursue your own ends in an ethical manner. In fact, if you are self-interested, in the best sense of the phrase, your behavior often falls naturally into conformation with sound, workable ethics. It is people who are confused about their own desires and purposes who generally cause the most havoc, not the self-interested ones.

Phyllis Penn, "Morals, Ethics, and that Cosmo Girl," *Cosmopolitan*, February 1975.

With the evolution of humans, however, environmental complexity increased out of all proportion to the genetic and neuronal changes distinguishing us from our simian ancestors. This was due partly to the fact that our species evolved in a geologic period of great climatic flux—the Ice Ages—and partly to the fact that our behaviors themselves began to change our environment. The changed environment in turn created new problems to be solved. Their solutions further changed the environment, and so on. Thus, the discovery of fire led to the burning of trees and forests, which led to destruction of local water supplies and watersheds, which led to the development of architecture with which to build aqueducts, which led to laws concerning water rights, which led to international strife, and on and on.

Given such complexity, even the ability to learn new behaviors is, by itself, inadequate. If trial and error were the only means, most people would die of old age before they would succeed in rediscovering fire or reinventing the wheel. As a substitute for instinct and to increase the efficiency of learning, mankind developed culture. The ability to teach—as well as to learn—evolved, and trial-and-error learning became a method of last resort.

By transmission of culture—passing on the sum total of the learned behaviors common to a population—we can do what Darwinian genetic selection would not allow: we can inherit acquired characteristics. The wheel once having been invented, its manufacture and use can be passed down through generations. Culture can adapt to change much faster than genes can, and this provides for finely tuned responses to environmental disturbances and upheavals. By means of cultural transmission, those behaviors which have proven useful in the past can be taught quickly to the young, so that adaptation to life—say on the Greenland ice cap—can be assured.

Even so, cultural transmission tends to be rigid: it took over one hundred thousand years to advance to chipping *both* sides of the hand ax! Cultural mutations, like genetic mutations, tend more often than not to be harmful, and both are resisted—the former by cultural conservatism, the latter by natural selection. But changes do creep in faster than the rate of genetic change, and cultures slowly evolve. Even that cultural dinosaur known as the Roman Catholic church—despite its claim to be the unchanging repository of truth and correct behavior—has changed greatly since its beginning.

Incidentally, it is at this hand ax stage of behavioral evolution at which most of the religions of today are still stuck. Our inflexible, absolutist moral codes also are fixated at this stage. The Ten Commandments are the moral counterpart of the "here's-how-you-rub-the-sticks-together" phase of technological evolution. If the only type of fire you want is one to heat your cave and cook your clams, the stick-rubbing method suffices. But if you want a fire to propel your jet airplane, some changes have to be made.

So, too, with the transmission of moral behavior. If we are to live lives which are as complex socially as jet airplanes are complex technologically, we need something more than the Ten Commandments. We cannot base our moral code upon arbitrary and capricious fiats reported to us by persons claiming to be privy to the intentions of the denizens of Sinai or Olympus. Our ethics can be based neither upon fictions concerning the nature of mankind nor upon fake reports concerning the desire of the deities. Our ethics must be firmly planted in the soil of scientific self-knowledge. They must be *improvable* and *adaptable*.

Where then, and with what, shall we begin?

The Principle of Enlightened Self-Interest

The principle of "enlightened self-interest" is an excellent first approximation to an ethical principle which is both consistent with what we know of human nature and is relevant to the problems of life in a complex society. Let us examine this principle.

First we must distinguish between "enlightened" and "unenlightened" self-interest. Let's take an extreme example for illustration. Suppose a person lived a totally selfish life of immediate gratification of every desire. Suppose that whenever someone else had something he wanted, he took it for himself.

"She is going for the Scriptures! Quick, let's make a run for it!"

Scott Masear. Reprinted with permission.

It wouldn't be long at all before everyone would be up in arms against him, and he would have to spend all his waking hours fending off reprisals. Depending upon how outrageous his activity had been, he might very well lose his life in an orgy of neighborly revenge. The life of total but unenlightened self-interest might be exciting and pleasant as long as it lasts—but it is not likely to last long.

The person who practices "enlightened" self-interest, by contrast, is the person whose behavioral strategy simultaneously maximizes both the *intensity* and *duration* of personal gratification. An enlightened strategy will be one which, when practiced over a long span of time, will generate ever greater amounts and varieties of pleasures and satisfactions.

176

How is this to be done?

It is obvious that more is to be gained by cooperating with others than by acts of isolated egoism. One man with a rock cannot kill a buffalo for dinner. But a group of men or women, with a lot of rocks, can drive the beast off a cliff and—even after dividing the meat up among them—will still have more to eat than they would have had without cooperation.

Cooperation

But cooperation is a two-way street. If you cooperate with several others to kill buffalo, and each time they drive you away from the kill and eat it themselves, you will quickly take your services elsewhere, and you will leave the ingrates to stumble along without the Paleolithic equivalent of a fourth-for-bridge. Cooperation implies reciprocity.

Justice has its roots in the problem of determining fairness and reciprocity in cooperation. If I cooperate with you in tilling your field of corn, how much of the corn is due me at harvest time? When there is justice, cooperation operates at maximal efficiency, and the fruits of cooperation become ever more desirable. Thus, "enlightened self-interest" entails a desire for justice. With justice and with cooperation, we can have symphonies. Without it, we haven't even a song.

Because we have the nervous systems of social animals, we are generally happier in the company of our fellow creatures than alone. Because we are emotionally suggestible, as we practice enlightened self-interest, we usually will be wise to choose behaviors which will make others happy and willing to cooperate and accept us—for their happiness will reflect back upon us and intensify our own happiness. On the other hand, actions which harm others and make them unhappy—even if they do not trigger overt retaliation which decreases our happiness—will create an emotional milieu which, because of our suggestibility, will make us less happy.

Because our nervous systems are imprintable, we are able not only to fall in love at first sight, we are able to love objects and ideals as well as people. We are also able to love with variable intensities. Like the gosling attracted to the toy train, we are pulled forward by the desire for love. Unlike the gosling's "love," however, our love is to a considerable extent shapable by experience and is educable. A major aim of "enlightened self-interest," surely, is to give and receive love, both sexual and non-sexual. As a general—though not absolute—rule, we must choose those behaviors which will be likely to bring us love and acceptance, and we must eschew those behaviors which will not.

Another aim of enlightened self-interest is to seek beauty in all its forms, to preserve and prolong its resonance between the world outside and that within. Beauty and love are but different facets of the same jewel: Love is beautiful, and we love beauty.

The experience of love and beauty, however, is a *passive* function of the mind. How much greater is the joy which comes from creating beauty! How delicious it is to exercise *actively* our creative powers to engender that which can be loved! Paints and pianos are not necessarily prerequisites for the exercise of creativity: Whenever one transforms the raw materials of existence in such a way that he leaves them better than they were when he found them, he has been creative.

Conclusion

The task of moral education, then, is not to inculcate by rote great lists of do's and don'ts but rather to help people to predict the consequences of actions being considered. What are the long-term and immediate rewards and drawbacks of the acts? Will an act increase or decrease one's chances of experiencing the hedonic triad of love, beauty, and creativity?

Thus it happens, that when the Atheist approaches the problem of finding natural grounds for human morals and establishing a non-superstitious basis for behavior, it appears as though nature has already solved the problem to a great extent. Indeed, it appears as though the problem of establishing a natural, humanistic basis for ethical behavior is not much of a problem at all. It is in our natures to desire love, to seek beauty, and to thrill at the act of creation. The labyrinthine complexity we see when we examine traditional moral codes does not arise of necessity: It is largely the result of vain attempts to accommodate human needs and nature to the whimsical totems and taboos of the demons and deities who emerged with us from our cave dwellings at the end of the Paleolithic Era—and have haunted our houses ever since.

"Money is the main, moving force of human life at the present stage of civilization."

Money Is Life's Present Guide

Jacob Needleman

Jacob Needleman is a professor of philosophy at San Francisco State University. His book *Money and the Meaning of Life*, from which the following viewpoint is excerpted, received national attention from NBC News, CNN, and Bill Moyers's PBS program "A World of Ideas." Needleman argues that "the art of living is to be engaged in the money game without being devoured by it." He believes that because money controls so many human endeavors, understanding money is necessary if one is to understand life.

As you read, consider the following questions:

1. What evidence does the author present to support his contention that "money is the main moving force of human life?" Do you agree?
2. Needleman maintains that money should be secondary in life. What does he think should be first?

One of the commonest views of money today is that it is a form of energy. Certainly, money is the main, moving force of human life at the present stage of civilization. Our relationships to nature, to health and illness, to education, to art, to social justice, are all increasingly permeated by the money factor.

It is not a question of regretting this fact; it is solely a question of understanding it. We live in the same world, metaphysically, cosmically speaking, as did Pythagoras, Gautama Buddha, St. Augustine, or Moses. The same forces are at play on this plane of being called earth, human life on earth. The Greeks gave the names of gods to these forces—Apollo, Aphrodite, Kronos. Today such forces are given names derived from modern psychology or science—for example, entropy, libido, homeostasis—which, however, convey only a pale reflection of their real power in human life and the cosmic scheme. And, in our time, the forces that define human life on earth manifest themselves through money.

Money Is the Primary Force in Our Culture

In other times and in other cultures, money has not played this role—but there has always been the same play of forces. What has changed is the medium through which these forces have flowed. In some cultures the "currency"—that is to say, the medium through which the main energies of human life has passed—has been land, or livestock, or human slaves, or a natural substance such as water or salt or iron, or weapons, or even ideas and symbolic forms, such as "beauty" or "honor." Walk into any museum, study any good book of history, look at any ancient document, and you will see that mankind has always put its main energy into one or another kind of thing, substance, or form.

We do not create the art of the Renaissance or medieval Europe; we do not worship the state as did ancient Rome; we do not build as did the Egyptians. But neither the Egyptians, nor the medieval Europeans, nor the peoples of the Renaissance— nor, for that matter, the cultures of ancient China, Greece, or Persia, nor the inhabitants of the North American continent before the white man—none of these created the immense global mechanism of finance whose penetration into every aspect of human life has been the chief feature of our contemporary culture. In other times and places, not everyone has wanted *money* above all else; people have desired salvation, beauty, power, strength, pleasure, propriety, explanations, food, adventure, conquest, comfort. But now and here, money—not necessarily even the things money can buy, but *money*—is what everyone wants. The outward expenditure of mankind's energy now takes place in and through money. . . .

For anyone who seeks to understand the meaning of our human life on earth, for anyone who wishes to understand the meaning of his own individual life on earth, it is imperative that one understand this movement of energy. Therefore, if one wishes to understand life, one *must* understand money—in this present phase of history and civilization. . . .

How to Find Meaning in a Money-Dominated Culture

I held a seminar a few weeks ago and I asked them what their questions were, and almost all of them had the same question: "How do I engage in making a living and still keep my soul?" They feel that the world of money, the world they are forced to live in, is sucking their soul dry and they cannot keep their self-respect, or their sense of inner worth, and still participate in the money world. They want meaning. People come for meaning.

There's this idea, "Do what you love, the money will follow." I think it's one of the New Age fantasies. Many people say, "No, I have found that when I'm there making my living, making money, I am completely wasted on meaning. My life is meaningless. I'm manufacturing widgets or I'm selling this or I'm writing these things that are totally without any nourishment to my inner life and I come away from that tired and exhausted. I have no time for anything that I consider meaningful. Now, how can I relate to money in a way that doesn't destroy me in some way?" Almost all of the questions are of one variation or another of that. One thing that helps them is to hear great ideas of the ancient traditions, restated in ways they can understand. When these great ideas are really given in the real way, they come in touch with another world. This is the world of ideas. If people come in touch with that they immediately feel a shock of recognition. It opens something, a part of themselves that they haven't been in touch with. And it may not be spiritual realization in any grand sense, but it's the beginning of a contact with a part of themselves that isn't concerned just with making money.

Jacob Needleman in *A World of Ideas:* II, 1990.

The thesis of this viewpoint is that the chief representative of "life on earth," the world of birth and death, the world we are born to, but not necessarily destined to die in—that chief representation is now *money.* Our task, then, is to search for contact with something far greater than we can imagine, while participating rightly and truly in the forces of life on earth. . . .

The challenge of our lives is to face the money question without disappearing into it or running away from it. We must take money seriously. If we wish to live a human life, this can mean only that we participate humanly in all the forces of life—or, to

*"Religious freedom is my immediate goal, but my
long-range plan is to go into real estate."*

put it another way, that we allow all the forces of life to participate in ourselves, to be embraced by our consciousness. We enter hell only when our consciousness is devoured, when we are absorbed by the outward-directed energy that constitutes only part of our true nature.

To be obsessed by money is certainly to be in hell. But there is another kind of hell, which we must also now acknowledge. We live in that hell when we refuse to participate in the realities of life, when dreams and fantasies, spiritual or otherwise, take the place of a real inner search. Let us now look at this other apartment in hell. . . .

Wizard of Id / By Brant Parker and Johnny Hart

By permission of Johnny Hart and Creators Syndicate, Inc.

Our challenge is to bring money back to the place where it belongs in human life. It is not a question of getting more money, although for you or me that may be necessary. It is not a question of giving up money, although, again, for you or me that may be necessary up to a point. It is not even a question of ordering one's life—tidying up one's affairs, necessary though that may be for you or me sometimes. It is solely a question of restoring money to its proper place in human life. And that place is *secondary*. Our aim is to understand what it means to make money secondary in our lives. . . .

Our only realistic aim can be the attainment of this power of discrimination, this unique quality of self-knowledge and inner freedom. And if money is to be secondary in our lives, *it can only mean that money serve the aim of self-knowledge.*

Here, at last, we have found our question. Here we find the key to the place that money can—and must—occupy in our lives. Money must become an instrument of the search for self-knowledge. Money must become a tool in the only enterprise worth undertaking for any modern man or woman seriously wishing to find the meaning of their lives: we must use money in order to study ourselves as we are and as we can become.

a critical thinking activity

Constructing Moral Rules

Hägar the Horrible / By Dik Browne

Hagar the Horrible, reprinted with permission from King Features Syndicate, Inc.

The moral rules that Hagar the Horrible lives by are probably ideal for one who makes his living by sacking and pillaging. However, if everyone in contemporary society lived by these moral guidelines life would be unbearable for all.

Each of us lives by a moral code whether or not we have taken the time to write it down or methodically think it through. Some people live by the simple code of "an eye for an eye." Others use the golden rule that forms the core of all major religions. This activity will give you an opportunity to think through the moral rules you live by.

Consider the ten moral rules listed below, taken from the book *The Moral Rules* by Bernard Gert. Gert suggests these ten rules as the basic or fundamental rules of morality. Do you agree with them? List the moral rules you live by.

THE MORAL RULES

The First Five

1. Don't kill.
2. Don't cause pain.
3. Don't disable.
4. Don't deprive of freedom or opportunity.
5. Don't deprive of pleasure.

The Second Five

6. Don't deceive.
7. Keep your promise.
8. Don't cheat.
9. Obey the law.
10. Do your duty.

"The church contributes to the ethical life by focusing our ethical concerns upon something more adventurous than self-preservation and personal security."

The Church Promotes Moral Behavior

William H. Willimon

William H. Willimon, a United Methodist minister, serves at Duke University in Durham, North Carolina. The following viewpoint is taken from his book *What's Right with the Church*. Willimon states that moral actions are the result of good moral habits. He contends that ethics are learned, like language. Because of the positive moral vision the church provides, those who attend church learn good habits and generally become good moral citizens.

As you read, consider the following questions:

1. Willimon argues that the moral habits the church promotes are based on a vision of life's meaning. What is this vision?
2. Willimon uses the example of the church women of Pine Mountain to prove that the church instills positive moral values. Do you agree? Why or why not?

It all started harmlessly enough. A group of church women were looking for a service project within the community. Someone suggested that they might do something at the local jail. . . .

So someone in the church suggested that it might be nice if a group of the church members made something for the people in the jail. Perhaps a toiletries kit would be good—a toothbrush and toothpaste, soap, shampoo, a piece of candy to make their stay a little brighter. . . .

Corrupt Practices

This is when the trouble started. When the women began spending more time at the jail, they saw things that few citizens of Pine Mountain had seen. They noticed the attitude of the police toward their work. They saw signs of excessive force being used on prisoners. They heard rumors of money changing hands in order to get people lighter sentences.

"I knew we were asking for trouble when we let you women stick your noses into things," the jailer said when a delegation from the women's newly formed Task Force on Local Prisons met with him to ask questions. "You women ought to stay out of what is none of your business," he advised. "What goes on here is really no concern of yours. Why don't you stick to church work and leave the legal work to us."

"This *is* church business," shouted Myrtle Thompson as she pounded her fist on his desk. "And therefore this is a concern of ours. If we don't get good answers from you and if we don't get them fast, we are calling the State Law Enforcement Division to look into the situation here."

The jailer refused to cooperate. "You ought to stick to religion, stick to saving souls, and let me handle the criminal element," he said.

"You're going to find out what a mistake you made when you began messing around with a group of Christians," Florence Smith muttered to the jailer as the meeting ended. "Some of our best friends spent time in jail."

To make a long story short, the police refused to cooperate. The women did indeed call the State Law Enforcement division. Then they drew up a formal complaint against the jailer and his jail at their Spring General Meeting. An investigation was launched. The city was charged with improprieties. All this eventually led to the jailer's resignation. Things changed at the jail.

This is a small example of what can happen when people begin messing around with the church. Christians, by simply being about their proper business and keeping their attention focused in the right direction, can be a light to a dark world.

Many people who think of the church picture it as a kind of ethical improvement society founded by Jesus: "The purpose of the church is to help us live better lives." In other words, the church is a means to an end, an organization whose purpose is to do some minor adjustment and fine-tuning on our lives. . . .

The church is an end in itself, the visible result of God's gracious intercourse with the world. The church exists, not to enable people to be better, but because God wills it. Whenever the church is seen as essentially a means of improving society, or producing better people, or fostering a love of good music, or giving the youth something wholesome to do on a Saturday night, the church is whittling itself down to scale as one more human organization that is content to be useful in doing things that other human organizations may do better.

Churches Are Teachers

Perhaps the most important advantage in church membership is the sharing of values and meaning. Churches are teachers. They transmit meanings for life and the values that people have found essential for their fulfillment. Not only do the churches frequently take the task of introducing meanings and values to the young if parents fail to do so, but they also continue to reinforce these meanings and values throughout the entire lifespan of the individual.

Andrew Panzarella, *Religion and Human Experience*, 1974.

The moral significance of the church is a more complex phenomenon; it is not simply a place to urge nice people to be nicer. The moral significance of the church arises as a kind of gracious by-product of a people who are first satisfied to be before they attempt to be good, a people who, in celebrating what God is doing in Jesus Christ, are surprised to find that God is doing something to them as well. . . .

It can be said that the church contributed to the moral direction and motivation of the women of Christ Church who rattled the bars of Pine Mountain jail. . . .

The Church Instills Good Moral Habits

What ought I to do? may not be the most pressing moral question. Who do I want to be? may be more to the point. Although decision and choice are important, so many of the "ethical" things we do or avoid doing arise, not by reference to a rule or out of agonized decisions, but simply out of habit. Our decisions arise from somewhere. The choices we make are interesting not only for their consequences but because of what our choices tell us about who we are and who we are becoming. Moral life is not simply deciding this or that; it is a complex of factors that form us into certain sorts of people who decide in certain ways because of who we are. Our actions flow from our identity. So we do well to inquire first, not into how we decide what to do, but how we become who we want to be. . . .

Ethics Is a Social Phenomenon

All ethics is social ethics, the result of living in a social framework. We learn our ethics as we learn language, as incidental to growing up with certain people, not because someone sat us down and taught it to us.

The assertion that none of us can say what is right in this situation unless we were there ourselves, rather than discrediting the power of our moral socialization, proves that we have been socialized into the American system's values of freedom, individualism, self-reliance, and contempt for history.

Our moral lives are cumulative and social. Debate over "right," "wrong," "good," or "bad" is impossible except as a debate in the context of a society that values certain things more than others and that grows through experience. "Let your conscience be your guide," automatically forecloses ethical discussion and protects us from the scrutiny of the community. Religion, we assure ourselves, is "a private affair." How dare you question my motives?

The church is the social matrix where Christian ethics arise. We do not act like Christians by natural inclination because we are made, not born. We are formed into Christians in the crucible of the church lest there be any misunderstanding that this is a thoroughly social faith. Our minds are stretched through the tradition of the church; our moral possibilities are broadened; and our present actions are placed in a larger context than what merely seems right to us in the moment.

The women of Christ Church came to a head-on collision with the jailer not simply because he was an evil person (which in a way he was) but because they had been socialized into a different set of values. They valued things differently than he did. Their community (the church) had taught them to act and react to certain things and not others. Their behavior was a social product.

Ethics Is a Matter of Habit

Aristotle was first to note that it was too much to expect ordinary people to be good. About the most that one could hope for is that we might develop good habits. In our daily lives we do not agonize over most decisions. We do not steal, we do not kill, not because we have consciously decided on anything, but out of "second nature." These habits are no less ethical because they have become part of us; in fact, they are the very qualities that make us people of character and fidelity. "That's just what I would have expected her to do" is an everyday observation of habits that form character. . . .

For the Christian, ethics is not simply a matter of deciding what suits the situation, or even what seems right. Ethics is an expression of discipleship—disciplining our lives in congruence with our Master. The church does so many things ritually and habitually, because it senses that its vision is so odd, so against the grain of the wider society, that only constant attentiveness and lifelong cultivation of that vision will enable it to endure in the lives of those who are Christ's disciples.

Morality Arises Out of Vision

My actions are not simply a matter of deciding between option A and option B on the basis of past experience. Actions also arise out of my vision of the future. This vision gives life coherence and direction, even though it may not specify the specific steps along the way.

We Need Organized Religion

We need organized religion for the same reason we need organized political parties, or any organized social movement. . . . The foundations of morality in the West are religious. Though a moral individual may be irreligious, he acquired his moral values from his ancestors who in all likelihood were religious, and/or from Western civilization which adheres (or at least pays lip service) to moral values formulated by Judaism and communicated by Christianity. The ethical secularist is essentially living by moral values inherited from thousands of years of religion.

Consequently, we ask whether the ethical secularist is capable of bequeathing a moral legacy to the next generation, now that he has cut them off from religion as the ultimate source of morality. The answer, as history has shown, is no. The existence of righteous individual secularists notwithstanding, the legacy of ideologies which attempt to destroy religion has been unparalleled human suffering.

Dennis Prager and Joseph Telushkin, *The Nine Questions People Ask About Judaism*, 1981.

Talk of right or wrong can only be meaningful in the context of some vision of the sort of world I want to live in and the kind of person I hope to be. . . .

The images, stories, sacraments, and work of the church give shape to the Christian vision, refurbish that vision in our people, and pass it on to our young. Without such vision, Christians might stop agonizing over what is right and true and settle for well-intentioned kindness, or decency in general, rather than Christian ethics in particular.

Life in the wider American society can never foster the countercultural vision that discipleship demands. The surrounding culture has its own secular view of what ought to be, a vision that is seductive to those who neglect the development of specifically Christian character and are careless about whose altar they bow before. . . .

So the church is morally significant not simply as a place to learn the right rules but in a more dynamic sense as a place that urges us to look in the right direction. In the church's worship, our vision is sharpened, clarified, and given vitality. Thus the church is a place full of symbols and images, for this faith is so complex and rich that it cannot be apprehended save through the richest of metaphors.

We make Christians by telling them stories of bad little boys like Jacob who got saved anyway and about a Savior who came via a cow stable, and by showing them a cross and asking them to shoulder it, and reminding them, as did the women of Christ Church, that "some of our best friends spent time in jail.". . .

In the church we gather to envision a "new heaven and a new earth" where the deaf hear, the blind see, and outcasts come to a feast. So, in a sense, the church contributes to the ethical life by focusing our ethical concerns upon something more adventurous than self-preservation and personal security. . . .

Church Gives Us God

Christian ethics is thus complementary to Christian worship. Both activities have to do with learning to pay attention. The church confesses that, until we are attentive to God, our selves remain mired in illusion, self-hate, self-defensiveness, and the anxiety that occurs when we assume that we are forced to create and sustain our own significance rather than its coming as a gift of God.

Sometimes the church gives us certain rules or helpful guides for behavior. Sometimes it gives us a forum for ethical debate and decision. It is right for the church to give its people help in discerning what it means to be a Christian. But the main thing the church gives us is God. That gift makes all the difference in who we are and what we do. . . .

The women of Christ Church were not extraordinary ethical heroes or moral virtuosi. They were just ordinary people who had learned to pay attention to something extraordinary. They lacked sophisticated insight but possessed a profound spiritual vision.

"Indoctrination with Christian god-talk is incompatible with the psychological growth and moral development of human beings."

Religion Does Not Promote Moral Behavior

Wendell W. Watters

Wendell W. Watters is professor emeritus in psychiatry at Mc-Master University in Hamilton, Canada, and the author of *Compulsory Parenthood: The Truth About Abortion*. He specializes in family therapy, couple sex therapy, and psychotherapy. Based on his experience as a psychotherapist, Watters asserts in the following viewpoint that Christian religious teachings do not build moral character. In fact, he thinks that Christians who do lead decent moral lives do so in spite of their religious indoctrination.

As you read, consider the following questions:

1. What point does the author make with his statement that "Christianity is literally the house that guilt built"?
2. How does Watters think Christians misdirect the emotion of anger and why does he think it is harmful?
3. What proof does the author present to back his contention that religion impedes moral behavior?

From Wendell W. Watters, "Moral Education: Homo Sapiens or Homo Religiosus?" *Free Inquiry*, Winter 1989/1990. Reprinted with permission.

If one were to make a list of the ten most powerful myths operating in Western society, at the top of that list would be the notion that religious indoctrination and religious affiliation contribute to or are positively correlated with moral behavior in human beings. So powerful is this myth that for many Christian god-talkers the word "moral" is synonymous with the word "religious."

I submit that this is not only one of the most powerful myths operating today, but one that is most in need of critical examination. In fact, I would like to make a case for the opposite hypothesis, namely that indoctrination with Christian god-talk is incompatible with the psychological growth and moral development of human beings, individually and collectively; that, in effect, those Christians who do lead decent moral lives do so despite their religious indoctrination and because of the kind of human beings they are and their critical and meaningful interactions with other human beings in early life.

Self-Fulfilling Prophecies

Conversely, we must not forget that many, if not most, of the residents of our penal institutions come from Christian backgrounds of one sort or another. Is it possible that they really and truly believed it when the Sunday-school teacher, priest, or minister repeated—week after week—that they were innately evil creatures born into a state of original sin? If so, did they then gradually make their behavior conform to the self-concept they were encouraged to develop?

In the area of health promotion, Christian indoctrination, rather than having a healing effect on human beings, in fact promotes unnecessary suffering and illness-inducing behavior. Other behavioral scientists have come to similar conclusions. Albert Ellis even goes so far to state that the adherents of religion are emotionally disturbed—"usually neurotic but sometimes psychotic." . . .

There are many other pathogenic features of Christian doctrine, including the belief in original sin, Christ's sacrifice on the cross to save us from the consequences of our innate wickedness, the belief that Christ/God is the source of all human strength, wisdom, and goodness, and that such characteristics are present only in those human beings who grovel abjectly at the feet of this celestial worthy. Because of our innate evil and despite the fact that Christ's sacrifice was meant to redeem us, Christians still have it drummed into them that they are worthless creatures who must reject human supports, and prostrate themselves at the feet of the divine big daddy. They are encouraged to embrace suffering in emulation of Christ's suffering on the cross, this masochistic self-flagellation being a strategy

192

for currying favor with a capricious, sadistic deity. If you think I exaggerate, I suggest you read or reread the book that is reputed to have had more influence in promoting Christianity than any other book save the Bible: *Imitation of Christ*, by the German ecclesiastic Thomas á Kempis. It is full of exhortations to Christians to reject their fellow human creatures, to think of themselves as worse than nothing, to turn their backs on knowledge, and to suffer, suffer, suffer; not simply to endure suffering when it occurs, but to seek it as a means of storing up brownie points in heaven.

"To me, religion is a state of mind . . . kind of like mental illness."

Reprinted by permission from *American Atheist*.

Central to all of this is the issue of guilt. Christianity is literally the house that guilt built. As George H. Smith put it in *Atheism: The Case Against God*, "Guilt, not love, is the fundamental emotion that Christianity seeks to induce—and this is symptomatic of a viciousness in Christianity that few people care to acknowledge.". . .

When it comes to the use of guilt in controlling the sheep in the flock, the founding fathers of Christianity developed most of their leverage in two areas of human life: sexuality and dysphoric affects (or emergency emotions), particularly anger. . . .

The Misdirection of Anger

One emergency affect—anger—reached the lofty status of one of the seven deadly sins, and for centuries the Christian approach to anger has shaped our social attitudes to this emotion, whether or not we are card-carrying Christians. Such attitudes are embedded deeply and widely in the social woodwork. I am reminded of Emerson's statement to the effect that the name of Jesus Christ was not so much written as ploughed into the history of the Western world. Our collective social approach toward what is essentially a normal human emotion is illustrated in the advice given by one Christian psychologist who, reinforcing the view that experiencing negative emotions indicates a lack of trust in Divine Providence, suggests that the best way to deal with anger is to swim fifty yards, run a mile, or do thirty push-ups. He says nothing about trying to express the anger openly and directly to the person with whom one is angry in an attempt to resolve the underlying issue itself. . . .

After twenty-five years working in the field of psychotherapy with individuals, couples, and families, I would say that problems in coping with anger are at the bottom of most individual emotional difficulties and relationship stresses. Because of deeply engrained social attitudes toward this emotion, we have not yet learned to deal with it adaptively but tend rather to defend excessively against it; nonetheless, it is usually expressed in covert destructive ways that increase relationship static. I wish I had a dollar for every couple that has told me—with pride, mind you—that they never fight or get angry at each other. These unfortunate people are paying for this unreal, inhuman equanimity with utterly joyless relationships.

Whether we are speaking of individual health, relationship health, or moral health, what is the actual mechanism involved? How does Christian indoctrination about anger contribute to self-destructive, violent, or other kinds of immoral behavior?

The Consequences of Suppressing Anger

This is an oversimplified account of what happens in a society so highly imbued with Christian notions about anger. Anger is a normal human emotion, a response to frustration of one kind or another. At the best of times anger is an unpleasant emotion, one we would rather not feel. The general tendency is to train children from an early age to believe that they are bad, evil people for feeling this way, for not being able to suppress this unpleasant emotion and prevent it from emerging in the first place. I submit that this attitude generates intense conflict between what the child actually feels and what the child "should" feel in order to be accepted by the caretaking group. Such conflicts are intensified if a child witnesses angry or violent outbursts in the caretakers, who themselves have not been trained to deal with these feelings in an adaptive way. The child's confusion is compounded when such violent behavior is directed toward him or her by the very caretakers who have tried to train the child to suppress such emotions entirely.

Religion and Cruelty

The more intense has been the religion of any period and the more profound has been the dogmatic belief, the greater has been the cruelty and the worse has been the state of affairs.

Bertrand Russell.

Conflicts of this sort generate anxiety, which in its extreme form is a very unpleasant emotion indeed. To avoid this unpleasant affect, humans develop what psychiatrists call "defense mechanisms." These are simply attitudinal and behavioral responses designed to ward off the unacceptable feeling that gives rise to the anxiety. Thus to deal with the conflict between the real feeling and the prescribed feeling, the child may simply deny the unacceptable anger (hence the term "denial"). The child, unacceptably angry at mother or father, may vent the anger on a younger sibling or the family dog (a mechanism we call "displacement"). The child may bend over backward to prove that he or she really is not angry at mother or father and become over-attentive and solicitous (a mechanism we call "reaction formation"). Or the child may distort the reality of the situation and insist that it is not he or she who is angry at the parent, but rather the parent who is angry at the child (this we call "projection").

In performing the task of keeping unacceptable angry feelings out of awareness, an individual's defenses may work for some time. But under some circumstances these defenses break down, and the unacceptable feeling threatens to break through into awareness. This may produce the kind of symptoms that may take the individual to a doctor or even a psychiatrist, or it may contribute to relationship disharmony. At other times the breakthrough of the unwelcome emotion occurs in a manner that leads to overt antisocial violent behavior. If the individual believes that he or she is basically evil even to feel angry, when the feeling erupts from behind brittle defenses, it may be expressed in a form that confirms the Christian view of anger as a violent, destructive act. This explosion-effect reinforces the impression that anger is a feeling that human beings should avoid at all costs—that it is indeed one of the seven deadly sins. . . .

As a society we are slowly coming to realize the contribution of Christian doctrine to our stunted, warped, antihuman attitudes toward sexuality. It is time we recognized that the impact of Christian teachings in many other areas has been equally devastating, and the task of designing educational programs to reverse and overcome these effects is formidable. In the area of teaching human-to-human communication and negotiation skills, we have made less progress than in the area of sex education. Indeed, we have not yet recognized that teaching children how to communicate and negotiate with one another should be more important than teaching them how to communicate with a computer or with a deity. No amount of religious indoctrination or computer training will help the growing child learn to be at home with emotions, to be comfortable in communicating with others, or to negotiate with others, especially in the presence of conflicting needs, aspirations, and priorities.

We should not dismiss the notion that our educational system could play a role in helping young people to learn communication and negotiation skills, particularly where angry feelings make such learning difficult. Much—if not most—of the work of psychotherapists, family therapists, and couple therapists consists of helping people to cope with anger. . . .

We Need a Human-Centered World

In our present God-centered world, it is a violation of all we know about psychology to believe that people can be helped to lead moral lives by manipulating their guilt and fear in the way that Christianity does. In the human-centered world, the child would be encouraged to develop a sense of the importance of human-to-human interdependency in this global village of ours. Religions, with their emphasis on the God-human connection, inevitably work against the formation of strong human-to-human supports—notwithstanding all of their hollow rhetoric about fellowship. Daily news reports from Northern Ireland, India, Lebanon, and elsewhere tell us just how much fellowship religion actually promotes.

In a humanist orientation toward life, individuals would be prepared to take responsibility for their moral choices. No more would people be able to justify oppressing other human beings as "doing the will of God," or to explain away antisocial behavior with "the devil made me do it."

196

In order for human beings to make the best moral choices possible, they must be well and accurately informed on all aspects of the issues on which they must make such choices. Since the Renaissance, Christianity has been the implacable foe of real learning, fighting science tooth and claw at every step of the way, even going so far as to establish Christian universities in order to keep as much control of the human mind as possible.

No Tie Between Faith and Actions

What then, can we surmise about the likelihood of someone's being caring and generous, loving and helpful, just from knowing that he or she is a believer? Virtually nothing, say psychologists, sociologists and others who have studied that question for decades.

Alfie Kohn, *Psychology Today*, December 1989.

In a humanist educational approach, it is essential that religion in general and Christianity in particular become the subject of critical study—not religious indoctrination and not the reverential, uncritical examination of religion that comes under the rubric of comparative religion—but *critical* evaluation.

Many Christians worry about what takes place currently in the public schools, where they think their children are being filled with all manner of diabolical secular humanist propaganda; this is the argument they use to justify building their own schools. The truth is that most public schools try to teach children to think for themselves about most things, although few public schools encourage this vigorously in the area of religion. Nonetheless, any child who is encouraged to think for himself or herself about anything is a loose cannon to the fundamentalist Christians; hence, the need to build their own schools, where doctrinal straitjackets can be applied to youthful minds.

Religion Must Be Examined

In reality, the public-school system should be doing the very job that fundamentalists accuse it of—helping children to think critically about religion just as they are encouraged to think critically about every other aspect of their lives. . . .

The humanist alternative will be alive and well only when religion can be examined critically in all schools—when the various myths can be explored, including the myth that religious affiliation promotes moral behavior. Other myths might also be examined: the myth that Christ died for us on the cross to save us from our sins; the myth that traditional Christian attitudes

197

about sexuality and reproduction have anything whatsoever to do with the teachings of Jesus of Nazareth; the myth that God has reserved a place for us in heaven if we only accept what the Christian snake-oil salesmen tell us.

The more our children and grandchildren come to appreciate that the fate of the world is in human rather than divine hands, the more likely they are to get on with the task of forging the human-to-human links that must be forged if we human beings are to develop the problem-solving strategies that might save us from the extinction toward which god-talk is hurling us at a great rate.

"How would you rate your own ethics compared to most other persons?"

Examine Your Ethical Attitudes

The Josephson Institute of Ethics

The Josephson Institute of Ethics, founded by Michael Josephson, conducts more than one hundred workshops a year for many influential organizations, including the Internal Revenue Service, the Department of Defense, the American Red Cross, the Girl Scouts, and state legislators and judges. Its goal is to improve the ethical quality of society. The questions that follow have been put to hundreds of participants in Josephson Institute workshops. They provide important information on attitudes and beliefs about your own ethics. Answer the questions in part I, then read parts II, III, and IV.

I

1. Who is the most ethical person you know? List three or four characteristics you associate with that person.

2. If people who know you well were asked the above question, what proportion do you think would name you?
   - A. Almost all.
   - B. Most.
   - C. About half.

From "Your Ethical Attitudes," page 5 of the July/August 1989 issue and "Ethical Values and Principles," page 69 of the Winter 1988 issue of *Ethics: Easier Said than Done*. Reprinted by permission of the Josephson Institute of Ethics.

D. Very few.

E. I have no idea.

3. How important to you is it that those who know you well respect you for your ethics?

A. Very important.

B. Somewhat important.

C. Somewhat unimportant.

D. Unimportant.

4. How would you rate your own ethics compared to most other persons?

A. Much higher.

B. Higher.

C. About the same.

D. Lower.

E. Much lower.

II. How Others Answered These Questions

1. There is a surprising consensus as to the characteristics of ethical persons. By far the most common characteristic listed is *honesty* (though some use related terms like truthful and straightforward). Other attributes listed most frequently: *integrity* (principled, courage of convictions, honorable); *trustworthy* (reliable, responsible, candid, keeps commitments); *fairness* (just, open, treats people equally); and *caring* (compassionate, kind, considerate, giving). Finally, *loyal, respectful,* and *accountable* are common.

2. Most people (60%-80%) think that almost all or most of the people that know them well would list them.

3. Over 90% of all participants surveyed say it is very important to them to be respected for their ethics.

4. Most (65%-85%) think that their ethics are higher than others.

III. Analysis

The consensus as to the characteristics of ethical persons rebuts the claim that ethics means different things to different people. In fact, almost everyone agrees that honesty, integrity, trustworthiness, fairness and caring are very essential to the notion of ethics.

The unrealistically high percentage of people who think they are more ethical than others reveals the tendency for self-delusion when it comes to assessing our own ethics. Almost everyone thinks he or she is more ethical than everyone else and virtually no one thinks he/she is less ethical. Most of us need a good dose of ethical humility—we are not nearly as good as we think we are and others are not as bad.

A major source of moral self-aggrandizement is rationalization. We tend to judge ourselves by our good *intentions* and our most noble moments. On the other hand, we usually judge others by what they do, especially the bad things they do.

Too many people consider the fact that their conscience doesn't bother them as confirmation that they have acted morally. Yet our consciences are frequently convinced by our self-justifying rationalizations. Many people who do bad things have no trouble sleeping or looking at themselves in the mirror. Self-righteous end-justifies-the-means reasoning frequently disarms the conscience.

Ethics is most definitely easier said than done because there is no shortage of temptations to shortcircuit moral reasoning and, the smarter we are, the more creative we become in finding "good" reasons to be less honest, fair, caring or principled than we ought to be.

People often tell us that they are "basically honest" or that they "hardly ever lie." This usually means that they are honest and truthful—except when it costs too much or is inconvenient. We are apt to label our transgressions as petty and our deceits as "white lies" yet we are not so generous when others are dishonest to us. The perspective of the person lied to is often very different than that of the liar.

Finally, since it is so important to our self-esteem to believe we are ethical, it is easy to allow our wishful thinking to make us less than objective about our true performance. If we really want to be thought of as one of the most ethical people, we probably have to be much more rigorous in our moral reasoning and more committed to our ethical values. Being ethical is a lifelong quest that gives meaning and value to life in a very special way.

IV. Ethical Values and Principles

The following list of ethical principles incorporates the characteristics and values that most people associate with ethical behavior.

Honesty. Be truthful, sincere, forthright, straightforward, frank, candid; *do not* cheat, steal, lie, deceive, *or act* deviously.

Integrity. Be principled, honorable, upright, courageous *and* act on convictions; *do not be* two-faced, *or* unscrupulous *or adopt an* end-justifies-the-means *philosophy that ignores principle.*

Promise-Keeping. Be worthy of trust, keep promises, fulfill commitments, abide by the spirit as well as the letter of an agreement; *do not interpret agreements in an* unreasonably technical or legalistic manner *in order to rationalize noncompliance or create excuses and justifications for breaking commitments.*

201

Loyalty (Fidelity). Be faithful *and* loyal *to family, friends, employers, clients and country; do not* use or disclose information learned in confidence; *in a professional context,* safeguard the ability to make independent professional judgments *by scrupulously* avoiding undue influences and conflicts of interest.

Fairness. Be fair *and* open-minded, *be willing to admit error and, where appropriate, change positions and beliefs, demonstrate a commitment to* justice, *the* equal treatment *of individuals,* tolerance for and acceptance of diversity, *do not* overreach *or* take undue advantage of another's mistakes or adversities.

Caring for Others. Be caring, kind *and* compassionate; share, *be* giving, *be of* service to others; help those in need *and* avoid harming others.

Respect for Others. Demonstrate respect for human dignity, privacy, *and* the right to self-determination *of all people; be* courteous, prompt, *and* decent; provide others with the information they need to make informed decisions about their own lives; *do not* patronize, embarrass *or* demean.

Responsible Citizenship. Obey just laws; *if a law is unjust, openly protest it;* exercise all democratic rights and privileges responsibly *by* participation *(voting and expressing informed views),* social consciousness *and* public service; *when in a position of leadership or authority,* openly respect *and* honor democratic processes of decision making, avoid unnecessary secrecy *or* concealment of information, *and* assure that others have all the information they need to make intelligent choices and exercise their rights.

Pursuit of Excellence. Pursue excellence *in all matters; in meeting your personal and professional responsibilities,* be diligent, reliable, industrious, *and* committed; *perform all tasks to the* best of your ability, *develop and maintain a* high degree of competence, *be* well informed *and* well prepared; *do not be* content with mediocrity; *do not* "win at any cost."

Accountability. Be accountable, accept responsibility for decisions, *for the* foreseeable consequences of actions and inactions, *and for* setting an example for others. *Parents, teachers, employers, many professionals and public officials have a special obligation to* lead by example, *to* safeguard and advance the integrity and reputation of their families, companies, professions and the government itself; *an ethically sensitive individual* avoids even the appearance of impropriety, *and* takes whatever actions are necessary to correct or prevent inappropriate conduct of others.

Making a Moral Decision

Part of being human is being forced to make moral decisions. We are all frequently confronted with situations where we have to choose between alternatives. Rarely is the choice easy.

The following moral dilemma is presented to give you practice in determining how others would react when confronted with a difficult moral problem. The ability to empathize, to see life and its problems through another person's eyes, is a skill that can be helpful when confronted with difficult situations.

Consider the following situation that actually occurred during the Second World War.

A Case of Adultery*

As the Russian armies drove westward to meet the Americans and British at the Elbe, a Soviet patrol picked up a Mrs. Bergmeier foraging food for her three children. Unable even to get word to the children, and without any clear reason for it, she was taken off to a prison camp in the Ukraine. Her husband had been captured in the Bulge and taken to a POW camp in Wales.

When he was returned to Berlin, he spent weeks and weeks rounding up his children; two (Ilse, twelve, and Paul, ten) were found in a detention school run by the Russians, and the oldest, Hans, fifteen, was found hiding in a cellar near the Alexander Platz. Their mother's whereabouts remained a mystery, but they never stopped searching. She more than anything else was needed to reknit them as a family in that dire situation of hunger, chaos, and fear.

*From *Situation Ethics* by Joseph Fletcher, pp. 164-65. Copyright © MCMLXVI, by W.L. Jenkins, The Westminster Press. Used by permission.

Meanwhile, in the Ukraine, Mrs. Bergmeier learned through a sympathetic commandant that her husband and family were trying to keep together and find her. But the rules allowed them to release her for only two reasons: (1) illness needing medical facilities beyond the camp's, in which case she would be sent to a Soviet hospital elsewhere, and (2) pregnancy, in which case she would be returned to Germany as a liability.

She turned things over in her mind and finally asked a friendly Volga German camp guard to impregnate her, which he did. Her condition being medically verified, she was sent back to Berlin and to her family. They welcomed her with open arms, even when she told them how she had managed it. When the child was born, they loved him more than all the rest, on the view that little Dietrich had done more for them than anybody.

When it was time for him to be christened, they took him to the pastor on a Sunday afternoon. After the ceremony, they sent Dietrich home with the children and sat down in the pastor's study, to ask him whether they were right to feel as they did about Mrs. Bergmeier and Dietrich. Should they be grateful to the Volga German? Had Mrs. Bergmeier done a good and right thing?

Try to imagine how the following individuals would react if they were Mrs. Bergmeier. What reasons do you think they would give for their choices? What would you do? What would be your reasoning?

1. Joseph Fletcher—using love and situation ethics as his guide.
2. Milton Rudnick—using scripture as his guide.
3. Frank Zindler—using self-interest as his guide.
4. You—using your philosophy as your guide.

Periodical Bibliography

The following articles have been selected to supplement the diverse views in this chapter. Because the subject matter of all chapters in this book is closely related, it may be helpful to examine the other chapter bibliographies when doing further study.

Joseph Alper   "The Roots of Morality," *Science*, March
                                1985.

Steven Cory   "Rerouting Ayn Rand's 'Virtue of
                                Selfishness'," *Christianity Today*, June 18,
                                1982.

Frederick Edwords   "The Human Basis of Laws and Ethics," *The
                                Humanist*, May/June 1985.

Joseph Fletcher   "A Secular Humanist Confession," *Free
                                Inquiry*, Summer 1987. Available from PO
                                Box 5, Buffalo, NY 14215-0005.

Joseph Fletcher   "Humanism and Theism: A Conflict?" *The
                                Witness*, February 1988.

Free Inquiry   "Ethics & Religion," Summer 1982.

Margaret Halsey   "What's Wrong with 'Me, Me, Me'?"
                                Newsweek, April 17, 1978.

Daniel R. Heischman   "Adolescents' Moral Compass, Adults' Moral
                                Presence," *The Christian Century*, January 30,
                                1991.

John Howard   "There Is a Difference Between Right and
                                Wrong," *Vital Speeches of the Day*, February
                                25, 1974.

S. Guernsey Jones   "How Deep Are Your Convictions?" *Vital
                                Speeches of the Day*, June 1, 1987.

Marvin Kohl and   "Morality Without Religion," *Free Inquiry*,
Joseph Fletcher   Winter 1980-81.

Alfie Kohn   "Do Religious People Help More? Not So
                                You'd Notice," *Psychology Today*, December
                                1989.

John Lachs   "Dogmatist in Disguise," *The Christian
                                Century*, November 16, 1966.

Leonard C. Lwein   "Ethical Aptitude Tests," *Harper's*, October 1976.

Albert Lyngzeidetson   "Why an Atheist Ethic Is Superior to a Religious Ethic," *American Atheist*, June 1990.

Richard A. McCormick   "Why Moral Decisions Shouldn't Be Left to Chance," *U.S. Catholic*, February 1990.

Myron Magnet   "The Money Society," *Fortune*, July 6, 1987.

Richard J. Neuhaus   "Ethics on Trial," *The American Legion*, September 1989.

Jacob Neusner   "Prescription for Moral Order," *National Review*, March 31, 1972.

Madalyn O'Hair   "Religion and Morality," *American Atheist*, September 1982.

Frederick E. Rowe Jr.   "Crossing the Line," *Forbes*, November 26, 1990.

C.J. Silas   "A Question of Scruples," *Vital Speeches of the Day*, May 15, 1989.

John Snarey   "A Question of Morality," *Psychology Today*, June 1987.

Lloyd H. Steffen   "On Honesty and Self-Deception: 'You Are the Man'," *The Christian Century*, April 29, 1987.

Paul Surlis   "Is Religion the Only Basis for Morality?" *Christianity & Crisis*, October 29, 1984.

Christopher L. Tyner   "A Generation in Search of Ethics," *Ethics: Easier Said than Done*, Number 10, 1990. Available from 310 Washington St., Suite 104, Marina del Rey, CA 90292.

Frank R. Zindler   "Religiosity as a Mental Disorder," *American Atheist*, April 1988.

5 CHAPTER

How Should
One Live?

Constructing a Life
PHILOSOPHY

Chapter Preface

The self-help section is one of the largest in most bookstores because people are continually searching for advice to help them lead better lives. As M. Scott Peck points out in chapter one, life is difficult and it takes courage to live successfully. It also takes introspection and thoughtful planning and the often difficult implementation of those plans and principles. It is unlikely that any of us will be visited by a ghost, as Scrooge was in Dickens's *Christmas Carol*, to be shown the error of our ways. We have to get it right the first time.

In Thornton Wilder's classic play *Our Town*, a young woman who died in childbirth is allowed to return to earth for one day. She chooses the day of her sixteenth birthday party. She is sadly disappointed when she discovers that no one besides her savors the wonder of life and the uniqueness of this special day, being too caught up in the activities of the moment. As she exits the stage she turns to the stage manager and asks: "Tell me, does anyone on earth ever realize life while he lives it . . . every minute?" "No . . .," he replies.

The contributors in this chapter have given more thought than the average person to the meaning of life and how it should be lived. There may not be a viewpoint here that will stir you. But, if nothing else, the chapter will help you reflect on the direction of your life and begin answering the most important question you will ever be asked. How should one live?

"Looking out for Number One is important because it leads to a simple, uncomplicated life in which you spend more time doing those things which give you the greatest amount of pleasure."

Look Out for Number One

Robert J. Ringer

Robert J. Ringer's first book, *Winning Through Intimidation,* sold over a million copies in the first few years after its publication in 1973. It made Ringer an instant celebrity. *Looking Out for Number One,* from which the following viewpoint was taken, was published in 1977 and spent a year on the *New York Times* Bestseller List. In the following viewpoint, Ringer argues that everyone's main objective in life is to feel good. With this in mind, he suggests that "man's primary moral duty lies in the pursuit of pleasure so long as he does not forcibly interfere with the rights of others."

As you read, consider the following questions:

1. What does the author mean when he uses the term "Looking Out for Number One"?
2. What is the author's definition of selfishness? Do you agree?
3. How do you think Ringer would answer the question "What is the meaning of life?"

Before moving forward, it will be extremely helpful to you to attempt to clear your mind of all preconceived ideas, whether they concern friendship, love, business or any other aspect of life. I realize this is easier said than done, but do try to make the effort; it will be worth your while. . . .

Clear your mind, then. Forget foundationless traditions, forget the "moral" standards others may have tried to cram down your throat, forget the beliefs people may have tried to intimidate you into accepting as "right." Allow your intellect to take control as you read, and, most important, think of yourself—Number One—as a unique individual. . . .

What Is It?

Looking out for Number One is the conscious, rational effort to spend as much time as possible doing those things which bring you the greatest amount of pleasure and less time on those which cause pain. Everyone automatically makes the effort to be happy, so the key word is "ration." . . .

Because people always do that which they *think* will bring them the greatest pleasure, selfishness is not the issue. Therefore, when people engage in what appear to be altruistic acts, they are not being selfless, as they might like to believe (and might like to have you believe). What they are doing is acting with a lack of awareness. Either they are not completely aware of what they're doing, or they are not aware of why they're doing it, or both. In any case, they are acting selfishly—but not rationally. . . .

What's the Payoff?

Why is it important to act out of choice? What's in it for you? You already know: more pleasure and less pain—a better life for Number One.

In everyday terms, it means feeling refreshed instead of tired. It means making enough money to be able comfortably to afford the material things you want out of life instead of being bitter about not having them. It means enjoying love relationships instead of longing for them. It means experiencing warm friendships instead of concentrating your thoughts on people for whom you harbor negative feelings. It means feeling healthy instead of lousy. It means having a relatively clear mind instead of one that is cluttered and confused. It means more free time instead of never enough time.

Looking out for Number One is important because it leads to a simple, uncomplicated life in which you spend more time doing those things which give you the greatest amount of pleasure. . . .

When you experience pleasure or an absence of pain, you know one thing: you're *feelin' good.*

When you boil it all down, I think that's what everyone's main objective in life really is—to feel good. Happiness isn't a mysterious condition that needs to be dissected carefully by wordologists or psychologists. It's your state of mind when you're experiencing something pleasurable; it's when you feel good.

"Sure enough, when winter came, the carefree, hedonistic grasshopper died. But the ant died, too, without ever really having lived at all."

Drawing by Ed Fisher; © 1971, The New Yorker Magazine, Inc. Reprinted with permission.

We sometimes lose sight of the fact that our primary objective is really to be as happy as possible and that all our other objectives, great and small, are only a means to that end. . . .

Is looking out for Number One "right?" As a preface, I find it necessary to describe an old nemesis of mine—a creature who's been running around loose on Planet Earth over the millennia, steadily increasing in number. He is the Absolute Moralist. His mission in life is to whip you and me into line. Like Satan, he disguises himself in various human forms. He may appear as a politician on one occasion, next as a minister, and still later as your mother-in-law.

Whatever his disguise, he is relentless. He'll stalk you to your grave if you let him. If he senses that you're one of his prey—that you do not base your actions on rational self-choice—he'll punish you unmercifully. He will make guilt your bedfellow until you're convinced you're a bad guy.

The Absolute Moralist is the creature—looking deceptively like any ordinary human being—who spends his life deciding what is right for *you*. If he gives to charity, he'll try to shame you into "understanding" that it's your moral duty to give to charity too (usually the charity of his choice). If he believes in Christ, he's certain that it's his moral duty to help you "see the light." (In the most extreme cases, he may even feel morally obliged to kill you in order to "save" you from your disbelief.) If he doesn't smoke or drink, it takes little effort for him "logically" to conclude that smoking and drinking are wrong for you. In essence, all he wants is to run your life. There is only one thing which can frustrate him into leaving you alone, and that is your firm decision never to allow him to impose his beliefs on you.

Eliminate Moral Opinions of Others

In deciding whether it's right to look out for Number One, I suggest that the first thing you do is eliminate from consideration all unsolicited moral opinions of others. Morality—the quality of character—is a very personal and private matter. No other living person has the right to decide what is moral (right or wrong) for you. I further suggest that you make a prompt and thorough effort to eliminate from your life all individuals who claim—by words or actions, directly or by inference—to possess such a right. You should concern yourself only with whether looking out for Number One is moral from your own rational, aware viewpoint.

Looking out for Number One means spending more time doing those things which give you pleasure. It does not, however, give you carte blanche to do whatever you please. It is not hedonistic in concept, because the looking-out-for-Number-One philosophy does not end with the hedonistic assertion that man's primary moral duty lies in the pursuit of pleasure.

Looking out for Number One adds a rational, civilized tag: man's primary moral duty lies in the pursuit of pleasure *so long as he does not forcibly interfere with the rights of others.* . . .

There is a rational reason why forcible interference with others has no place in the philosophy of looking out for Number One. It's simply not in your best interest. In the long run it will bring you more pain than pleasure—the exact opposite of what you wish to accomplish. It's possible that you may, on occasion, experience short-term pleasure by violating the rights of others, but I assure you that the long-term losses (i.e., pain) from such actions will more than offset any short-term enjoyment. . . .

With absolute morality and hedonism out of the way, I perhaps can best answer the question *Is it right?* by asking you one: Can you see any rational reason why you *shouldn't* try to make your life more pleasurable and less painful, so long as you do not forcibly interfere with the rights of others?

It Is Virtuous to Love Yourself

If it is a virtue to love my neighbor as a human being, it must be a virtue—and not a vice—to love myself, since I am a human being too. . . .

The love for my own self is inseparably connected with the love for any other being.

From this it follows that my own self must be as much an object of my love as another person. *The affirmation of one's own life, happiness, growth, freedom is rooted in one's capacity to love,* i.e., in care, respect, responsibility, and knowledge. If an individual is able to love productively, he loves himself too; if he can love *only* others, he cannot love at all.

Eric Fromm, *The Art of Loving,* 1956.

You have but one life to live. Is there anything unreasonable about watching over that life carefully and doing everything within your power to make it a pleasant and fulfilling one? Is it wrong to be aware of what you're doing and why you're doing it? Is it evil to act out of free choice rather than out of the choice of others or out of blind chance?

Remember, selfishness is not the issue. So-called self-sacrifice is just an irrationally selfish act (doing what you think will make you feel good) committed under the influence of a low awareness level. The truth is that it won't make you feel good—certainly not in the long run, after bitterness over what you've "sacrificed" has had a chance to fester within you. At its extreme, this bitterness eventually can develop into a serious case of absolute moralitis. A person's irrational decision to be self-sacrificial can lead to a bitterness so great that it can be soothed only by his preaching to others the virtue of committing the same error.

You may mean well, but don't try so hard to sacrifice for others. It's unfair to them and a disaster for you. The sad irony is that if you persist in swimming in the dangerous and uncivilized waters of self-sacrifice, those for whom you "sacrifice" often

213

will be worse off for your efforts. If instead you spend your time looking out for Number One, those people for whom you care most will benefit by your actions. It's only when you try to pervert the laws of Nature and make the other person's happiness your first responsibility, relegating yourself to the Number Two position, that you run into trouble. It has never worked, and it will not work for you. It's a law of Nature. The idea that self-sacrifice is virtuous is a law of *man*. If you're going to expend your energies fighting laws, fight man-made laws; they are worth resisting. The laws of Nature will not budge an inch no matter how great your efforts.

That looking out for Number One brings happiness to others, in addition to Number One, is one of the beautiful realities of life. At best, it benefits you and one or more other persons. At worst, it benefits only you and interferes with no one else. Even in the latter case, it actually is a benefit to others because the happy individual is one more person on this earth who does not represent a potential burden to the rest of the population.

That, in my opinion, is enough to make it right. If you practice the principles of looking out for Number One, you'll find it easier to develop rewarding relationships with other human beings, both friends and lovers. It will enhance your ability to be a warm and sensitive person and to enjoy all that life has to offer.

"He sought the welfare of others to such an extent that He was oblivious of Himself if only He might do some good to others."

Live for Others as Jesus Did

Ole Hallesby

Ole Hallesby, one of Norway's leading Christian teachers and writers, was a seminary professor in Oslo until his death in 1961. In the following viewpoint, taken from Hallesby's book Why I Am a Christian, *the author presents his reasons for choosing to follow Jesus. In contrast to the author of the preceding viewpoint, who places the pursuit of pleasure first, Hallesby finds meaning in a life that is dedicated to service to others. He claims "when our consciences are confronted by Jesus, we are compelled to accord Him our full and unqualified approval."*

As you read, consider the following questions:

1. Why does the author think that Jesus is different from the founders of other religions?
2. Why does Hallesby find in Jesus a model he can follow?

From Ole Hallesby, *Why I Am a Christian*. Minneapolis: Augsburg Publishing House, © 1930, 1958. Reprinted with permission.

Human life has its own peculiar characteristics, which make it human. And this life develops only under certain conditions and in certain environments.

One of the characteristics of human life, among others, is that it must discover its own peculiarity, that is, discover the meaning of life. In all other living beings the innate life unfolds itself automatically, by means of the instincts. In man, however, the unfolding of life takes place consciously and deliberately.

Man himself must know what it means to be a man, and will to be it. He himself must select the environment in which his own peculiar life can unfold itself. And this is what men have been working at down through the ages as far back as we have any historical records of human life. The best men and women of each generation have been the ones who have sacrificed the most time and energy to ascertain the meaning of life.

The Founding of Religions

One day a quiet, good man came forth and said: "I have found it."

Men crowded around him and listened. After they had heard him to the end, they said: "Verily, we have found it!"

And a religion had been founded upon earth.

Now, all life is supplied with a peculiar apparatus which we call sensitiveness or feeling. It constitutes a very important factor in life. It serves life both positively and negatively. It serves positively by making the living organism aware of those things or conditions which will promote its existence. Even in plants we can clearly discern a "sensitiveness" of this kind. If a tree, for instance, is growing in lean earth and there is better earth a short distance away, we notice that the tree practically moves away from the lean earth by sending its roots over into the good earth.

The feelings serve the living organism negatively by making it aware of everything in its surroundings which is detrimental to its existence. Thus, for instance, the sensitiveness of our skin. It helps us to protect our bodies against dangerous cold or heat. If we touch a hot iron, our feelings give instant warning and we withdraw our hand, thereby escaping greater injury. . . .

Our soul-life, too, has its apparatus for feeling, the function of which is to serve this life by pointing out those things in our environment which are conducive to the well being of the soul and by warning against those things which are detrimental to it. This apparatus of the soul we usually call the conscience. It is a part of that life which is peculiar to man, and a very important part, because it is the life-preserving and life-protecting function of the soul.

Its task is to prove all things both from without and within which affect our spiritual life and to determine whether they are benefi-

216

cial or detrimental to the soul. If the conscience is permitted to function normally, nothing reaches the soul before the conscience has expressed its opinion concerning it.

When the quiet, good man had spoken, and men had heard from him what the meaning of life was, conscience immediately began its work. It proved all things. But gradually the number of those grew greater and greater who said to themselves and later to others: this is not the meaning of life.

The Loss of Self

The cult of "I," has taken hold with the strength and impetus of a new religion. But the joker in the pack is that it is all based on a false idea. . . .

A long time ago, in a book called *Civilization and Its Discontents* Freud pointed out that there is an unresolvable conflict between the human being's selfish, primitive, infantile impulses and the restraint he or she must impose on those impulses if a stable society is to be maintained. The "self" is not a handsome god or goddess waiting coyly to be revealed. On the contrary, its complexity, confusion and mystery have proved so difficult that throughout the ages men and women have talked gratefully about losing themselves. They lose the self in contemplating a great work of art, or in nature, or in scientific research, or in writing poetry, or in fashioning things with their hands or in projects that will benefit others rather than themselves.

The current glorification of self-love will turn out in the end to be a no-win proposition, because in questions of personality or "identity," what counts is not who you are, but what you do. "By their fruits, ye shall know them." And by their fruits, they shall know themselves.

Margaret Halsey, "What's Wrong with 'Me, Me, Me,'" *Newsweek*, April 17, 1978.

And they began anew to try to find the answer to the old problem.

One day another man came forth. He, too, was a quiet and a good man. He, too, said: "I have found it."

And people listened and said: "In truth, now we have found it."

And another new religion had been founded on earth.

Thus it continued through hundreds and thousands of years. But the conscience of man was not satisfied with any of the solutions.

Then Came Jesus

Then came Jesus.

He showed us what the meaning of life is. When Jesus came, we saw for the first time on earth what a real man is. He called himself the *"Son of Man."*

The others, who had preceded Jesus, could only tell us how a

217

man should be. Jesus, however, exemplified it in His own life. He did not only point out the ideal, as others had done; He Himself was the ideal, and He actually lived it out before our very eyes.

Permit me to mention two things in connection with this ideal. In the first place, Jesus, too, directs His appeal to our consciences. Furthermore, He seeks no other following but that which the consciences of men will grant Him.

Many think that Jesus forces men to follow Him. In so doing they reveal how little they know about Him.

Let me call your attention to one incident in the life of Jesus. It was during the great awakening in Galilee. The people were streaming together and almost trampling one another down. One day Jesus stopped and looked at all these people. And He seemed to ask Himself this question: I wonder if they have understood me? Then He turned and cried out once again to the multitudes: "No man can be my disciple without renouncing all that he hath, yea, even his own life" (Luke 14:25-33).

A man who speaks to the people in that way does not expect to gain any other adherents but such as are convinced in their hearts that both the man and his message are trustworthy and that they, therefore, are inwardly bound to follow him, regardless of what it may cost them.

This is the remarkable thing that happens. When our consciences are confronted by Jesus, we are compelled to accord Him our full and unqualified approval. At least, He received the approval of my conscience. No matter in what situation I see Jesus, my conscience says: Verily, that is the way a man should be. . . .

Jesus Lived for Others

What, then, was the life of Jesus like?

Large volumes, both scientific and devotional, have, of course, been written about this. I must be brief and shall, therefore, mention only a couple of the fundamental traits, the two which, to my mind, most clearly distinguish the life of Jesus from that of all other people.

In the first place, Jesus never had to grope His way to find the meaning of life, as everybody else has had to do, both before and after His time. Unerringly He discerned it and lived in harmony with it, to Him a perfectly natural way of living. We can not discover that He was ever in doubt, not even during His temptation or His passion.

The unique thing about Jesus, however, that which impresses us most, was, without comparison, His intimate and unbroken fellowship with the Father. He Himself knew that this was the secret of his life. . . .

In the second place, I would mention the life Jesus lived among men.

218

The unique thing about this aspect of His life, as contrasted with our lives, was that He sought the welfare of others to such an extent that He was oblivious of Himself if only He might do some good to others.

Jesus has had many enemies, both among His contemporaries and since, and they have scrutinized His life very closely. None of them, however, has been able to point to a single instance in which Jesus acted from selfish motives.

True Love Is Selfless

True love is an emotion which discharges itself in an activity that overcomes self-centredness by expending the self on people and on purposes beyond the self. It is an outward-going spiritual movement from the self towards the universe and towards the ultimate spiritual reality behind the universe.

There is a paradox here. This love that is a form of self-denial is the only true self-fulfillment, as has been pointed out by the founders of all the great historic religions.

Arnold Toynbee, *Surviving the Future*, 1971.

Jesus has given expression to this normal human life by saying: "Thou shalt love the Lord thy God above all else, and thy neighbor as thyself." . . .

I Had to Choose

Permit me at this point to mention the two things which came to mean most to me.

In the first place, concerning the life of Jesus with which I had now come in contact, my conscience compelled me to say: Verily, that is the way a man should be. I began to feel also that the life of Jesus was a condemnation of my own life. . . .

I now saw how inhuman the life was which I had been living. Jesus lived His life for others. I had lived my whole life for myself, in petty selfishness, pride, and pleasure. . . .

In the second place, the life of Jesus attracted me with a power which I had never before felt in all my life.

I saw before my eyes that pure, good, beautiful, and strong life which God had intended that I should live. It attracted me with a wonderful power.

I could understand now why so many young men were drawn to Jesus. All He had to say to them was: "Follow me," and they left all and followed Him. . . .

Jesus once said: "Everyone that is of the truth heareth my voice." Now I knew that Jesus was right. Every one who is confronted by Jesus and refuses to accept Him is untrue to himself.

I had formerly believed that people who became Christians had to deny their own convictions, if they were people who did their own thinking, but now I saw that I had to become a Christian if I was not to be untrue to myself and my most sacred convictions.

Then came the choice.

I had to choose. . . .

I could not endure being untrue to myself, both for time and for eternity. I could not enter upon a life of unequivocal falsehood, such as would have been the case if, after having been confronted with Jesus, I had continued to live as before.

So I chose to follow Jesus.

"It is well to seem merciful, faithful, humane, sincere, religious, and also to be so; but you must have the mind so disposed that when it is needful to be otherwise you may be able to change to the opposite qualities. "

Develop a Devious Mind

Niccolo Machiavelli

Niccolo Machiavelli was born in Florence, Italy, in 1469 and spent much of his working life as an administrator for Florentine politicians. Always concerned with how to achieve results, he became a student of power and influence. *The Prince*, from which the following viewpoint was excerpted, was intended as practical advice to the Medici princes to aid them in governing. Machiavelli opposed Christianity because it glorified the weaker aspects of human behavior like humility, pacifism, and idealism.

As you read, consider the following questions:

1. Under what circumstances does Machiavelli suggest that a ruler not keep faith?
2. What does the author mean when he says "the end justifies the means"?
3. What kind of personal life philosophy do you think Machiavelli would recommend for you in today's society?

From Niccolo Machiavelli, *The Prince*. Luigi Ricci, trans. Revised by E.R.P. Vincent. Reprinted by permission of Oxford University Press.

How laudable it is for a prince to keep good faith and live with integrity, and not with astuteness, every one knows. Still the experience of our times shows those princes to have done great things who have had little regard for good faith, and have been able by astuteness to confuse men's brains, and who have ultimately overcome those who have made loyalty their foundation.

You must know, then, that there are two methods of fighting, the one by law, the other by force: the first method is that of men, the second of beasts; but as the first method is often insufficient, one must have recourse to the second. It is therefore necessary for a prince to know well how to use both the beast and the man. This was covertly taught to rulers by ancient writers, who relate how Achilles and many others of those ancient princes were given to Chiron the centaur to be brought up and educated under his discipline. The parable of this semi-animal, semi-human teacher is meant to indicate that a prince must know how to use both natures, and that the one without the other is not durable.

A Character of Man and Beast

A prince being thus obliged to know well how to act as a beast must imitate the fox and the lion, for the lion cannot protect himself from traps, and the fox cannot defend himself from wolves. One must therefore be a fox to recognize traps, and a lion to frighten wolves. Those that wish to be only lions do not understand this. Therefore, a prudent ruler ought not to keep faith when by so doing it would be against his interest, and when the reasons which make him bind himself no longer exist. If men were all good, this precept would not be a good one; but as they are bad, and would not observe their faith with you, so you are not bound to keep faith with them. Nor have legitimate grounds ever failed a prince who wished to show colourable excuse for the non-fulfillment of his promise. Of this one could furnish an infinite number of modern examples, and show how many times peace has been broken, and how many promises rendered worthless, by the faithlessness of princes, and those that have been best able to imitate the fox have succeeded best. But it is necessary to be able to disguise this character well, and to be a great feigner and dissembler; and men are so simple and so ready to obey present necessities, that one who deceives will always find those who allow themselves to be deceived.

I will only mention one modern instance. Alexander VI did nothing else but deceive men, he thought of nothing else, and found the occasion for it; no man was ever more able to give assurances, or affirmed things with stronger oaths, and no man observed them less; however, he always succeeded in his deceptions, as he well knew this aspect of things.

It is not, therefore, necessary for a prince to have all the above-named qualities, but it is very necessary to seem to have them. I

222

would even be bold to say that to possess them and always to observe them is dangerous, but to appear to possess them is useful. Thus it is well to seem merciful, faithful, humane, sincere, religious, and also to be so; but you must have the mind so disposed that when it is needful to be otherwise you may be able to change to the opposite qualities. And it must be understood that a prince, and especially a new prince, cannot observe all those things which are considered good in men, being often obliged, in order to maintain the state, to act against faith, against charity, against humanity, and against religion. And, therefore, he must have a mind disposed to adapt itself according to the wind, and as the variations of fortune dictate, and, as I said before, not deviate from what is good, if possible, but be able to do evil if constrained.

Keeping Faith

A prudent ruler ought not to keep faith when by so doing it would be against his interest, and when the reasons which make him bind himself no longer exist. If men were all good, this precept would not be a good one; but as they are bad, and would not observe their faith with you, so you are not bound to keep faith with them.

Niccolo Machiavelli, *The Prince,* 1532.

Appearance of Integrity

A prince must take great care that nothing goes out of his mouth which is not full of the above-named five qualities, and, to see and hear him, he should seem to be all mercy, faith, integrity, humanity, and religion. And nothing is more necessary than to seem to have this last quality, for men in general judge more by the eyes than by the hands, for every one can see, but very few have to feel. Everybody sees what you appear to be, few feel what you are, and those few will not dare to oppose themselves to the many, who have the majesty of the state to defend them; and in the actions of men, and especially of princes, from which there is no appeal, the end justifies the means. Let a prince therefore aim at conquering and maintaining the state, and the means will always be judged honourable and praised by every one, for the vulgar is always taken by appearances and the issue of the event; and the world consists only of the vulgar, and the few who are not vulgar are isolated when the many have a rallying point in the prince. A certain prince of the present time, whom it is well not to name, never does anything but preach peace and good faith, but he is really a great enemy to both, and either of them, had he observed them, would have lost him state or reputation on many occasions.

"Whenever you are to do a thing tho' it can never be known but to yourself, ask yourself how you would act were all the world looking at you, and act accordingly."

Develop an Honest Heart

Thomas Jefferson

During Thomas Jefferson's astoundingly creative life he only wrote one book, *Notes on the State of Virginia*. Much of what is known about Jefferson comes from the thousands of letters he wrote. He said that the letters of a man "form the only genuine journal of his life." The following viewpoint, excerpted from a letter written by Jefferson to his fifteen-year-old nephew and ward, Peter Carr, offers vastly different advice than does the previous viewpoint by Machiavelli. Although written for a schoolboy rather than a ruler, Jefferson's advice provides a clear alternative based on honesty, scholarship, and effort for those who want to live a moral life.

As you read, consider the following questions:

1. What does Jefferson mean when he suggests one develop an "honest heart"?
2. What course of action does Jefferson suggest when "faced with difficulties and perplexing circumstances"?
3. After an honest heart, what does Jefferson claim is most important?

From Thomas Jefferson's letter to his nephew and ward Peter Carr, August 19, 1785.

Time now begins to be precious to you. Every day you lose, will retard a day your entrance on that public stage whereon you may begin to be useful to yourself. However the way to repair the loss is to improve the future time. I trust that with your dispositions even the acquisition of science is a pleasing employment. I can assure you that the possession of it is what (next to an honest heart) will above all things render you dear to your friends, and give you fame and promotion in your own country. When your mind shall be well improved with science, nothing will be necessary to place you in the highest points of view but to pursue the interests of your country, the interests of your friends, and your own interests also with the purest integrity, the most chaste honour. The defect of these virtues can never be made up by all the other acquirements of body and mind. Make these then your first object.

Develop an Honest Heart

Give up money, give up fame, give up science, give [up] the earth itself and all it contains rather than do an immoral act. And never suppose that in any possible situation or under any circumstances that it is best for you to do a dishonourable thing however slightly so it may appear to you. Whenever you are to do a thing tho' it can never be known but to yourself, ask yourself how you would act were all the world looking at you, and act accordingly. Encourage all your virtuous dispositions, and exercise them whenever an opportunity arises, being assured that they will gain strength by exercise as a limb of the body does, and that exercise will make them habitual. From the practice of the purest virtue you may be assured you will derive the most sublime comforts in every moment of life and in the moment of death. If ever you find yourself environed with difficulties and perplexing circumstances, out of which you are at a loss how to extricate yourself, do what is right, and be assured that that will extricate you the best out of the worst situations. Tho' you cannot see when you fetch one step, what will be the next, yet follow truth, justice, and plain-dealing, and never fear their leading you out of the labyrinth in the easiest manner possible. The knot which you thought a Gordian one will untie itself before you. Nothing is so mistaken as the supposition that a person is to extricate himself from a difficulty, by intrigue, by chicanery, by dissimulation, by trimming, by an untruth, by an injustice. This increases the difficulties tenfold, and those who pursue these methods, get themselves so involved at length that they can turn no way but their infamy becomes more exposed. It is of great importance to set a resolution, not to be shaken, never to tell an untruth. There is no vice so mean, so pitiful, so contemptible and he who permits himself to tell a lie once,

Strengthen Your Moral Faculties

He who made us would have been a pitiful bungler if he had made the rules of our moral conduct a matter of science. For one man of science, there are thousands who are not. What would have become of them? Man was destined for society. His morality therefore was to be formed to this object. He was endowed with a sense of right and wrong merely relative to this. This sense is as much a part of his nature as the sense of hearing, seeing, feeling; it is the true foundation of morality. . . . The moral sense, or conscience, is as much a part of man as his leg or arm. It is given to all human beings in a stronger or weaker degree, as force of members is given them in a greater or less degree. It may be strengthened by exercise, as may any particular limb of the body . . . and/above all things lose no occasion of exercising your dispositions to be grateful, to be generous, to be charitable, to be humane, to be true, just, firm, orderly, couragious &c. Consider every act of this kind as an exercise which will strengthen your moral faculties, and increase your worth.

Thomas Jefferson in a letter to Peter Carr on August 10, 1787.

---

finds it much easier to do it a second and third time, till at length it becomes habitual, he tells lies without attending to it, and truths without the world's believing him. This falsehood of the tongue leads to that of the heart, and in time depraves all its good dispositions.

An honest heart being the first blessing, a knowing head is the second. It is time for you now to begin to be choice in your reading, to begin to pursue a regular course in it and not to suffer yourself to be turned to the right or left by reading anything out of that course. I have long ago digested a plan for you, suited to the circumstances in which you will be placed. This I will detail to you from time to time as you advance. For the present I advise you to begin a course of ancient history, reading every thing in the original and not in translations. First read Goldsmith's history of Greece. This will give you a digested view of that field. Then take up ancient history in the detail, reading the following books in the following order. Herodotus. Thucydides. Xenophontis Hellenica. Xenophontis Anabasis. Quintus Curtius. Justin. This shall form the first stage of your historical reading, and is all I need mention to you now. The next will be of Roman history. From that we will come down to Modern history. In Greek and Latin poetry, you have read or will read at school Virgil, Terence, Horace, Anacreon, Theocritus, Homer. Read also Milton's *Paradise Lost*, Ossian, Pope's works, Swift's works in order to form your style in your own language. In morality read Epictetus, Xenophontis' memorabilia, Plato's Socratic dialogues, Cicero's philosophies.

In order to assure a certain progress in this reading, consider what hours you have free from the school and the exercises of the school. Give about two of them every day to exercise; for health must not be sacrificed to learning. A strong body makes the mind strong. . . .

Never think of taking a book with you. The object of walking is to relax the mind. You should therefore not permit yourself even to think while you walk. But divert your attention by the objects surrounding you. Walking is the best possible exercise. Habituate yourself to walk very far. . . .

Our Moral Instinct

I sincerely, then, believe with you in the general existence of a moral instinct. I think it the brightest gem with which the human character is studded, and the want of it as more degrading than the most hideous of the bodily deformities.

Thomas Jefferson in a letter to Thomas Law on June 13, 1814.

There is no habit you will value so much as that of walking far without fatigue. I would advise you to take your exercise in the afternoon. Not because it is the best time for exercise for certainly it is not: but because it is the best time to spare from your studies; and habit will soon reconcile it to health, and render it nearly as useful as if you gave to that the more precious hours of the day. A little walk of half an hour in the morning when you first rise is advisable also. It shakes off sleep, and produces other good effects in the animal oeconomy. Rise at a fixed and an early hour, and go to bed at a fixed and early hour also. Sitting up late at night is injurious to the health, and not useful to the mind.

"We need to develop a system of personal values against which to measure ourselves."

Develop a System of Values

Charles W. Anderson

This viewpoint was originally delivered as a commencement address to the graduating class of George S. Parker High School in Janesville, Wisconsin, June 6, 1972. At the time, Charles W. Anderson was the coordinator of the Alcoholism and Drug Abuse Service at Rock County Hospital in Janesville. In this viewpoint, Anderson addresses the question of "how to develop a system of values in a valueless society." He suggests that everyone needs to develop a system of personal values against which to measure themselves. At the core of this personal value system should be self-love, self-knowledge, and a willingness to share and show emotions.

As you read, consider the following questions:

1. Why does the author believe that knowledge of self is important?
2. In Anderson's opinion, how has society made life more difficult by stifling emotions?
3. Why does the author feel love is the most important emotion in developing values?
4. How does Anderson suggest the individual develop a system of values in "America's valueless society"?

From Charles W. Anderson, commencement address to George S. Parker High School graduating class of June 6, 1972, Janesville, Wisconsin. Reprinted with permission.

I would like to address myself to how you can develop a system of values in a valueless society.

I work in an alcoholic treatment center which is housed in a mental institution complex. Each day I see what society can do to those human beings who are less resilient than those of us who are usually but not necessarily correctly referred to as "normal" people. My interest in these less fortunate people was developed as the result of my own experiences of many years as a drinking alcoholic and my experiences also as the son of an active alcoholic who ultimately died from it.

Know Thyself

There was a Jesuit philosopher who wrote wisely about the phenomenon of man and the future of man. Pierre Teilhard de Chardin argued that the evolutionary process on earth has stopped as far as man's physical development is concerned and that the earth's evolutionary capacity is concerned now with the growth of the human spirit. Teilhard maintained that man will continue to grow in spiritual capacity and one day he will become one with his fellow man and be then aware of God as never before. He believed that at the ultimate point, man would not lose his individuality but, rather, gain it. He would gain it through evaluation of his thoughts and their influence for good on other human beings.

This was not a new idea. Socrates urged his audience to "know thyself." Plato learned from him and taught the same. Plutarch and Solon advised similarly. Alfred Lord Tennyson said it too in a favorite poem of mine.

> Flower in the crannied wall,
> I pluck you out of the crannies.
> I hold you here, root and all, in my hand,
> Little flower—but if I could understand,
> What you are, root and all, and all in all,
> I should know what God and man is.

Obviously, wise men through the ages felt that knowledge of self was a prerequisite to understanding others. Unfortunately, we spend so little time doing that in our go-go world. And when we do, so infrequently, we measure ourselves against a societal model. I believe we need to develop a system of personal values against which to measure ourselves.

I'd like to share with you today, two things that are based on and are the product of my very personal experiences. First, I wish to share my feelings with you. Emotions are things we are taught to control or, better yet, to hide; we are told they are only for very private occasions—the intimacy of the family, or the bedroom; we are taught they should never be displayed in public. We are told there is something shameful and even unmanly about them. Men tend to excuse emotional displays in women

as the result of some type of inferior mental mechanism or, il-
logically, to an inherent lack of logic in women. Many women,
in reaction to this unjust and unwise attitude, attempt to stifle a
quality that truly puts them above men in the ongoing process
of human spiritual development.

The Examples of Socrates and Jesus

We ought, I think, to study such men as Socrates and Jesus.
These two men had genius in the examination of the spiritual
life. Each was a thinker of the highest order. Just as Galileo,
Newton, Darwin, Loeb, excel in intellectual mastery of the world
of outer fact, so do these two surpass their fellows in the search
for human wisdom. . . .

It is recorded of the great Greek and of the great Jew that they
went about among their fellows, talking with them of the values
which they had found in human experience then pondering,
meditating upon what they had seen and heard. . . .

Both of them sought acquaintance with men and their intentions.
Both tried to weave this information into a scheme of meaning, to
understand, to interpret human purposes in ways of which they
found those purposes to be sorely in need.

Out of these two studies there came what are, I think the two
most fruitful insights which Western civilization has known. For
men who are forever asking, "What shall I be and do?" Socrates
summed up his wisdom in the phrase, "Be intelligent; act critically." And Jesus, likewise pondering on human action, said to
his fellows, "Be kind." And in terms of sheer domination over the
mind of the Western world no other pair of intellectual achieve-
ments can equal these two. . . .

Out of them came the two great practical tests which we apply to
any proposal of action, any social institution, any individual attitude. First we demand, with Socrates, "Is it intelligent or is it
stupid?" Second we ask with Jesus, "Does it spring from hate and
indifference, or does it come from love?"

Alexander Meiklejohn, *What Does America Mean?*, 1935.

Society tends to cripple our emotions each day. We are taught
to hold back. Did you ever hear people laugh uncomfortably at
an emotional scene in a movie? Think of how on television a
scene can be developing, perhaps involving the very soul of a
human being, and it is interrupted insensitively to have the
virtues of a motor oil or panty hose extolled. Emotions are not
allowed to be nurtured. If you are a boy and you cry, you are a
sissy. If a girl cries, you are told to expect such nonsense from
women. . . .

People with "crippled" or suppressed emotions tend to become neurotic, they often seek escape from tensions with drugs and alcohol. Some have the psychological and spiritual strength to survive this endless process and battle for some peace of mind in an insane world that allows little respite. However, our mental institutions and alcoholic treatment centers are filled with those who are not quite so strong. I hasten to add this strength comes not from will power, personally developed, but from a combination of genetic factors and fortuitous environmental influences in the formative years. None of us can truly take for granted being outside these institutions. All of us are, ultimately, vulnerable.

I choose not to cripple my emotional life any more than it has already been by society. I tell you therefore how I feel. I am thrilled that you should ask me to speak at your commencement. I am hopeful that I can say something worthwhile. I've thought long and hard for I want to leave a lasting impression. I could cry when I think of the millions of young people who are turned off by what they face. Who truly believe there is no hope for a better world. This is why I so deeply desire that you will respond with a determination to be someone with values and someone of value in this value-less society of ours. There is a future for all of us, if we just open our hearts.

This brings me now to those thoughts I wish to share. Hopefully my thoughts will change from time to time—hopefully, also, they will always change for the better. Never, I hope, will my thoughts be based on anything other than my own values. These values I hope will always be reflected in my behavior and emotions. Emotions or thoughts without a system of values are value-less. We must seek therefore to develop a system of values.

Love Thyself

Love in my judgment is the most basic emotion yielding good to the individual and society, and it is the bedrock for all our other values. It is unfortunate that we have equated love with sex for love transcends sex. Men may love men, women may love women and not be homosexual. Man should love man. Christ urged us all to do unto others as we would have them do unto us. Man has made the mistake of thinking that obeying such an injunction will put him in the class of the martyr. Nothing could be farther from the truth. Think of those things which make you feel good. Do you feel best when you do something good for someone else or when you hurt someone? If you answer the latter, you had best beware for you haven't looked deeply enough. All evidence indicates good acts, acts of kindness, integrity, loyalty, produce good personal feelings about self. As we do good things we develop a love of self, not a selfish love of demanding and getting, but the love of self which comes from knowing you have done right. Feeling worthy is what William Glasser the proponent of reality therapy would call it.

True North Principles

Certain principles govern human effectiveness. The six major world religions all teach the same basic core beliefs—such principles as "You reap what you sow" and "Actions are more important than words." I find global consensus around what "true north" principles are. These are not difficult to detect. They are objective, basic, unarguable: "You can't have trust without being trustworthy" and "You can't talk yourself out of a problem you behave yourself into."

There is little disagreement in what the constitutional principles of a company should be when enough people get together. I find a universal belief in fairness, kindness, dignity, charity, integrity, honesty, quality, service, and patience.

Consider the absurdity of trying to live a life or run a business based on the opposites. I doubt that anyone would seriously consider unfairness, deceit, baseness, uselessness, mediocrity, or degradation as a solid foundation for lasting happiness and success.

Stephen R. Covey, *Principle-Centered Leadership*, 1991.

It is from this love of self that love for others flows. Alcoholics have a suicide rate which is 58 times greater than the average. Their hate for themselves is of the deepest intensity. And they all feel alienated—unable to love others, though they yearn to so desperately. When they discover they are the victims of a disease and are not moral weaklings, the first opportunity for self love develops, and miracle of miracles, they learn they can love others too.

We cannot love others if we hate ourselves; we can hardly teach others to love if our own hearts are empty. How then do we develop love for self. I repeat, we do it through doing things which make us feel good. I am not speaking of things we may say make us feel good after only superficial and shallow thought like buying a bigger house, a swimming pool, a new car. We must dig deep into our minds and hearts and know ourselves as we are. Shakespeare wrote:

This above all: To thine own self be true,
And it must follow as the night the day,
Thou canst not then be false to any man.

True to self thus true to others; love for self, thus love for others, follows as the night the day.

I know some cynics will sneer and say we delude ourselves. Love conquers all things we are told but they know it is not true. Love has not conquered all things. We know it too. But we can hope that love *will* conquer all things. Hate is a destructive force; it tears one apart against others and these actions may be successful at the moment. Hitler was successful and conquered many—his hate killed millions of humans. But it also destroyed him. I do not equate his ultimate demise with the deaths of millions as far as justice is concerned. They were innocent and justice was not theirs. But Hitler never found what he sought, which was happiness for himself. He became in fact a madman. And that unfortunately is where our world is headed. Mass paranoia, schizophrenia, depression, alcoholism and drug abuse are already here. Escapism is the order of the day. Each of us is alone and withdrawing more and more. But John Donne warned us:

> No man is an island, entire of itself; every man is a piece of the continent, a part of the main and also any man's death diminishes me, because I am involved in mankind; and therefore never send to know for whom the bell tolls; it tolls for thee.

If the world is allowed to go to hell, it goes to hell for all of us.

Let me warn you not to depend on society to serve as your guide for developing values. Society cheats us every day. It urges us to get away from self rather than to seek self. Booze and pills will relieve your tension, take away your fear, help you sleep, help you with sex. Television and endless sports spectacles numb your mind. Forget, forget is the subliminal chant of the entertainment entrepreneurs whose only interest is money, not you.

Society tells us to avoid truthfulness, if need be. Politicians take polls on issues and then tell you what you want to hear, not what they believe. President John Kennedy, a victim of our sick society, wrote a book called *Profiles in Courage*. He extolled a handful of men for putting their integrity above political expediency. What a sad commentary that so few could be found. The message of today is do not search for truth but for opinion. In a speech to the Electors of Bristol, in 1774, Edmund Burke said: "Your representative owes you, not his industry only, but his judgment; and he betrays instead of serving you if he sacrifices it to your opinion."

Business tells us to buy its endless parade of goods, and to think only of material things and the satisfaction of our wants not our needs. Poor quality and planned obsolescence is routine procedure. Profit is king. Business, especially through Madison Avenue, lies to us each day and pays our neighbors to do it. And

233

students, beware, for it is prepared to pay you too! William
Wordsworth said it long ago.

> The world is too much with us; late and soon,
> Getting and spending, we lay waste our powers;
> Little we see in Nature that is ours. . . .

Conclusion

How then can we develop a system of values that will serve
us and society well; that will truly make us, as individuals
happy? *One,* beware of the corporate gods bearing gifts—comfort is pleasant but luxury is decadent. We do not need an endless array of electric toothbrushes, electric blankets, electric
mixers, electric fans, electric thises and electric thats, washers
and dryers, and three, not two cars, and television sets for every
person in the family. I suggest we have been oversold on reliev-
ing ourselves of physical chores. We are urged to join health
clubs and country clubs to get exercise and then we use motor
driven cycles or electric golf carts to take the physical effort out
of exercise. Paradox after paradox fills our lives.

Two, look for the truth about yourself; it is not easy to find but
it's worth looking hard for. *Three,* fill your heart with emotions
that are good for you. Then show them to others. Do not be
ashamed of them. Tell your fellow man—I love you. Feel worthwhile about yourself, love yourself and then love others.

Remember if we want to make a better world, we must first
make better selves. If we ourselves are filled with greed and
hate, how can we teach generosity and love?

Let us all change only ourselves. That is not an insurmount-
able task. If each of us would change ourselves, the whole
world would be changed. But even if only we change, we at
least are the victors. Develop your values for yourself and the
world will be better for it.

Integrity in business and politics can become the rule rather
than the exception. Men and women can look at each other
with trust rather than suspicion. Your children can look to the
future as a challenge rather than an impending doom.

Fill your hearts with the wonder of life and the joys it can
bring. Don't let anyone tell you it can't be done, tell them it will
be done.

"It was about this time I conceived the bold and arduous project of arriving at moral perfection. I wished to live without committing any fault at any time."

Aim for Perfection

Benjamin Franklin

Benjamin Franklin was a jack-of-all-trades and master of many, including printer, scientist, banker, inventor, merchant, soldier, patriot, philosopher, and statesman. In his autobiography, from which the following viewpoint is taken, he reveals his formula for attaining perfection. Although he approached the acquisition of virtue in the same methodical manner he used at his workbench, he discovered that the self is difficult material to work. Franklin never attained perfection, but in this viewpoint he does suggest a way to self-improvement.

As you read, consider the following questions:

1. Why did Franklin place temperance at the top of his list of virtues to acquire?
2. What virtue did he overlook but add to his list, at the suggestion of a friend?

From Benjamin Franklin's autobiography, 1700.

It was about this time I conceived the bold and arduous project of arriving at moral perfection. I wished to live without committing any fault at any time; I would conquer all that either natural inclination, custom, or company might lead me into. As I knew, or thought I knew, what was right and wrong, I did not see why I might not always do the one and avoid the other. But I soon found I had undertaken a task of more difficulty than I had imagined. While my care was employed in guarding against one fault, I was often surprised by another; habit took the advantage of inattention; inclination was sometimes too strong for reason. I concluded, at length, that the mere speculative conviction that it was our interest to be completely virtuous was not sufficient to prevent our slipping; and that the contrary habits must be broken and good ones acquired and established before we can have any dependence on a steady, uniform rectitude of conduct. For this purpose I therefore contrived the following method. . . .

Virtues to Acquire

I concluded under thirteen names of virtues all that at that time occurred to me as necessary or desirable and annexed to each a short precept which fully expressed the extent I gave to its meaning.

These names of virtues with their precepts were:

1. TEMPERANCE

Eat not to dullness; drink not to elevation.

2. SILENCE

Speak not but what may benefit others or yourself; avoid trifling conversation.

3. ORDER

Let all your things have their places; let each part of your business have its time.

4. RESOLUTION

Resolve to perform what you ought; perform without fail what you resolve.

5. FRUGALITY

Make no expense but to do good to others or yourself; i.e., waste nothing.

6. INDUSTRY

Lose no time; be always employed in something useful; cut off all unnecessary actions.

7. SINCERITY

Use no harmful deceit; think innocently and justly, and, if you speak, speak accordingly.

8. JUSTICE

Wrong none by doing injuries or omitting the benefits that are your duty.

9. MODERATION

Avoid extremes; forbear resenting injuries so much as you think they deserve.

10. CLEANLINESS
Tolerate no uncleanliness in body, clothes or habitation.

11. TRANQUILLITY
Be not disturbed at trifles, or at accidents common or unavoidable.

12. CHASTITY
Rarely use venery but for health or offspring, never to dullness, weakness, or the injury of your own or another's peace or reputation.

13. HUMILITY
Imitate Jesus and Socrates.

My intention being to acquire the *habitude* of all these virtues, I judged it would be well not to distract my attention by attempting the whole at once, but to fix it on one of them at a time; and, when I should be master of that, then to proceed to another, and so on, till I should have gone through the thirteen; and, as the previous acquisition of some might facilitate the acquisition of certain others, I arranged them with that view as they stand above. Temperance first, as it tends to procure that coolness and clearness of head which is so necessary where constant vigilance was to be kept up and guard maintained against the unremitting attraction of ancient habits and the force of perpetual temptations. This being acquired and established, Silence would be more easy; and my desire being to gain knowledge at the same time that I improved in virtue, and considering that in conversation it was obtained rather by the use of the ears than of the tongue, and therefore wishing to break a habit I was getting into of prattling, punning, and joking which only made me acceptable to trifling company, I gave Silence the second place. This and the next, Order, I expected would allow me more time for attending to my project and my studies. Resolution, once become habitual, would keep me firm in my endeavors to obtain all the subsequent virtues; Frugality and Industry freeing me from my remaining debt, and producing affluence and independence, would make more easy the practice of Sincerity and Justice, etc., etc. Conceiving then that agreeably to the advice of Pythagoras in his Golden Verses daily examination would be necessary, I contrived the following method for conducting that examination.

I made a little book in which I allotted a page for each of the virtues. I ruled each page with red ink so as to have seven columns, one for each day of the week, marking each column with a letter for the day. I crossed these columns with thirteen red lines, marking the beginning of each line with the first letter of one of the virtues, on which line and in its proper column I might mark by a little black spot, every fault I found upon examination to have been committed respecting that virtue upon that day.

I determined to give a week's strict attention to each of the virtues successively. Thus in the first week my great guard was to avoid even the least offense against Temperance, leaving the other virtues to their ordinary chance, only marking every evening the faults of the day. Thus, if in the first week I could keep my first line, marked T, clear of spots, I supposed the habit of that virtue so much strengthened and its opposite weakened that I might venture extending my attention to include the next, and for the following week keep both lines clear of spots. Proceeding thus to the last, I could go through a course complete in thirteen weeks and four courses in a year. . . .

Ordering My Day

The precept of Order requiring that *every part of my business should have its allotted time,* one page in my little book contained the following scheme of employment for the twenty-four hours of a natural day.

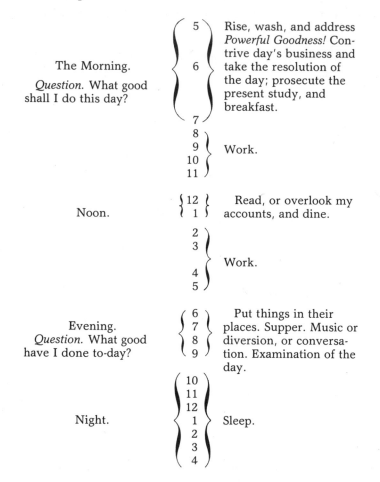

The Morning. *Question.* What good shall I do this day?	5 6 7	Rise, wash, and address *Powerful Goodness!* Contrive day's business and take the resolution of the day; prosecute the present study, and breakfast.
	8 9 10 11	Work.
Noon.	12 1	Read, or overlook my accounts, and dine.
	2 3 4 5	Work.
Evening. *Question.* What good have I done to-day?	6 7 8 9	Put things in their places. Supper. Music or diversion, or conversation. Examination of the day.
Night.	10 11 12 1 2 3 4	Sleep.

238

I entered upon the execution of this plan for self-examination and continued it with occasional intermissions for some time. I was surprised to find myself so much fuller of faults than I had imagined; but I had the satisfaction of seeing them diminish. To avoid the trouble of renewing now and then my little book, which, by scraping out the marks on the paper of old faults to make room for new ones in a new course, became full of holes, I transferred my tables and precepts to the ivory leaves of a memorandum book on which the lines were drawn with red ink that made a durable stain, and on those lines I marked my faults with a black-lead pencil, which marks I could easily wipe out with a wet sponge. After a while I went through one course only in a year, and afterward only one in several years, till at length I omitted them entirely, being employed in voyages and business abroad with a multiplicity of affairs that interfered; but I always carried my little book with me.

A Speckled Axe Was Best

My scheme of Order gave me the most trouble. . . . I was almost ready to give up the attempt and content myself with a faulty character in that respect, like the man who, in buying an axe of a smith, my neighbor, desired to have the whole of its surface as bright as the edge. The smith consented to grind it bright for him if he would turn the wheel; he turned while the smith pressed the broad face of the axe hard and heavily on the stone, which made the turning of it very fatiguing. The man came every now and then from the wheel to see how the work went on, and at length would take his axe as it was, without farther grinding. "No," said the smith, "turn on, turn on: we shall have it bright by-and-by; as yet, it is only speckled." "Yes," says the man, *"but I think I like a speckled axe best."* . . .

In truth, I found myself incorrigible with respect to Order; and now I am grown old and my memory bad, I feel very sensibly the want of it. But on the whole, though I never arrived at the perfection I had been so ambitious of obtaining, but fell far short of it, yet I was by the endeavor a better and a happier man than I otherwise should have been if I had not attempted it.

I Added Humility to My List

My list of virtues contained at first but twelve; but a Quaker friend having kindly informed me that I was generally thought proud; that my pride showed itself frequently in conversation; that I was not content with being in the right when discussing any point, but was overbearing, and rather insolent, of which he convinced me by mentioning several instances; I determined endeavoring to cure myself, if I could, of this vice or folly among the rest, and I added Humility to my list, giving an extensive meaning to the word.

Franklin's Log and Virtues

TEMPERANCE.							
EAT NOT TO DULLNESS; DRINK NOT TO ELEVATION.							
	S.	M.	T.	W.	T.	F.	S.
T.							
S.	*	*		*		*	
O.	**	*	*		*	*	*
R.			*			*	
F.		*			*		
I.			*				
S.							
J.							
M.							
C.							
T.							
C.							
H.							

These names of virtues with their precepts were:

TEMPERANCE
Eat not to dullness.
Drink not to elevation.

SILENCE
Speak not but what may benefit others or yourself.
Avoid trifling conversation.

ORDER
Let all your things have their places. Let each part of your business have its time.

RESOLUTION
Resolve to perform what you ought. Perform without fail what you resolve.

FRUGALITY
Make no expense but to do good to others or yourself; i.e., waste nothing.

INDUSTRY
Lose no time. Be always employed in something useful. Cut off all unnecessary actions.

SINCERITY
Use no hurtful deceit. Think innocently and justly; and, if you speak, speak accordingly.

JUSTICE
Wrong none by doing injuries or omitting the benefits that are your duty.

MODERATION
Avoid extremes. Forbear resenting injuries so much as you think they deserve.

CLEANLINESS
Tolerate no uncleanness in body, clothes or habitation.

TRANQUILLITY
Be not disturbed at trifles or at accidents common or unavoidable.

CHASTITY
Rarely use venery but for health or offspring—never to dullness, weakness, or the injury of your own or another's peace or reputation.

HUMILITY
Imitate Jesus and Socrates.

I cannot boast of much success in acquiring the *reality* of this virtue, but I had a good deal with regard to the *appearance* of it. I made it a rule to forbear all direct contradiction to the sentiments of others and all positive assertion of my own. I even forbade myself, agreeably to the old laws of our Junto, the use of every word or expression in the language that imported a fixed opinion, such as "certainly," "undoubtedly," etc., and I adopted, instead of them, "I conceive," "I apprehend," or "I imagine" a thing to be so or so; or it "so appears to me at present." When another asserted something that I thought an error, I denied myself the pleasure of contradicting him abruptly and of showing immediately some absurdity in his proposition; and in answering I began by observing that in certain cases or circumstances his opinion would be right, but in the present case there *appeared* or *seemed* to me some difference, etc. I soon found the advantage of this change in my manner; the conversations I engaged in went on more pleasantly. The modest way in which I proposed my opinions procured them a readier reception and less contradiction; I had less mortification when I was found to be in the wrong, and I more easily prevailed with others to give up their mistakes and join with me when I happened to be in the right. . . .

In reality there is, perhaps, no one of our natural passions so hard to subdue as Pride. Disguise it, struggle with it, beat it down, stifle it, mortify it as much as one pleases, it is still alive, and will every now and then peep out and show itself; you will see it, perhaps, often in this history; for even if I could conceive that I had completely overcome it, I should probably be proud of my humility.

"A church which encourages you to think will . . . help you to develop a set of beliefs uniquely your own to guide your living."

Join a Church That Encourages You to Think

Ruth Truman

Ruth Truman has a Ph.D. in education from the University of California at Los Angeles and has been a college instructor and counselor. The following viewpoint is taken from her book *How to Be a Liberated Christian*. In it, she advocates a process of liberation that emphasizes a Christ-directed life based on personal responsibility, self-acceptance, and independent thinking. At the time she wrote this viewpoint she was chairperson for the Commission on the Status and Role of Women for the Pacific Southwest Conference of the United Methodist Church.

As you read, consider the following questions:

1. What characteristics does the author recommend looking for in a church?
2. What role should women have in a church, in the author's opinion?

From Ruth Truman, *How to Be a Liberated Christian*. Nashville: Abingdon Press, 1981. Reprinted with permission.

If you want to begin living the Christian life, let me suggest that you start by looking in a *yes* church.

In any religion that goes back almost two thousand years there are bound to be many offshoots of thought and practice, and Christianity is no exception. You can find the complete emotional spectrum in churches, from shouting and dancing in the aisles to solemn worship services where everything is preplanned and no variations are allowed. You can find people and leaders who are so fanatic that all of life is prescribed: how you should pray, what you should think, how your marriage should be conducted, and so on. At the other extreme will be people who attend church and never mention it outside the sanctuary doors.

What I call a *yes* church has some special characteristics that separate it from the extremes. Among them are the following:

- you are encouraged to think out your faith;
- scripture is studied in its context and times;
- Christ is presented positively as the encourager of fullness of life;
- you are presented a positive image of yourself as a child of God; and
- you are constantly encouraged to grow both as a Christian and as an individual through opportunities to realize and use your God-given talents and abilities.

These may seem like qualities that should be common to all churches; yet in my forty-nine years of church-going (I started at four weeks) I have come to believe they are unique to churches which liberate the individual Christian. Let's take a closer look.

Join a Church That Encourages You to Think

A church which encourages you to think will present more than one way of interpreting scripture. It will not prescribe how you should live, but will rather help you to develop a set of beliefs uniquely your own to guide your living. This is not to say that it will have no concepts of scriptural interpretation or guidelines for Christian living, but rather that it will expect you to think about, discuss, and examine its teachings, *and will accept you as a Christian even if you disagree*. This church will want you to bring your complete mental abilities to the consideration of scripture and will be comfortable if you challenge its thought. It will expect you to approach life in the same way. In short, if you are in a church which tells you what you *must* believe to be a Christian, if that church's way is the only way to get to heaven and all who do not follow it are doomed, you are not in a *yes* church.

Supporting the first characteristic but separate from it is the second: a *yes* church dares you to study scripture in its context and times. It has been said that you can prove anything by using

243

(or abusing) the Bible, but to do so you must use the selective scripture approach: you simply select the scripture passages which support what you want to prove. For example, there is a small sect of Christianity that handles poisonous snakes to demonstrate faith, and they use Mark 16:17-18 to support their activities. A less extreme but more insidious illustration is the twisting of Paul's teaching on mutual submission of all Christians to one another in order to prove that women are ruled by and must remain submissive to men. (More about this later.)

In both of these illustrations scripture has been lifted out of its context and time. It is transplanted into this age without an understanding of the people to whom the scripture was written and the events then occurring which provoked the writing. Even more dangerous, scripture is not only literally translated but *lit-*

H. Brown/*Catholic Standard*

erally applied, as if no differences exist between the first and the twentieth centuries. A church that says *yes* to an abundant Christian life will be careful to teach scripture in its totality and will help you to understand its historical framework.

Join a Church That Emphasizes the Positive

The Christ presented by a *yes* church will have a positive image—the third characteristic. Christ was a reformer in his day, not an effeminate, weak teacher. He preached a message so threatening to the religious establishment that they maneuvered his death. He made the individual important. He gave women a place of value equal to men. He crossed the barriers of race and religion. He condemned sacrilege in the temple and in its place encouraged sacrifice of the spirit.

By breaking traditional barriers Jesus set a new order of relationships between God, humankind, and individual persons. He established love as the factor defining his followers: love for God, love for others, and love for self. He envisioned love as the power to unleash the downtrodden, encourage the suffering, cleanse the sinner, and develop the saint.

So when you're looking for a *yes* church, the third consideration is to listen closely to what they say about Christ. If he is your condemner, if his chief function is to initiate guilt within you, if his prime purpose is to return to judge mankind, you are not in a *yes* church. Christ does convict us of our sins through his teachings, and we *are* apt to experience guilt for our shortcomings and misdoings, but the positive church will point to the forgiving love and amazing grace of God in Christ. Christ will become your leader into ever-expanding avenues of life, giving you not only a positive image of God but also a positive image of yourself as a child of the Almighty.

Join a Church That Teaches Self-Acceptance

A child of God is loved and cared for by the Father of whom Christ spoke. This child is cherished, is so important that the Father sent his son Jesus to teach and to lead all of us into "salvation." A church that emphasizes the positive elements of Christianity will teach a many-faceted salvation whose ultimate conclusion is the acceptance of self and of others. For example, salvation can mean that we are forgiven by God for all the wrong things we have ever thought or done. Obviously that takes a load off our backs and makes us feel better about ourselves. But salvation is more. Christ saves us *from* ourselves if we let him, from our characteristics and/or habits that make us unhappy with ourselves. But to be saved from something is to be saved *to become* something else. The self becomes a part of God's self.

If we are filled with hate and we ask the God/Christ to forgive us for hating, we are asking to have a powerful negative emotion removed from our lives. If at the same time we determine to "love our enemies" or to "love your neighbor as yourself" as Christ taught, we have taken the first step toward the positive emotion of love and freedom from hate. We may even recognize the need to come to terms with loving our "self" so that in turn we are better able to love others.

The Church Improves Society

It is often suggested that there are better ways of improving society than through the influence of the church. But the fact is that wherever the church is firmly planted, life becomes more honest, more just, more humane, and more reasonable. Darkness recedes; righteousness flourishes. Communities become happier places in which to live. . . .

The church improves society. When Eskimos became Christians, the first thing they did was to stop killing off their aged parents. When certain tribes of Zaire became Christians, they ended constant warring against their neighbors. As communities on the American frontier became Christians, they began schools and colleges.

Donald McGavran, *Christianity Today,* April 7, 1978.

The *yes* church will encourage such a salvation of love that produces a positive image of yourself, but it will probably go further. This church will help you understand that by being free of hate you free those around you as you begin to practice loving them. You are then "saved" from hurtful relationships because you bring Christ's love to life's unkindness. As others experience your love they respond to you in different patterns, so that slowly you build new relationships that return love; and in loving and being loved you begin to feel good about yourself, and you extend this "salvation" to others.

Join a Church That Treats Women as Equals

The *yes* church will encourage and help you recognize these changes and then take you one step further: it will provide opportunities for you to develop your talents and abilities regardless of your gender. This characteristic is of supreme importance to a Christian woman. Churches have always encouraged members to participate in organization, administration, and ministry. Not all churches, however, encourage full participation of women at all and/or any level of activity. Some reserve the priesthood or clergy roles only for men. Others do not allow or at least do not encourage women to serve in top administrative positions and councils. Some blatantly confine women to home and servant tasks.

Such churches not only present negative self-images to women, but also put barriers between male and female Christians. They justify their actions by arguing from the teachings of Paul as he ministered to the people of the first century. They forget that Christ accepted women and men for what they really were: living spirits spun off by God and housed in gendered bodies. The positive church will recognize with Paul that we are all "one in Christ Jesus" (Gal. 3:28), and will help us understand the contextual reasons for male disciples and early church leaders. It will open wide its doors—and its offices of leadership—to all who would follow Christ. This church will thereby unite men and women as co-workers, liberating both to use their talents as Christians.

When you look for this characteristic in a church, you will want to pay more attention to its actions than its words. Pronouncements of acceptance of women are fine and to be desired, but are meaningful only if these resolves are carried into the life of a church. It is easy to *say* that men and women are equal in Christ and then to apply first-century polity that allows only men to have active roles in the administrative and clerical church life. So look for a changing church: one that is saying the right things and has begun to take the proper actions. Actualized equality in a church frees both men and women, for by sharing the work of Christ, the organizational load becomes lighter for both sexes, and the joyous task of caring for others can be more easily accomplished.

Becoming a Liberated Christian

In summary, a *yes* church encourages you to think, studies scripture in context, presents a positive Christ and thereby encourages a positive *you*, and offers opportunity for full personal growth, regardless of gender. These characteristics will make it easier for you to investigate, find, and develop your potential as a liberated Christian.

What Qualities Do You Admire in Others?

MISS PEACH by Mell Lazarus. Reprinted by special permission of North America Syndicate.

In the cartoon above, Arthur places a price tag on qualities to admire in others. Do you agree with Arthur, or do you weigh other considerations when making value judgments? Assign the number 1 to the quality below you most admire in others. Assign the number 2 to the second-most admired quality, and so on, until all the qualities have been ranked. Add any qualities, not listed, that you think should be included.

ADMIRABLE QUALITIES

financial success
inner peace
an adventurous life-style
open to change
service to others
commitment to a cause
physical attractiveness
peer group admiration

Periodical Bibliography

The following articles have been selected to supplement the diverse views in this chapter. Because the subject matter of all chapters in this book is closely related, it may be helpful to examine the other chapter bibliographies when doing further study.

Rita Mae Brown	"Surrender to Life," *Free Inquiry*, Summer 1987. Available from PO Box 5, Buffalo, NY 14215-0005.
Richard G. Capen Jr.	"Ethical Values," *Vital Speeches of the Day*, September 1, 1990.
Beverly Chiodo	"Choose Wisely," *Vital Speeches of the Day*, November 1, 1987.
Katherine Cook	"But Francis; You've Got to Be Crazy," *The Other Side*, August 1984. Available from 300 W. Apsley St., Philadelphia, PA 19144.
Theodore E. Dobson	"How God Found Me: My Personal Journey," *New Catholic World*, March/April 1986. Available from Paulist Press, 997 Macarthur Blvd., Mahwah, NJ 07430.
Tom Molone	"Self-Fulfillment Through Service to Others," *The Humanist*, January/February 1989.
Ashley Montagu	"As If Living and Loving Were One," *Free Inquiry*, Summer 1987.
David G. Myers	"The Secrets of Happiness," *Psychology Today*, July/August 1992.
Newsweek	"Another Ringer," July 25, 1977.
Henri Nouwen	"The Selfless Way of Christ," *Sojourners*, June 1981.
W.E. Odom	"Changes and Choices," *Vital Speeches of the Day*, June 1, 1991.
David Rockefeller	"The Values by Which We Live," *Vital Speeches of the Day*, December 1, 1979.
Al Santoli	"You Can Find the Courage," *Parade Magazine*, April 8, 1990.
Alexander M. Schindler	"Pursue Not Just the Material," *Vital Speeches of the Day*, August 15, 1987.
John R. Snortum	"Ben Franklin's Pursuit of Perfection," *Psychology Today*, April 1976.
Gerald S. Strober	"My Life as a Christian," *Commentary*, June 1982.
Robert Weier	"Are You Too Materialistic?" *Success*, January 1984. Available from Accent Publications, 12100 W. Sixth Ave., Denver, CO 80215.

Annotated Book Bibliography

Peter Angeles, ed.   *Critiques of God.* Buffalo, NY: Prometheus Books, 1976. Seventeen famous individuals present a variety of arguments against belief in God.

Erick C. Barret and David Fisher   *Scientists Who Believe.* Chicago: Moody Press, 1984. Twenty-one scientists present their arguments for believing in God.

Phillip L. Berman, ed.   *The Courage of Conviction.* New York: Ballantine Books, 1986. Thirty-three prominent people reveal their beliefs and how they act on them.

Joseph Campbell   *An Open Life.* New York: Harper & Row, 1989. Using examples from legends, literature, mythology, and religion, Campbell talks about his beliefs.

Joseph Campbell   *The Power of Myth.* New York: Doubleday, 1988. This book expands on the six-hour PBS Bill Moyers interview of Campbell, taking material from the full twenty-four hours of filming.

Riane Eisler   *The Chalice and the Blade.* New York: Harper & Row, 1987. Argues that a partnership model of society, rooted in the worship of goddesses, is the true foundation of civilization. It further contends that these peaceful female-based societies have been supplanted by a dominator culture worshipping male deities.

Clifton Fadiman, ed.   *Living Philosophies.* New York: Doubleday, 1990. Thirty-six eminent men and women express their ultimate beliefs and doubts.

Louis Finkelstein   *The Jews: Their History, Culture and Religion.* New York: Schocken Books, 1970. A comprehensive overview of Judaism, tracing its roots, beliefs, and practices.

Joseph Fletcher   *Situation Ethics: The New Morality.* Philadelphia: Westminster Press, 1966. The author contends that there is only one moral absolute—to do whatever increases love.

Matthew Fox   *Creation Spirituality.* New York: HarperCollins, 1991. The founder of the Institute in Culture and Creation Spirituality outlines a spirituality that melds Christian mysticism with social justice, feminism, and environmentalism.

Viktor Frankl   *Man's Search for Meaning.* New York: Simon and Schuster, 1984. As a result of his work and imprisonment in a Nazi death camp, a psychiatrist presents his theory, called logotherapy, that all people need meaning in their lives to provide purpose and the will to survive.

Eric Fromm — *The Art of Loving.* New York: Harper & Row, 1956. Argues that one must cultivate the habit of loving, "the art of loving," beginning with the love of oneself.

Naomi R. Goldenberg — *Changing the Gods.* Boston: Beacon Press, 1979. The author states that Western society and religion will be changed as religious feminism gains ground. She says life's meaning will take on new significance as the present patriarchal system is discredited.

Billy Graham — *Peace with God.* Waco, TX: Word Books, 1984. A traditional Christian presents his case for Christianity.

Arnold D. Hunt and Robert Crotty — *The Ethics of World Religions.* San Diego, CA: Greenhaven Press, 1991. Examines the ethics and religious philosophies of Judaism, Christianity, Islam, Hinduism, Buddhism, and Confucianism.

Sam Keen — *Your Mythic Journey: Finding Meaning in Your Life Through Writing and Storytelling.* Los Angeles: Jeremy Tarcher, Inc., 1989. A book of exercises and personal stories designed to help individuals discover and direct their personal mythic stories.

Paul Kurtz — *Eupraxophy: Living Without Religion.* New York: Prometheus Books, 1989. One of America's foremost advocates for humanism outlines his theory that one can lead a good and ethical life without the practice of religion.

Corliss Lamont — *The Philosophy of Humanism.* New York: Continuum, 1990. The honorary president of the American Humanist Association presents a classic explanation and defense of humanism.

Niccolo Machiavelli — *The Prince.* New York: Random House, 1950. A political-bureaucrat, opposed to Christianity and convinced that human nature responds more effectively to fear than love, suggests practical advice to a ruler in fifteenth-century Italy.

Donald E. Miller — *The Case for Liberal Christianity.* San Francisco: Harper & Row, 1981. A college professor presents a liberal Christian alternative to conservative Christianity or secular humanism.

Stephen Mitchell — *The Gospel According to Jesus.* New York:

HarperCollins, 1991. A translation of the essential Gospel teachings of Jesus that attempts to delete the polemical and legendary additions of the early Christian church.

Hugh S. Moorhead   *The Meaning of Life: According to Our Century's Greatest Writers and Thinkers*. Chicago: Review Press, 1989. Over 250 great thinkers respond to the question "What is the meaning or purpose of life?"

LaVonne Neff, ed.   *Practical Christianity*. Wheaton, IL: Tyndale House, 1988. Seventy-four prominent Christians, in hundreds of articles, offer their thoughts on subjects ranging from the church and love to spiritual discipline.

Kai Nielsen   *Ethics Without God*. Buffalo, NY: Prometheus Books, 1990. The author presents a case that life can have meaning and people can act ethically without believing in a god.

M. Scott Peck   *The Road Less Traveled*. New York: Simon and Schuster, 1978. A practicing psychiatrist presents a way to confront life and its problems with examples from his patient histories.

Milton L. Rudnick   *Christian Ethics for Today*. Grand Rapids, MI: Baker Book House, 1979. An evangelical argues for moral absolutes and suggests biblical norms to use as guidelines when confronted with the ambiguity of contemporary moral issues.

David Sharpe   *So What Makes You Tick?* Berkeley, CA: Ten Speed Press, 1990. More than one hundred notable people respond to the question that forms the book's title.

Benjamin Shield and Richard Carlson, eds.   *For the Love of God*. San Rafael, CA: New World Library, 1990. Twenty-six of the world's leading spiritual and psychological figures, in short essays, write about their personal relationships with God.

John Snelling   *The Buddhist Handbook*. Rochester, VT: Inner Traditions, 1991. A comprehensive and nonsectarian survey of Buddhist teaching, practice, schools, and history with very helpful appendices of Buddhist books, journals, and biographical sketches of who's who in Buddhism.

John Shelby Spong   *Rescuing the Bible from Fundamentalism*. New York: HarperCollins, 1991. An Episcopal bishop presents the latest biblical scholarship for the laity in an attempt to present an alternative to literal and conservative readings of the Bible.

Michael Toms	*At the Leading Edge.* New York: Larson Publications, 1991. Fourteen creative individuals from the fields of science, spirituality, ecology, consciousness, cosmology, and evolution present their world views.
Dan Wakefield	*The Story of Your Life: Writing a Spiritual Autobiography.* Boston: Beacon Press, 1990. Drawing on the techniques he uses in conducting his workshops and the autobiographical sketches of the participants, the author directs the reader to construct a spiritual autobiography.
William H. Willimon	*What's Right with the Church.* New York: Harper & Row, 1985. A United Methodist minister presents a case for the Christian church by focusing upon particular experiences within a mainline Protestant denomination.

Helpful Periodicals

The following is a list of periodicals readers will find helpful for further research. Readers should write for current subscription rates and policies.

America
106 W. 56th St.
New York, NY 10019

This Roman Catholic weekly has been published since 1909 by the Jesuit religious order.

American Atheist
PO Box 140195
Austin, TX 78714

This journal of atheist news and thought is published monthly by American Atheists, Inc.

Business Ethics
1107 Hazeltine Blvd., Suite 530
Chaska, MN 55318

This bimonthly's goal is to promote ethical business practices and to serve professionals striving to live and work in responsible ways, while at the same time helping these professionals create financially healthy companies.

The Christian Century
5615 W. Cermak
Cicero, IL 60650

This biweekly, published by the Christian Century Foundation, has a mainline Protestant point of view.

Christianity & Crisis
PO Box 6415
Syracuse, NY 13217

Published twice a month, the magazine's purpose is "to apply a Judeo-Christian ethical perspective to the contemporary study of history."

Christianity Today
PO Box 11618
Des Moines, IA 50340

This magazine, published fifteen times a year, has an evangelical Christian point of view.

Christian Social Action
100 Maryland Ave. NE
Washington, DC 20002

This monthly is published by the United Methodist church and deals primarily with social justice issues.

Commonweal
15 Dutch St.
New York, NY 10038

This Roman Catholic magazine reviews public affairs, religion, literature, and the arts, and is published biweekly.

Creation Spirituality
160 E. Virginia St., #290
San Jose, CA 95112

This bimonthly is published by Friends of Creation Spirituality, Inc., which describes itself as striving to "awaken authentic mysticism, revitalize Western religion and culture, and promote social and ecological justice by mining the wisdom of ancient spiritual traditions and the insights of contemporary science."

Ethics: Easier Said than Done
310 Washington Blvd., Suite 104
Marina del Rey, CA 90292

This magazine is published quarterly by the Josephson Institute of Ethics, which "seeks to increase the nation's awareness of ethical issues and to provide individuals with the skills to make their behavior more ethical."

Free Inquiry
PO Box 664
Buffalo, NY 14226

This magazine is published quarterly by the Council for Democratic and Secular Humanism.

Friends Journal
1501 Cherry St.
Philadelphia, PA 19102

Published monthly by Friends Publishing Corp., this journal features articles on Quaker thought and life today.

The Humanist
7 Harwood Dr.
PO Box 146
Amherst, NY 14226

Published six times yearly by the American Humanist Association, this magazine "presents a nontheistic, secular, and naturalist approach to philosophy, science, and broad areas of personal and social concern."

The Human Quest
1074 23rd Ave. N
St. Petersburg, FL 33704

This bimonthly describes itself as "a journal for the religious liberal."

Moody
PO Box 2064
Marion, OH 43305

Published monthly by the Moody Bible Institute, this magazine presents a Protestant evangelical perspective.

New Dimensions
PO Box 410510
San Francisco, CA 94141

This quarterly is received by members of New Dimensions Foundation, a nonsectarian organization that explores human consciousness and spirituality from a variety of perspectives. In addition to feature articles, the magazine offers a wide variety of audio programs.

New Oxford Review
1069 Kains Ave., Rm. 573
Berkeley, CA 94706

This ecumenical monthly is edited by lay Catholics.

The Other Side
300 W. Apsley St.
Philadelphia, PA 19144

This bimonthly Christian publication has the goal of promoting social justice through Christian practices.

Parabola
656 Broadway
New York, NY 10012

This quarterly, which is subtitled "The Magazine of Myth and Tradition," explores the central questions of human existence through the writings of leading thinkers from a variety of disciplines.

Sojourners
PO Box 29272
Washington, DC 20078

A monthly, this independent Christian magazine is published by a community of Christians who describe themselves as "a diverse, ecumenical, and extended community of faith seeking spiritual and social transformation."

Tricycle: The Buddhist Review
Dept. TRI
PO Box 3000
Denville, NJ 07834

As the title suggests, this quarterly is a review of Buddhist life and thought.

Index

abortion, 159-161
alcoholism, 229, 231, 232, 233
American Humanist Association, 91
Anderson, Charles W., 228
anger, 194-196
animals, 69, 74, 75, 106, 110-111,
  127, 172-173, 174, 222-223
  native American beliefs about,
  131, 132
antinomianism, 157, 161
archaeology, 49, 50, 51
art, 101, 180
  humanist advocacy for, 92
  liberal Christian view of, 115
atheists
  as virtuous, 40-41
  definition of, 102
  ethical decision making of, 171
  opposition to school prayer, 100-101
Auca Indians, 43-44
Augustine, Saint, 67, 75, 146, 149,
  180

beauty, 177-178
Beckwith, Burnham P., 40
Bellah, Robert, 120
Bible, 43, 44, 45, 132
  divine inspiration of, 108, 118-119,
  163
  Genesis creation story in, 64, 67,
  108
  Judaism and, 84, 86
  liberal Christian view of, 117-118,
  120
  parts of, 108
  should guide ethical decisions,
  162-169
  studying in context, 243-245
Bradley, Preston, 166
Brown, Rita Mae, 24
Bruno, Giordano, 144, 145
Buddha, Siddhartha, 57, 137, 180
Buddhism, Zen, 159
  concept of God, 136
  founder of, 137
  goals of, 141-142
  koan study, 139-140
  meditation's role in, 137-141
  teacher's role in, 138-139, 140
Bultmann, Rudolf, 117, 158

Campbell, Joseph, 122, 126, 128
Catholicism, 67

myth in, 125
  persecution of scientists, 144-145
  position on abortion, 160-161
cave allegory, Plato's, 25-29
children
  anger and, 194-195
  education for, 196-198
  view of parents, 20-22
  see also youth
Christianity
  conservative, 107-113
  fundamentalist, 197
  gives life meaning, 46-47, 187
  con, 40
  importance of cross to, 45, 46, 112,
  192
  improves society, 187-188, 246
  con, 57, 197
  influence on education, 197-198
  liberal, 114-121
  moral decisions in, 157, 159
  promotes ethical decisions, 185-190
  con, 191-198
  promotes human evolution, 70
  promotes low self-esteem, 192-193
  con, 243
  social activism in, 114, 117
  suppresses normal anger, 194-195
  variety of churches within, 243-247
  women's role in, 186, 187, 188, 190,
  245, 246-247
civilization
  human weakness and, 43-44
  on other planets, 65
  prehistoric, 49, 52
Covey, Stephen R., 232
creation-centered spirituality, 143-149

Dalai Lama, 141
death, 104-105, 111-112, 123
decisions, ethical
  Bible should guide, 162-169
  business's lack of, 233-234
  characteristics of, 200-202
  churches promote, 185-190
  con, 171, 191-198
  conscience's role in, 172
  end justifies the means, 221-223
  examining motives in, 167-168
  heart should guide, 224-227
  humanist beliefs about, 90-91,
  196-197
  Jewish teachings on, 82

258

nervous system of, 171, 173, 177
reasoning power of, 74, 75, 90
resistance to change, 57, 60
social nature of, 171-172, 177
struggle for knowledge, 63
humility, 239, 241
Huxley, Julian, 91

India, 73, 74
Indians, American. *See* native
Americans
international relations, 22

jail, 186, 187, 188, 190, 192
Jains, 74, 159
Jefferson, Thomas, 224, 226, 227
Jesus, 44, 45, 46, 57, 98, 113, 118,
159, 198
as guide for life, 230, 245
description of, 218-219
provides meaning for life, 217-218
Jewish creed, 87-88
Josephson Institute of Ethics, 199
Judaism
beliefs of, 82, 87, 159
difference between Reform and
Orthodox, 87
membership in, 82-83, 87
rabbis, 86
relationship to government, 83-84
religious writings of, 82
study of Mosaic Law developed by,
84-86
Jung, C.J., 31, 33, 148

Kant, Immanuel, 106
Keen, Sam, 30, 32, 34
Kempis, Thomas à, 146, 193
Kobler, John, 66
Kohn, Alfie, 197
Krishnamurti, Jiddu, 56

Lamont, Corliss, 89
Landers, Ann, 166
Law of Complexity-Consciousness,
69
legalism, 157, 160, 161
life, 24
creation of, 64, 110
meaning of
ecofeminist worldview explains,
48-53
futility of searching for, 38-41,
123
con, 216
God-directed evolution explains,
66-70, 229
humanism explains, 89-93

individuals must seek on their
own, 56-61, 128
Jesus Christ explains, 42-47,
217-218
money and, 181
scientific evolution explains,
62-65
through love, creation, and
understanding, 71-76
on other planets, 63-64
termination of, justification for,
160-161
ways of living
deceitfulness, 221-223
honesty, 224-227
placing others first, 215-220
placing self first, 209-214
positive church roles for, 242-247
values' guidance for, 228-234,
235-241
life path, choosing a
by examining myth, 30-34
by facing unpleasant truths, 17-24
cave allegory and, 25-29
difficulty of, 18-19
is a false concept, 58
love, 70, 219
Buddhist view of, 141
creation-centered spirituality's
beliefs about, 144, 146
definition of, 72-73
gives meaning to life, 72, 231-233,
234
humanist beliefs about, 91
Jesus' teachings about, 245-246
of oneself, 213, 232-233
should guide moral decisions,
156-161, 177-178

McGavran, Donald, 246
Machiavelli, Niccolo, 221, 223
Mackay, John A., 43
McLuhan, Marshall, 33
Mahabharata, 159
materialism, 103-104, 105-106
Medicine Eagle, Brooke, 130
Meiklejohn, Alexander, 230
mental illness, 159-161, 229, 231
Christianity promotes, 192-196
reason for, 20
Miller, Donald E., 114
money, 179-184, 210
morality
absolute, 211-212
common principles of, 232
developing instinct for, 227
must be individually determined,
210, 212

261

Sherdskov, Vladislav, 172
Short, Robert, 118
Sikhism, 159
sin, 110, 111
  explains human misery, 43-44, 112
  is overemphasized, 146, 147, 148,
    192
  Jesus' death for, 45, 112, 169
    as pathological, 192-193, 197
  overcoming, 164, 165
Snelling, John, 139
social order, 114, 117, 127, 146, 246
  dominator vs. partnership, 50-52
Socrates, 25, 229, 230
soul, 110-111, 112, 149, 216-217
spirit, 110, 111, 112
  native American beliefs about,
    130-134
spirituality
  connection to humans, 131
  connection with nature, 51-52, 128,
    132, 146-147
  creation-centered, 143-149
  fall/redemption, 146-149
Stone, Merlin, 49
suicide, 232
symbolism
  atheists must create, 41
  Goddess, 53
  in Bible, 120-121
  in myths, 123, 126, 128

Talmud, 84-86
technology, 52, 144
Teilhard de Chardin, Pierre, 66, 68,
  70, 229
Telushkin, Joseph, 189
Ten Commandments, 172, 175
Tennyson, Alfred Lord, 229
Tillich, Paul, 119
Toynbee, Arnold, 71, 219
transference, 20, 22
Truman, Ruth, 242
trust, 20-21
truth, 18, 29, 58
  Buddhist meditation on, 140-141
  challenges and, 23-24
  impossibility of finding, 106
  is embodied in Jesus, 45, 219-220
  love of, 73

UFOs, 65

universe
  creation-centered spirituality's
    understanding of, 148
  God's role in, 67-70, 109
  humans should seek to change, 75
  other forms of life in, 63-64
  understanding through myth, 127,
    144

values
  developing, 229, 231-232
  B. Franklin's efforts toward,
    236-241
  society's attitude toward, 233-234
Vedas, 95
vice, 225-226

Wald, George, 62, 64
Walker, Mort, 21, 23
Watters, Wendell W., 191
Western culture, 73-74, 145
Whale, J.S., 43
Whitehead, Alfred North, 45
William J. Murray III vs. John N.
  Curlett, 102
Williams, James M., 164
Willimon, William H., 185
wisdom, 144-148
women
  and emotions, 230
  Apostle Paul's teachings on, 118,
    244, 247
  devaluation of, 52, 53, 147
  in Christianity, 186, 187, 188, 190,
    245, 246-247
  in prehistoric societies, 49, 50
Wordsworth, William, 234
worldview (*Weltanschauung*), 18
  myth's role in shaping, 31-32
  of dominator vs. partnership
    societies, 50-52
  of scripture authors, 117
  revising, difficulty in, 19, 22

youth
  developing values in, 228-234
  lack of modern rituals for, 124
  rebellion, 45-46
  search for meaning, 72, 190

Zindler, Frank R., 170
Zoroastrianism, 126, 159